"The early years of the ASB transformed concepts and practice in financial reporting, setting an example that was followed globally. The authors of *The UK Accounting Standards Board, 1990–2000* led this transformation; there is nobody better to tell the story."

**Prof. Richard Barker,** *Member, International Sustainability Standards Board*

"We all have a clear interest in company accounts painting a true picture of their financial position, which in the 1980s they often did not. The three authors of *The UK Accounting Standards Board 1990–2000* paint a personal and fascinating picture of how they succeeded in radically reforming standards, dealt with technical and political challenges, overcame opposition and established the independence of the standard setting board."

**Sir Bryan Nicholson GBE,** *Deputy Chairman of the Financial Reporting Council, 1993–1996 and Chairman 2001–2005*

"The interview format used in *The UK Accounting Standards Board, 1990–2000: Restoring Honesty and Trust in Accounting* by Tweedie, Cook and Whittington brings a stimulating period of accounting standards history to life. The authors' innovative ideas on accounting have stood the test of time."

**Pauline Wallace,** *Chair, UK Endorsement Board*

# The UK Accounting Standards Board, 1990–2000

In the late 1980s, financial accounting in Britain was in disarray. 'Creative' accounting was rife. The authority of the industry's standard-setters had been drastically compromised when their rules for inflation accounting were first ignored by many firms and then abandoned. There were calls for government to replace the accountants' self-regulation with a tough regulatory regime close to the American model. Also, rapid change in the financial industry was generating complex new financial schemes for which existing accounting standards were inadequate. This book tells the story of the next decade: the problems the standard-setters faced, both technical and political, the resistance they met, the solutions they developed, and the durability of their work. Innovations they developed have become part of global accounting standards.

The story is told in the words of three board members, all of whom had spent their careers in accounting, one as the senior technical partner of a Big 4 audit firm, one as an executive in major multinational businesses, one as a university professor: respectively, the Chairman, Sir David Tweedie; the Technical Director, Allan Cook; and the academic board member, Professor Geoffrey Whittington. The medium is for the most part conversation, with the standard-setters questioned by Cambridge Professor Geoff Meeks, recorded over three years producing a more vivid picture of motivations and events. Also, in this technically demanding subject, it has the advantage of a simpler, more informal, and engaging conversational style and language.

The book will appeal not just to accountants interested in the origins of the rules they are following and students learning why those rules were adopted, but also to anyone interested in how, in spheres beyond accounting, to harness the expertise and support of business regulatees without suffering regulatory capture.

**David Tweedie** was an academic accountant, senior technical partner of KPMG and, latterly, the first Chairman of the UK's Accounting Standards Board (1990–2000) and of the International Accounting Standards Board (2001–2011).

**Allan Cook** brought to the ASB extensive experience of working with major accounting standard-setting bodies and, on behalf of his employers, Unilever then Shell, and other multinationals, pressing in international fora for convergence in accounting standards worldwide.

**Geoffrey Whittington** is an accountant and economist who has held chairs at Edinburgh, Bristol, and Cambridge universities and has also been closely involved in standard setting and the use of accounting information, as a member of regulatory bodies such as the Monopolies and Mergers Commission, the Technical Committee of the ICAEW, the ASB, and the IASB.

## Routledge Studies in Accounting

**43 Quality Management and Accounting in Service Industries**
A New Model of Quality Cost Calculation
*Wojciech Sadkowski and Piotr Jedynak*

**44 Artificial Intelligence in Accounting**
Organisational and Ethical Implications
*Othmar Lehner and Carina Knoll*

**45 The Financial Reporting Quality of Public Companies**
The Cultural Dimension
*Katarzyna Mokrzycka-Kogut*

**46 Strategic Pricing and Management Accounting**
*David Dugdale*

**47 Statutory Audits in Europe**
Latest Reforms and Future Challenges
*Michael Kend, Giulia Leoni, Cristina Florio and Silvia Gaia*

**48 The Privatisation of British Rail**
How Not to Run a Railway
*Sean McCartney and John Stittle*

**49 The UK Accounting Standards Board, 1990–2000**
Restoring Honesty and Trust in Accounting
*David Tweedie, Allan Cook and Geoffrey Whittington*

For more information about this series, please visit www.routledge.com/Routledge-Studies-in-Accounting/book-series/SE0715

# The UK Accounting Standards Board, 1990–2000

## Restoring Honesty and Trust in Accounting

**David Tweedie**
**Allan Cook**
**Geoffrey Whittington**

*in conversation with* Geoff Meeks
*with a foreword by* Robert Bruce

Routledge
Taylor & Francis Group
LONDON AND NEW YORK

ACCOUNTING
STANDARDS
BOARD

The Spire logo of the ASB is reproduced on the cover by kind permission of the Financial Reporting Council.

First published 2024
by Routledge
4 Park Square, Milton Park, Abingdon, Oxon OX14 4RN

and by Routledge
605 Third Avenue, New York, NY 10158

*Routledge is an imprint of the Taylor & Francis Group, an informa business*



*British Library Cataloguing-in-Publication Data*
A catalogue record for this book is available from the British Library

*Library of Congress Cataloging-in-Publication Data*
Names: Tweedie, D. P., author.
Title: The UK accounting standards board, 1990-2000 : restoring honesty and trust in accounting / David Tweedie, Allan Cook, Geoffrey Whittington ; in conversation with Geoff Meeks ; with a foreword by Robert Bruce.
Description: Abingdon, Oxon ; New York, NY : Routledge, 2023. |
Series: Routledge studies in accounting | Includes bibliographical references and index.
Identifiers: LCCN 2023001000 (print) | LCCN 2023001001 (ebook) | ISBN 9781032388151 (hbk) | ISBN 9781032388168 (pbk) | ISBN 9781003346920 (ebk)
Subjects: LCSH: Accounting Standards Board (Great Britain) |
Accounting—Great Britain.
Classification: LCC HF5616.G7 T93 2023 (print) | LCC HF5616.G7 (ebook) |
DDC 657.0941—dc23/eng/20230515
LC record available at https://lccn.loc.gov/2023001000
LC ebook record available at https://lccn.loc.gov/2023001001

ISBN: 978-1-032-38815-1 (hbk)
ISBN: 978-1-032-38816-8 (pbk)
ISBN: 978-1-003-34692-0 (ebk)

DOI: 10.4324/9781003346920

Typeset in Bembo
by codeMantra

**Authors' Note**

While the authorship of this book is shown as David Tweedie, Allan Cook, and Geoffrey Whittington in conversation with Geoff Meeks, the three of us believe that Professor Meeks is also equally an author. Geoff believes that as he wasn't a member of the ASB his contribution was not equal to ours. We disagree.

The interviewing format of the book was Geoff's idea; he acted not only as the interviewer but also as editor, transcribed the Zoom sessions, made constructive criticisms and suggestions at all stages of the work, and wrote several introductions and the final chapter. We respect his integrity and modesty in seeking only an acknowledgement for his work but believe that readers of this book should know the major role that Geoff played in its production. We were a team of four and Geoff was a key member of that team.

**David Tweedie**
**Allan Cook**
**Geoffrey Whittington**

# Contents

# Figures

# Tables

# Foreword

I must have first met David Tweedie at one of the extraordinary, and long-gone, annual events which went under the guise of the Summer School of the Institute of Chartered Accountants of Scotland. It was a gathering like no other. There was learned debate, guest speakers and plenary sessions, furious arguments, and the world was full of ideas, fuelled by the sea air and whisky. The onetime Chancellor of the Exchequer, Denis Healey, prefaced his contribution once with: "I'm from the opposition and I'm here to horrify you". But there was golf (this was St Andrews after all), dinners, one long evening of homemade entertainment, and bagpipes and dancing, that could happily last almost until breakfast and at that latitude and time of year daylight anyway seemed to stretch to dawn. As a gathering it typified the world from which David Tweedie and the ideas that underpinned the pioneering and revolutionary work of the Accounting Standards Board (ASB) emerged. He came from both the hard world of Glasgow accounting and the forthright thinking of Scots academics. His mentor, Professor David Flint, straddled both worlds. Ideas had to be rigorous. Actions had to be principled and extremely firm. A contemporary of Tweedie's in Glasgow had, as a junior auditor, questioned the accounts of the client he was working on, mentioned his suspicions to his senior partner, who in turn descended on the chairman of the client with the words that if ever this happened again he would personally come down and ram the accounts up his arse. If things were wrong you took no prisoners.

Small wonder that when he came down to London with the Scots firm of Thomson McLintock, Tweedie observed that "what was immoral in Edinburgh was frowned upon in the Midlands and was damn good business in the City of London". There were scandals and potential scandals all around. The 'Big Bang' and the loosening up of the world of financial institutions had brought US banks firmly into the equation. Their culture of a myriad of rules had led to what Tweedie saw as 'loopholing' and encouraged an astonishing level of creative accounting. The birth of the Accounting Standards Board, levered into an independent status from out of the control of the professional bodies, was down to Sir Ron Dearing, a saintly civil servant (and how we wish there were more of those around today). He designed its independent structure, drove it through, and saw to the installation of Tweedie and his triumvirate with Allan Cook and Geoff Whittington, as well as the hiring of its Holborn-based HQ.

The putting together of that team was the other catalyst. Whittington had been professor at Edinburgh University when a newly qualified Tweedie had first become a lecturer. Cook was the detail guru and technical director. They formed a united and determined team that in turn attracted other talents to the staff. Dearing had created the fortress and then stepped aside to give Tweedie and his team the space to lead the attack.

And attack they did. First in line was the disease afflicting much of financial reporting, what Tweedie termed the 'creeping crumple'. This was a blatant form of blackmail operated by the corporate sector. Audit firm X would tell client Y that it couldn't approve a specific accounting treatment. Client Y would then retort that it had sought an opinion from audit firm A and they had said they would allow it. The whole system was openly on the slide. Tweedie recalls refusing to accept a scheme and having the investment banker concerned look him in the eye and say: "You'll never stop us". "That really was", recalls Tweedie, "the incentive to stick it to them". And stick it to them was what the ASB did. Area after area, issue after issue, were patiently and persistently closed down. As each new ASB initiative was launched I would head up to hear what Tweedie and his team were unveiling. As a journalist I really had only one question to ask: "Who is going to hate this?". And that was your story in the bag. Another corporate sector was going to have to change its financial reporting practices.

It was, I have to say, enormous fun. And that, in part, was the secret of the ASB's success. Tweedie had the ability to boil each issue down to a short and, mostly, irrefutable nugget of common sense. And then to lodge it firmly in everyone's consciousness he would spin a joke around it to dramatise the issue. When they brought in changes to make what was known by commentators and investment analysts as 'the bottom line' more accurate and less misleading Tweedie announced that: "The bottom line was like a haggis: if you knew what was in it, you wouldn't touch it with a barge pole". When it came to arguments over goodwill and brands and the US argued that they should be written off over 40 years regardless, Tweedie retorted that: "In the UK we've got brands such as Gordon's Gin and Johnnie Walker that are actually older than the United States. And in my humble opinion they have done more for the sum of human happiness than the United States, and that personally I would amortise America before I'd ever write off Johnnie Walker Black Label".

It was all about giving people a simple solution that could be easily understood by them. In presentations on pensions obligations, Tweedie would go through a calculation that, as he demonstrated, produced something daft. He would look the audience in the eye and say: "Explain that to your granny. You may as well take the $10 million, divide it by the cube root of the number of miles to the moon and multiply it by your shoe size. The number doesn't mean a thing!". The point would be made. The audience would understand. And more to the point the audience would be on his side. He was also indefatigable. At conference after conference the same jokes, and explanations and exhortations would roll out. But, in the spirit of the Glasgow music hall, his timing was impeccable and his charm absolute.

But beyond the charm lay the toughness. You do not manage to reform a whole range of financial reporting rules through which the finance directors of some of the country's finest companies had been managing to drive a coach and horses on the basis of a good repertoire of jokes and a pleasant manner. Tweedie's secret lay in the combination of two factors. He was academically brighter than most accountants and he was, to most in the large accountancy firms, an outsider. That combination allowed him to note things that those who were more dependent on the culture of the firms would rather not. And it allowed him to refute the arguments of others in a logical way. They even faced down the Government when it came to the Chancellor, Gordon Brown, and the Private Finance Initiative, which imitated the same misleading off-balance-sheet financing that had brought the corporate sector into such disgrace.

The UK ASB presided over an extraordinary decade of reform and innovation. The obvious loopholes had been closed and the rules now forced people to look harder at what the figures meant. The reputation of financial reporting was enhanced. Research showed that between 1994 and 2000 inward portfolio investment in UK equities went up 20-fold. Inevitably when Tweedie and the team took the concepts to an international stage with the International Accounting Standards Board they eventually became diluted. But the ambition and objective to raise the quality and usefulness of financial reporting throughout the world remain.

by Robert Bruce

Robert Bruce was, for ten years, Editor of *Accountancy Age* and then for another decade a columnist with *The Times*, during which time he contributed 500 weekly columns.

# Preface

In the late 1980s, financial accounting in Britain was in disarray. The authority of the industry's standard-setters had been drastically compromised when their rules for inflation accounting were first ignored by many firms and then abandoned. 'Big Bang' had brought more aggressive ways of working in the financial sector, and this included circumventing accounting rules to flatter a company's accounts and mislead investors. A best-selling book had the sub-title, "How to make your profits what you want them to be". The users of accounts were losing confidence in the accounts prepared by businesses; accountants feared a loss of trust in their profession; and there were calls for government to replace the accountants' self-regulation with a tough regulatory regime close to the American model. In addition, rapid change in the financial industry was generating complex new financial schemes for which existing accounting standards were inadequate.

A committee chaired by the ingenious administrator Sir Ron (later Lord) Dearing proposed a new regime with more authority and more resources: the Accounting Standards Board. Neither purely private – self-regulation – nor arm's length public, it was designed to secure access to the technical expertise of the profession and the support from practitioners needed to achieve compliance – but without suffering regulatory capture. Inevitably it faced resistance from vested interests – investment bankers, lawyers, and executives used to manipulating the accounts. It was not clear in 1990 that the Board would succeed where its predecessors had been thwarted.

This book tells the story of the next decade: the problems the standard-setters faced, both technical and political, the solutions they developed, and the durability of their work. Many of their innovations have become part of global accounting standards. Its activities certainly aroused passions not usually associated with accounting, as illustrated by the headline in the *Scotsman* newspaper (in the figure below), which was directed at the ASB Chairman, David Tweedie:

The story is told in the words of three Board members, all of whom had spent their careers in accounting, one as the senior technical partner of a Big 4 audit firm, one as an executive in major multinational businesses, one as

A poster repeating the headline 'The most hated accountant', in the *Scotsman* newspaper of 3 March 1991 – accompanying an article profiling David Tweedie and the work of the ASB.

a university professor: respectively, the Chairman, Sir David Tweedie, the Technical Director, Allan Cook, and the academic Board member, Professor Geoffrey Whittington. The book consists primarily of three-cornered conversations. Like the oral history of wartime veterans, the colloquial style and vividly expressed opinions are intended to make the history readable and accessible, not just to accountants interested in the origins of the rules they are following and students learning why those rules were adopted but also to anyone interested in how to harness the expertise and support of business regulatees without suffering regulatory capture.

Tweedie went on to chair the new International Accounting Standards Board (IASB) whose rules were by his retirement in 2011 required or permitted by almost 120 countries. Whittington was also a founder member of the IASB.

They discuss the efforts to achieve the independence normally associated with a public body detached from special interest groups, at the same time as securing the expertise and buy-in of a private regulator peopled by regulatees. They reflect on the gulf between the aspirations of lawyers and those of accountants. And they illustrate the tension between, on the one hand, the short-term financial interest of executives (and their investment bankers, lawyers, and even their auditors) in being economical with the truth in their accounts, and, on the other, the honesty and transparency which are prerequisites of efficient markets and of effective monitoring of managers' stewardship of complex businesses.

The medium is for the most part conversation with the standard-setters, recorded over almost three years. (The COVID pandemic emerged soon after the start of this project, and the authors never met: all the conversations had to be conducted via Zoom. COVID also delayed and inhibited the search for materials and consultation with other people.) In this technically demanding subject littered with jargon, the approach has the advantage of a simpler, more informal, and accessible conversational style and language: spades are called spades. It makes it clear, too, that these are subjective perspectives and recollections which may not be shared by other participants in these events.

Crucially important in the accounting reforms were the other Board members and observers (see Appendix 1). They brought a wealth of experience and expertise to the Board. In addition, they kept the Board informed of what was currently happening in the market and the views of its participants. Their invaluable part-time role was not an easy one. While Tweedie and Cook were full-timers and Whittington was a member of faculty at Cambridge University, the other Board members, in dealing with controversial issues on the Board's agenda, had, on a daily basis, to face irate clients, partners, or colleagues who may have had serious reservations about the Board's decisions. While the Board met behind closed doors, the part-timers' views would be revealed on the publication of a standard when they would be identified as agreeing with its requirements or would be required to show their disagreement by dissenting. During the ten years covered by this book, during which 19 standards, many controversial, were published by the Board, there were only three dissents – in each case the dissentient was expressing a long-held conviction. The ASB owed much to its part-time members' undoubted skills, commitment, collegiality, and, above all, integrity.

For the first years of the ASB's existence, Sir Bryan Carsberg served as part-time Vice Chairman and played an active part in the Board's discussions. He resigned as Vice Chairman in 1992 and as a member in 1994, as a consequence of his appointment as Director General of Fair Trading, but later he played an important role in facilitating the transition of international standard setting from the IASC to the IASB.

While sitting in the background, Sydney Treadgold and Ann Wilks (Secretaries to the FRC) and Michael Butcher (Secretary to the ASB) oversaw the board's critical relationship with the Department of Trade and Industry where formerly they had been senior officials. Their diplomatic skills and governmental contacts smoothed the way for many of the board's reforms. All were accomplished wordsmiths and Michael's drafting skills were legendary – many staff members will remember their drafts being "butchered".

Attention should also be drawn to the support of Professor Robert Jack, the Board's legal adviser, who, with his sound common sense and desire to identify the substance rather than the letter of the law, assisted the Board in many of its controversial projects.

Finally, but crucially, the research and development of the standards was supported by a skilled professional staff, whose contribution is acknowledged below. This book is written from the perspective of Board members, who were ultimately responsible for policy decisions, but those decisions were informed and influenced by the information and ideas generated by the staff, each of whom would have their own interesting tale to tell.

Geoff Meeks

# Acknowledgements

We are very grateful to Andrew Lennard and Sandra Thompson for guidance on aspects of the ASB's work with which they were involved as staff members; to Jonathan Faasse, Len Skerratt, and the ICAEW Library for supplying information; and to Kristina Abbots and Christiana Mandizha from Routledge for excellent editorial advice and support. Geoff Meeks and Geoff Whittington wish to acknowledge the research support of the Cambridge Centre for Finance in the Judge Business School, where they are both research fellows.

While they were not directly involved with this book, we would also like to acknowledge the professionalism and enthusiasm of the board staff during the first ten years of the life of the ASB. They were critical to the work of the Board. Several members joined the ASB staff on a full-time basis. Others were seconded from auditing firms or industry for a period of two or three years. All were dedicated to the objectives of the ASB and without their research, willingness to debate the issues with market participants and desire to change financial reporting for the better, the pronouncements discussed below would not have emerged so quickly nor have been generally accepted.

We warmly thank artists and editors Nick Baker, Simon Farr, Aaran Fronda, and Graham High for permission to reproduce some of their images of the 1990s ASB.

# Authors

**Sir David Tweedie** was educated at Edinburgh University (BCom 1966, PhD 1969) and qualified as a Scottish Chartered Accountant in 1972. After teaching at Edinburgh University he became Technical Director of the Institute of Chartered Accountants of Scotland (ICAS) in 1978. In 1982, he was appointed national technical partner of Thomson McLintock & Co and later of KPMG. In 1990, he became the Chairman of the (then) newly created UK Accounting Standards Board after chairing the UK's Auditing Practices Committee in 1989. In January 2001, he was appointed the first Chairman of the International Accounting Standards Board. He then led the Board for ten years, retiring in 2011. He is a visiting Professor of Accounting at Strathclyde University and the Management School of Edinburgh University. He has received honorary degrees from nine British universities. He served on the Advisory Board of Cambridge Judge Business School. He was knighted in 1994 and was inducted into the Accounting Hall of Fame in 2013. He was President of the Institute of Chartered Accountants of Scotland from 2012 to 2013 and was Chairman of the International Valuation Standards Council from 2012 to 2019. He chaired the Royal Household Audit Committee for the Sovereign Grant and was also Chairman of the Board of Trustees of the Scottish Charities, Leuchie House, and the ICAS Foundation.

**Allan Cook** graduated from the London School of Economics in 1961, where he acquired an interest in the application of accounting techniques in industry as well as a desire to work in an international environment. He became a member of the Institute of Chartered Accountants in England and Wales in 1964 and after a further 18 months in public practice joined Unilever in 1966. Over the next 13 years, his experience included management accounting and data processing in a food retailing subsidiary, Accountant to the Central Pensions Department, and membership of a small team compiling the group's annual budgets and longer-term plans. In 1979–1981, he was seconded by Unilever as Secretary to the International Accounting Standards Committee, with responsibility for drafting both technical and strategic papers for the Board and its sub-committees. In 1981, he joined the Royal Dutch/Shell Group as Head of Accounting Research. In this role, he monitored and actively contributed to accounting developments in the UK, the Netherlands, and the US. For six years he led the BIAC (Business and Industry Advisory Committee) delegation on the OECD's Working Group on Accounting Standards. From 1988 to 1990, he was a member of the UK Accounting Standards Committee. In 1990, he joined David Tweedie as Technical Director of the newly formed UK ASB, being one of the two full-time members. From 2001 to 2005, he was a member of the Technical Expert Group of EFRAG (the European Financial Reporting Advisory Group) charged with advising the European Commission on the adoption of individual standards issued by the IASB. In 2005, he stepped down from both the ASB and EFRAG to join IASB as Coordinator of the IFRIC (the International Financial Reporting Interpretations Committee), where he served till taking retirement in 2007. He was awarded a CBE for services to the accounting profession.

**Geoffrey Whittington** is currently an Emeritus Professor of Financial Accounting at the University of Cambridge, a Life Fellow of Fitzwilliam College, and a Senior Research Fellow of the Judge Business School, in the Cambridge Centre for Finance. After graduating in economics and accounting from the London School of Economics, he trained as a Chartered Accountant in London and then studied for a doctorate in economics at Cambridge. From 1962 to 2001, he held full-time academic posts in economics, finance, and accounting, including chairs at Edinburgh, Bristol, and Cambridge Universities. He was also involved in policy-making and its implementation in both the public and private sectors, including acting as a part-time economic advisor to the Office of Fair Trading on the Stock Exchange case, which led to the 'Big Bang' reforms. From 2001 to 2006, he was a full-time member of the International Accounting Standards Board, and he was a part-time observer and member of the UK Accounting Standards Board from 1990 to 2009. Earlier, he was a part-time member of the UK Monopolies and Mergers Commission (1987–1996) and served on panels which investigated proposed mergers. Honours include a CBE for services to accounting, the British Accounting Association's Distinguished Academic of the Year Award, the Institute of Chartered Accountants in England and Wales Founding Societies' Centenary Award, and honorary doctorates from the universities of Edinburgh and Sussex.

***Interviewer Geoff Meeks*** is an Emeritus Professor of Financial Accounting at Cambridge University and Honorary Senior Research Associate at Cambridge Judge Business School (CJBS). He joined the School in 2003, having previously been employed by Price Waterhouse, Edinburgh University, and the Faculty of Economics at Cambridge, where he was Director of Graduate Studies. He has held visiting positions at Harvard Business

School, INSEAD, and London School of Economics; and has held a Fellowship at Darwin College, Cambridge, and an Academic Fellowship at the ICAEW. At CJBS he has served as Director of Teaching, Director of Research, Head of the Finance and Accounting Group, and Acting Dean. His research has mostly been on M&A, bankruptcy, accounting regulation, and integrating company accounts with national accounts.

# Acronyms and other abbreviations

| | |
|---|---|
| AAA | American Accounting Association |
| AICPA | American Institute of Public Certified Accountants |
| AIM | Alternative Investment Market (UK) |
| APB | Accounting Principles Board (US) |
| APC | Audit Practices Committee (UK) |
| ARB | Accounting Research Bulletin (US) |
| ASB | Accounting Standards Board (UK) |
| ASBJ | Accounting Standards Board of Japan |
| ASC | Accounting Standards Committee (UK) |
| BBA | British Banking Association (UK) |
| CAPEX | spending on buying or improving fixed assets such as land, buildings, and equipment |
| CBI | Confederation of British Industry |
| CCA | Current Cost Accounting |
| CCAB | Consultative Committee of Accountancy Bodies (UK) |
| CEO | Chief Executive Officer |
| CFO | Chief Financial Officer |
| DTI | Department of Trade and Industry (UK) |
| EBIT | Earnings before interest and taxation |
| EBITDA | Earnings before interest, taxation, depreciation, and amortisation |
| EC | European Commission |
| ED | Exposure Draft (UK) |
| EFRAG | European Financial Reporting Advisory Group (EU) |
| EPS | Earnings per share |
| ESMA | European Securities and Markets Authority (EU) |
| EU | European Union |
| FAS | Financial Accounting Standard (US) |
| FASB | Financial Accounting Standards Board (US) |
| FRC | Financial Reporting Council (UK) |
| FRED | Financial Reporting Exposure Draft (UK) |
| FRRP | Financial Reporting Review Panel |
| FRS | Financial Reporting Standard (UK) |

| | |
|---|---|
| FTSE | Financial Times Stock Exchange [100 Index] (UK) |
| GAAP | Generally Accepted Accounting Principles |
| GBP | British pound sterling |
| IASB | International Accounting Standards Board |
| IASC | International Accounting Standards Committee |
| IAS | International Accounting Standard |
| ICAEW | Institute of Chartered Accountants in England and Wales |
| ICAS | Institute of Chartered Accountants of Scotland |
| IFRS | International Financial Reporting Standard |
| IOSCO | International Organization of Securities Commissions |
| IP | Intellectual property |
| IPO | Initial Public Offering [of shares] |
| IVSC | International Valuation Standards Council |
| JANE | Joint Activity that is Not an Entity |
| M&A | Mergers and acquisitions |
| MD&A | Management Discussion and Analysis |
| P&L | Profit and Loss Account |
| QUANGO | Quasi-autonomous non-governmental organisation |
| ROE | Return on equity |
| RONA | Return on net assets |
| SEC | Securities and Exchange Commission (US) |
| SFAS | Statement of Financial Accounting Standards (US) |
| SME | Small and medium-sized enterprise |
| SSAP | Statement of Standard Accounting Practice (UK) |
| TR | Technical Release (UK) |
| TSR | Total shareholder return |

# 1 Origins

The first day of August 1990 the temperature in London rose to higher than anyone could remember – within a whisker of 40C. In Chartered Accountants' Hall in the City of London, the computers overheated and the staff had to be sent home. Meanwhile in an uninspiring office block just outside the City at the Holborn end of the Gray's Inn Road, six accountants and two secretaries took possession of their plain but air-conditioned rooms and began to fill the empty drawers, cupboards and filing cabinets. The same evening a dinner took place at the Goring Hotel at which three of those accountants joined their newly appointed fellow board members and observers at an informal gathering hosted by Sir Ron Dearing, the man who had designed the structure under which they were to work and chosen them for the task ahead. Even before they went in to dinner, a tropical storm broke directly overhead. So it was that under the auspices of thunder, lightning and flood the Accounting Standards Board was born.

Although not seen as such at the time, that storm could be regarded as a symbol of the pent-up energy that had been building up over the previous decade as efforts to grapple with the challenges of accounting for newly emerging problems were repeatedly thwarted by an inadequate regulatory structure. This chapter examines the background to those problems and may give some understanding of the burden of expectations assumed by the new bodies.

The Accounting Standards Board (ASB) of the UK and the Republic of Ireland was founded in 1990. It was the first accounting standard-setter in the British Isles to have the power to set standards which had the backing (albeit in a rather subtle way) of company law, and it inherited a raft of 'creative accounting' issues which its predecessor, the professionally sponsored Accounting Standards Committee (ASC), had been unable to resolve, due to its lack of authority. During the next ten years, under the leadership of its first Chairman, David Tweedie, the ASB issued 19 standards (plus the FRSSE: the Financial Reporting Standard for Smaller Entities, and a Statement of Principles) which addressed many of the most important problems that it had inherited and laid the foundation for future international developments.

DOI: 10.4324/9781003346920-1

By the end of that decade, the European Union (EU), of which the UK and the Republic of Ireland were members, was committed (by the Lisbon Agreement, 2000) to the adoption of international accounting standards, set by the new (2001) International Accounting Standards Board (IASB) for the accounts of companies listed on stock exchanges. This was implemented in 2005, thus reducing the ASB to the role of a commentator on the work of the IASB for listed companies and an adaptor of IASB standards for unlisted UK companies. J.R. Edwards, historian of financial reporting in Britain, describes the latter period as marking "the effective end of British regulation of company accounting practices" (Edwards, 2019, p.4). Thus, the first decade of the ASB's existence represented the most productive period of accounting standard-setting in the British Isles.

This book does not claim to be a comprehensive history of the ASB in its first ten years. It is not comprehensive, because it focuses on the standards which the authors consider to be most interesting or important, and it does not claim to be a history because three of the authors were participants in the work of the ASB and cannot therefore claim to be objective observers, as would befit historians. Rather, this is autobiographical: a series of discussions of topics by participants in the standard-setting process, in conversation with Geoff Meeks, based primarily on subjective recollections. It is therefore historical material but not history. However, in order to understand the working of the ASB and the origins of the problems which it faced, it is necessary to understand the historical background, and the remainder of this chapter provides a brief account of this. A comprehensive account of the early historical background will be found in Edwards (2019), and an authoritative history of the ASC, which was the ASB's immediate predecessor, is Rutherford (2007). Griffiths (1986) and Smith (1992) were campaigning books which exposed the extreme creative accounting practices of the 1980s. The Dearing Report (1988) proposed the new ASB structure and the Solomon's Report (1989) proposed a new conceptual framework for accounting standards in the British context.

## Financial reporting before 1970

Financial reporting has been required for as long as investors have trusted managers to invest and manage their funds. This is often described as a principal/agent relationship, investors being the principals and managers being the agents. Financial reports by the agents provide the principal with information about the honesty and efficiency of management. It is in the interests of the management that the reports give a favourable picture, and there is a temptation to provide an unduly favourable picture by means of 'creative accounting' devices which stretch current rules and conventions to their limit, and often beyond it. Auditors have been employed to detect and prevent such distortions, but with limited success: they have sometimes been 'captured' by management. These themes run through the history of financial reporting and are regularly highlighted by accounting 'scandals' often associated with corporate collapses (such as the railway company failures of the 1840s or the Royal Mail Steamship Company case of the 1930s). All of this sounds very familiar to the modern observer: corporate collapses and criticisms of the audit process are still with us, despite the efforts of the ASC, the ASB, and other regulators. However, this does not mean that the efforts of regulators have been in vain; contemporary financial reports and their audits are much more sophisticated than those of the nineteenth century (when, for example, consolidated accounts were unknown), as are the complex global corporations which they record. Financial reporting has changed in response to the needs of companies and their investors (now also representing global capital markets), but the tension between preparers and users of financial reports is a continuing theme.

The need for financial reports is obviously greatest when large numbers of investors are required to fund expensive projects such as infrastructure investments: a large shareholder community reduces the possibility of personal engagement of shareholders with management. In Britain, the canal building of the late eighteenth century, followed by the railway building of the early nineteenth century, required such investment, culminating in the 'railway mania' of the 1840s. Until that time, companies were created by Act of Parliament, and financial reporting was specified individually in each Act. In 1844, the creation of companies was streamlined by the introduction of registered companies, which were created by registration of documents with the Registrar of Companies, and most companies floated after this date were registered. One requirement for registration was the filing of accounts with the registrar. Although the requirements were minimal, this marked the beginning of the regulation of financial reporting by company law. In 1855, the reporting requirement to file accounts was withdrawn, and although the stock exchange required accounts of listed companies to be filed with it from 1890 onwards, company law did not reinstate the requirement until 1900. This illustrates the Victorian *laissez faire* attitude to financial reporting that prevailed until the 1948 Companies Act, which, for the first time listed the items to be recorded in accounts in some detail and required consolidated accounts for groups of companies.

This is not to say that the period between 1844 and 1948 was the 'Dark Ages' of financial reporting. The pressures of the capital market led many companies to go beyond the minimal disclosures required by statute, and a body of generally accepted accounting practices began to emerge, fostered by the emergent auditing profession. The leading professional bodies all had their origins in the second part of the nineteenth century: the first to receive a Royal Charter (in 1854) was the forerunner of the Institute of Chartered Accountants of Scotland (ICAS), and the Institute of Chartered Accountants in England and Wales (ICAEW) followed in 1880. However, progress was patchy and haphazard, and the freedom allowed by generally accepted accounting practice was not conducive to inter-company comparison. As pressure for tighter regulation of accounting practices grew, the ICAEW, which had previously supported the *laissez faire* approach, started to issue its Recommendations on Accounting Principles, the first of which appeared in 1942. These were recommendations rather than requirements, and they were distillations of what was judged to be the best current practice rather than attempts to introduce new, improved practice (Zeff, 2009). Nevertheless, they represented the first attempt to standardise accounting practice in Britain and were the forerunners of the ICAEW's subsequent attempts at professional regulation through the medium of the ASC.

The 1948 Companies Act enacted many of the Recommendations of the Cohen Committee Report (1945). For the first time, consolidated accounts were required for groups of companies; previously, non-consolidation had been a convenient vehicle for off-balance sheet transactions. The other major accounting innovation was the introduction of formats for the balance sheet and profit and loss account, with the balance sheet being the more detailed. The profit and loss account was less detailed and did not require sales to be disclosed: this had to await the 1967 Companies Act. The requirement that company accounts should show "a true and fair view" was also introduced for the first time. However, the Act did not specify the recognition criteria or measurement methods that accountants should use. Such matters were left to professional judgement, informed by generally accepted practice and the ICAEW's recommendations.

This system did not give rise to any notable problems in the first few years of its existence, which was a period of post-war recovery, in which rationing and restrictions on economic activity (including limits on capital issues) were the order of the day. However, by the late 1950s, there was a relaxation of restrictions and the free market was restored. This included removing restrictions on capital issues, and business combinations, often financed by new issues, became more common. This process continued into the 1960s, when business combinations became a matter of concern to policy makers (notably the Monopolies and Mergers Act, 1965, which added mergers to the scope of the Monopolies Commission) and to economists such as Marris (1964) and Galbraith (1967) who suggested that uncontrolled growth through take-over was not conducive to economic efficiency, a proposition supported empirically by Singh (1971) and Meeks (1977). This view was supported by the fact that creative accounting was being used by companies involved in take-overs, usually to boost reported profits either as a defence against take-over or, in the case of a bidding company, to boost the price of the shares offered as consideration. These activities came to a crisis point in the late 1960s, notably with the acquisition of AEI by GEC (1968), in which AEI's forecast profit of £10 million was reduced to £4.5 million by applying GEC's accounting practices. This was mainly due to different valuation practices, particularly in relation to stock and work in progress, which were all within the scope of generally accepted accounting practice. Similar issues were raised by the investigation into the aborted take-over of Pergamon by Leasco in 1969.

## The ASSC and ASC: 1970–1990

The public outrage at the laxity of professional requirements illustrated by these and other cases was expressed by Prof. Edward Stamp in a letter to *The Times* (1969), and a subsequent exchange (fully described and discussed in Stamp and Marley, 1970) with Sir Ronald Leach, the then current President of the ICAEW, which was responsible for the Recommendations on Accounting Principles. The outcome was that the ICAEW set up the Accounting Standards Steering Committee (ASSC) in 1970, formally as a sub-committee of the ICAEW but including members from and the support of the chartered institutes of Ireland and Scotland, and from 1972 the certified and management accounting institutes joined. The Chartered Institute of Public Finance Accountants (CIPFA) became the sixth and final member in 1976 when the title was shortened to the Accounting Standards Committee (ASC).

The ASSC was tasked with devising standards which would raise the quality of financial reporting and eliminate the lack of comparability revealed in recent cases. It was a committee of unpaid volunteers, with modest administrative and technical support, and its authority was limited to the professional discipline of the bodies that supported it. Accountants who were members of one of those bodies could be disciplined if they failed to comply with the standards. Also, like the earlier Recommendations, the new Standards would be evidence of generally accepted accounting practice but could be overruled by other evidence to the contrary.

Given this tenuous authority, its limited technical resources, and the difficult problems it faced, it is remarkable that the ASSC/ASC was so productive and survived for 20 years. By the end of 1975, 11 standards were published and, when the ASC was replaced by the ASB in 1990, the number had risen to 25, in addition to a considerable body of work in progress, including ten exposure drafts that had not become standards. A comprehensive account of its work is from Rutherford (2007). It represented the final attempt by the accounting profession to control accounting standards. During its life, it was reformed in 1983 to include non-accountant users of accounts, but its funding and management remained in the hands of professional bodies. Its successor, the ASB, retained the principle of being a private sector body, independent of government, but was not dependent on, or controlled by, professional bodies.

The ASC was hampered throughout its existence by the lack of legal authority for its standards. It therefore found it difficult to lead and innovate, but rather had to seek consensus amongst its constituents, particularly preparers of accounts. A notable example of this was inflation accounting, where its difficulties in enforcing a solution led it to seek a legal opinion, the Hoffman-Arden Opinion (1983), which asserted that the ASC's standards did have authority as evidence of what was generally accepted accounting practice (GAAP), but that this authority would not be sufficient to over-rule a situation in which most of the actual practice was at variance with a standard, as occurred in the case of the current cost accounting standard, SSAP16 (1980).

The ASC was also unfortunate in its economic environment. Two specific aspects of this exposed the weakness of the ASC's authority: inflation accounting and the rise of creative accounting, following the liberalisation of securities markets.

Inflation had been pervasive in the economy, following the Second World War, and its effects on accounts were a concern for accountants, but in the 1970s, when the ASSC was newly established, the rate of inflation increased and reached double-digit levels, peaking at more than 24% in 1975. The ASSC responded initially with an Exposure Draft (ED8, 1973) which adopted the relatively simple and conservative approach of providing a supplementary statement, applying a general purchasing power index to adjust historical cost. The Government clearly did not approve of this, possibly because it feared that the spread of general indexation would amplify 'cost push' pressures in the economy, so it responded by announcing the appointment of its own committee to investigate accounting for inflation. As a result of this, ED8 became only a provisional standard (PSSAP7, 1974): an early blow to the authority of the ASSC. The Sandilands Committee, as the government committee became known, was dominated by business people rather than (as in the case of the ASSC) professional accountants, and its Report (1975) rejected the whole concept of the general price level and advocated current cost accounting, based on replacement cost. The ASC (as it had just become) lacked the authority to oppose the Government and felt obliged to comply with its recommendation to adopt Sandilands' current cost proposal. This resulted in a tortuous debate about how to deal with monetary items. Furthermore, there was a rebellion by members of the ICAEW which passed a resolution that no form of inflation accounting should be adopted. In 1979, following a heroic effort by the ASC's Inflation Accounting Steering Group, a current cost accounting standard, SSAP16, applicable primarily to supplementary information, was issued at the very time when inflation was falling and had dropped to single-digit levels. Furthermore, the Government announced that it would not allow the current cost stock adjustment to profit for corporation tax purposes, thus removing one of the possible attractions of CCA for industry. The result was that there was never full compliance with SSAP16, and the rate of compliance fell rapidly after the first year, causing the ASC to seek the Hoffman-Arden Opinion. Eventually, the ASC accepted reality; SSAP16 was made voluntary rather than a requirement in 1985 and ultimately withdrawn entirely. This episode not only demoralised the ASC but also absorbed a large portion of its limited resources. It also left behind considerable confusion about the appropriate valuation basis and how to deal with inflation. These problems persist today.

Creative accounting activity increased over the life of the ASC and, in the mid-1980s, replaced inflation accounting as the principal concern of the ASC. Creative accounting means the use (or misuse) of accepted accounting practices to present a misleading (over-favourable) view of an entity's financial position or performance. This type of activity was not new: for example, the use of secret reserves to manipulate profit was a feature of the Royal Mail Case (1931). However, in the 1980s, the ingenuity and extent of creative accounting methods were unprecedented. This was encouraged by the liberalisation of capital markets by the Thatcher government (1979–1993), with such measures as the abolition of foreign exchange controls (1979) and the introduction of the 'Big Bang' reforms of the Stock Exchange (1986). As a result of such changes, London became an international financial centre with financial markets (including the Stock Exchange) dominated by investment banks and other financial institutions, many based in the US, where creative accounting was already flourishing. The environment became extremely competitive and the incentives to make the accounts give a favourable picture, whether to raise finance or to avoid take-over, were strong. The opportunities for creative accounting were also increased by the introduction of financial engineering (often devised by investment banks, who earned lucrative commission for their efforts) which created new forms of contract and financial instruments, enabling such practices as securitisation. The ASC responded bravely by trying to assert the principle of substance over form, asserting that accountants and auditors should look through the complex form of contracts to identify the substance of what was happening, but this had achieved only Exposure Draft status (ED49, 1990) by the end of the ASC's existence (1990).

The techniques of creative accounting were explained in Ian Griffiths' best-selling book *Creative Accounting* (1986), which was aptly sub-titled 'how to make your profits what you want them to be'. Subsequent surveys of creative accounting methods were the ICAEW survey by Skerratt and Tonkin (1989) and *Accounting for Growth* by Terry Smith (1992), sub-titled 'Stripping the Camouflage from Company Accounts'. An academic paper by two of the present authors (Tweedie and Whittington, 1990) also surveyed contemporary creative accounting practices and attempted to relate them to fundamental recognition and measurement issues which required clarification and consistency of application across standards.

The pervasive nature of creative accounting practices is captured by the broad classifications used in the latter paper: Off-Balance Sheet Schemes (including leasing, quasi-subsidiary vehicles, and contracts with repurchase options), Business Combinations (including the choice of merger or acquisition accounting, the treatment of acquired goodwill, reorganisation provisions, and equity accounting for associated companies), and Complex Capital Issues (including deep discount bonds and loan or preference stocks with options to convert to equity). The remedies suggested required the clarification of several issues such as the definitions of assets and liabilities and their consistent application across standards. This would be best achieved by having a clear and comprehensive conceptual framework, something which had already been attempted by the Financial Accounting Standards Board (FASB) in the US and the International Accounting Standards Committee (IASC), and which was proposed for the UK by the Solomons Report (1989).

Most of these issues were on the agenda of the ASC when it was replaced by the ASB in 1990.

Although companies that practised creative accounting saw benefits in it, not all corporates were happy with the *laissez faire* attitude to financial reporting that was becoming increasingly acceptable in the UK. Multinationals and other companies whose shares were widely held faced a growing problem in presenting their results in terms that were readily understood by different user groups and in different regulatory environments. The same principle applied within their domestic market. Companies that sought to provide the basis for an informed discussion with the users of their financial statements needed sound reporting standards for themselves and wanted their competitors to be held to the same high standards of reporting so that inter-company comparisons were made on a sound footing. This required accounting standards which would provide comparable, relevant and reliable information. Such considerations had begun to weigh with senior financial officers of leading UK companies, many of whom were therefore supportive of improved accounting standards. For example, the 100 Group of senior financial officers provided valuable constructive criticism and support to both the ASC and its successor, the ASB, and the ASB itself always had two senior finance directors amongst its nine members.

A further reason for improving the quality of UK financial reporting was the growing movement towards convergence in national accounting standards. The US financial market regulator, the Securities and Exchange Commission (SEC), had persuaded the IASC to undertake a tightening of its standards, eliminating options and improving disclosures, with a view to their becoming an acceptable basis for filing financial statements in the US without the requirement for reconciliation to American standards. While acknowledging the leadership role of the FASB in developing high-quality standards, many in the UK feared the excessive detail and rules-based approach that characterised much of its work and raised the possibility of 'loopholing' of the rules by creative accountants. If the UK were to play a part in developing standards less tied to specifics of the US domestic scene, it would need to restore its reputation for sound financial reporting based on the overriding obligation to provide a true and fair view.

## The Dearing Report and the Foundation of the ASB

In 1987, the Consultative Committee of Accountancy Bodies (CCAB), which sponsored the ASC on behalf of the six leading UK accounting institutes, recognised the difficulties facing the ASC by appointing a committee to review the standard-setting process. The ASC had previously sponsored its own internal reviews, notably the Watts Report (1981), which made some radical recommendations, including a body to supervise the enforcement of standards, the development of a conceptual framework, and greater resources to support the standard-setter. These recommendations were not adopted at the time, but by 1987 there was greater urgency, and the Watts proposals were more relevant than ever. The new committee was essentially an external review, reporting to the CCAB rather than the ASC and having a stronger representation from outside the accounting profession. Only 4 of the 16 members were accountants in public practice, indicating a wish to engage with the wider community of users and preparers. The Chairman was Sir Ron Dearing, a former senior civil servant and Chairman of the Royal Mail, who was a notable administrator and designer of administrative systems (amongst his later achievements was the creation of the Higher Education Funding Council, which ended the binary division of higher education into universities and other institutions).

From the outset, the Committee recognised that the two crucial issues it had to address were, first, the relationship between law and standards and, secondly, enforcement.

In researching the former issue, the Committee examined experience in Australia and Canada, two countries which had started with the UK model but moved away from it. In Australia, a separate body incorporated accounting standards into statute, shorn of explanatory material, and expressed in legal language. In Canada, the various Provinces required compliance with the accounting standards of the Accounting Profession. Members showed a preference for the Canadian solution because it avoided the trap of excessively legalistic standards.

On enforcement, the problem was not so much overt non-compliance with standards as the fact that the same firm of auditors would interpret a standard differently in what were essentially the same circumstances. There was widespread agreement that the existing criminal offence of failing to give a true and fair view was too blunt an instrument to be effective. The UK lacked an institution with the range of sanctions available to the SEC in the US, which could target the directors rather than the company itself. There was, however, one critical change in the law that the Committee felt able to recommend. In court proceedings over whether accounts gave a true and fair view the onus of proof should lie with the company to show that they did, notwithstanding that it had not complied with an accounting standard.

On sanctions, the Dearing Report was essentially pragmatic. It urged the investment institutions to bring their influence to bear in challenging doubtful accounting practices and pressed the CCAB bodies to enquire into the behaviour of their members both in industry and public practice.

It was later, in the drafting of the 1989 Companies Act, that the court was given the power to order that costs of a successful prosecution and recirculation of accounts be borne by such of the directors as were responsible for the defective accounts, although the recommendation on burden of proof was not implemented.

The Report, submitted in September and published in November 1988, bore the hallmarks of Sir Ron's pragmatic but effective approach to administrative reform, and he was appointed by the Department of Trade and

Industry (DTI) to oversee the implementation of his proposals (apart from a few minor details). This led to the creation of the ASB in 1990, its legal status being confirmed by amendments to the law by the Companies Act, 1989.

The Dearing system was designed to preserve private sector regulation, with its greater adaptability to new circumstances and problems (such as creative accounting) than could be provided by direct legislation. It sought to avoid the lack of authority that had plagued the ASC and to remove the vestiges of professional self-regulation. Independence from the accounting profession (each ASC standard had to be approved by each of the six CCAB professional bodies) was considered necessary for the new ASB to command respect, so the private sector was defined as being the full range of users and preparers of financial statements. The new body required greater legal support than that of the ASC. It also required greater resources supported by an income that was not wholly dependent on professional bodies, being derived from three separate sources, the Government, the financial community, and the accountancy profession.

These desirable properties were achieved by setting up a two-tier framework, which bore a formal resemblance to the system already in place in the US, although the UK system did not have the legal authority of the SEC to support its standards. At the top of the system was the Financial Reporting Council (FRC), which was responsible for financing, appointing, and overseeing the ASB's long-term programme, but not for intervening in its day-to-day operations. The Chairman of the FRC was to be appointed jointly by the Governor of the Bank of England and the Secretary of State for Trade and Industry, and the part-time members were to be drawn from a wide range of constituencies concerned with the preparation and use of accounts, e.g. the first council included the general secretary of a trade union. The ASB would set standards, without recourse to the FRC for approval. It was to have not more than nine members, including a full-time technical director and chairman and up to seven part-time members. All ASB members would be paid (unlike members of the ASC), and they would be supported by a full-time technical staff. The ASB would have a subsidiary committee, the Urgent Issues Task Force (UITF), which was to develop prompt guidance on the application of standards where conflicting interpretations or novel problems might seem to be emerging.

Thus, the new ASB would have greater independence and be better resourced than its predecessor. It would also have greater legal authority. The Dearing proposal was that accounting standards, issued by a body approved by the Secretary of State, should be recognised by company law, and departures from standards should be reported and explained. This was implemented by the 1989 Companies Act, and the ASB was subsequently recognised as the approved body. Compliance with the standards was not explicitly deemed to be necessary for accounts to give a "true and fair view", as required by the Act, but it would be authoritative evidence and strong contrary evidence would be required to over-rule the standards. Enforcement of the standards would be provided by the Financial Reporting Review Panel, a separate offshoot of the FRC which had the power to investigate cases of non-compliance. If the Review Panel found unjustified or unexplained non-compliance with accounting standards, the reporting company would be asked to issue corrected accounts, and if it failed to do this the Review Panel could take the company to Court on the ground that the accounts did not show a true and fair view. The Dearing proposal that the burden of proof should lie with the company was not adopted, but if the Court did find that the accounts were not 'true and fair', it could require the directors of the company to issue revised accounts at their own personal expense. The latter was possibly the most ingenious and effective innovation of the new arrangements. Placing the financial burden of non-compliance on the directors (who are the signatories of the accounts), rather than the deeper pocket of the company, proved to be an effective deterrent to non-compliance. During the first decade of the ASB's existence, with which we are concerned, all of the companies that received adverse findings from the Review Panel chose to issue revised accounts, at the company's expense, rather than contesting the ruling by going to Court and risking an order to re-issue at the directors' expense.

The new system was put in place in 1990, with Sir Ron Dearing as the first Chairman of the FRC, responsible for overseeing the system which he had devised and created. He was later (1996) succeeded by Sir Sydney Lipworth, a distinguished businessman, lawyer, and former Chairman of the Monopolies and Mergers Commission. The first Chairman of the ASB was David Tweedie, former Senior Technical Partner of the leading audit firm KPMG and Chairman of the Auditing Practices Committee (APC). He remained in post until he became Chairman of the newly formed International Accounting Standards Board (IASB) in 2001, and this is the period covered by this book. The Technical Director of the ASB was Allan Cook (formerly of Shell and the ASC) who remained in office until 2003 when his participation as a founder member in the expanding work programme of EFRAG caused him to step down from that office. He moved to the IASB in 2005. The third of our discussants, Geoffrey Whittington, was Academic Advisor to the ASB (attending all Board meetings) from its inception and subsequently a part-time Board member (from 1994). At the time of his appointment, he was Price Waterhouse Professor of Financial Accounting at the University of Cambridge. Appendix Table A1 lists all board members who served in the first decade of the ASB.

The new Board inherited the problems of creative accounting, and these were reflected in the work-in-progress that it inherited from the ASC, notably in the Exposure Draft ED49, *Reporting the substance of transactions in assets and liabilities*, which addressed a range of off-balance sheet schemes. It also inherited an exhortation from the Dearing Committee to set principles-based standards, and this would require a statement of principles, or conceptual framework, to provide the necessary frame of reference. The Solomons Guidelines (1989) provided one model for such a framework, and the incomplete FASB conceptual framework and the briefer IASC framework (largely derived from the FASB's work) provided practical examples, and perhaps warnings of the difficulties, of such frameworks. The ASB could not afford the luxury of developing its conceptual framework before commencing to set standards. Rather, the two developed side by side, and the Statement of Principles (as the conceptual framework was described) was eventually completed and published in December 1999.

Another challenge for the ASB was to engage constructively with the IASC, which, as mentioned above, was changing the emphasis of international accounting standards to be more prescriptive and less permissive, increasing the danger of conflict with national standards, but also increasing the possibility of a useful international language of accounting. From the beginning, the ASB worked closely with the IASC and David Tweedie was appointed one of the two UK and Irish representatives on the Committee in 1995. The ASB also became a member of the 'G4+1' group of national standard setters from Australia, Canada, the UK, and the US plus the IASC (the +1) and latterly New Zealand, which produced research and discussion papers on topics of common interest. Moreover, the new ASB standards contained statements of their compatibility with IASC standards.

One of the first acts of the ASB was to adopt the extant standards of the ASC (known as Statements of Standard Accounting Practice, or SSAPs). Subsequently, many of these were revised or completely replaced, and some completely new standards (known as Financial Reporting Standards, or FRSs) were developed. The ASC's current programme of work was selectively continued, notably that on ED49 (1990), which provided the foundation for FRS5. New projects were added, and by the end of the first ten years, many of the hopes of 1990 were fulfilled, although a changing world means that the standard-setter's work is never completed. The main body of the ASB's output up to December 2000 is contained in the ASB publication, *Accounting Standards* 2001/2002.

As stated earlier, our objective is not to provide a complete account or evaluation of the work of the ASB in its first decade, but to record our recollections of how certain standards, which we consider to be particularly interesting or important, developed. Chapter 2 sets the scene by providing recollections of the period in which the ASB was established. Each of the following chapters is devoted to one or a group of the selected standards. A brief introductory section provides the context of each standard and this is followed by a discussion between the three former ASB members, mediated by Geoff Meeks.

**Geoffrey Whittington**

## References

### *Books and articles*

Cohen Committee Report. (1945). *Report of the Committee on Company Law*, Board of Trade, Cmnd 6659.

Dearing Report (1988). *The Making of Accounting Standards*, London: ICAEW.

Edwards, J.R. (2019). *A History of Corporate Financial Reporting in Britain*, New York and London: Routledge.
Galbraith, J.K. (1967). *The New Industrial State*, Boston: Houghton Mifflin.
Griffiths, I. (1986). *Creative Accounting*, London: Unwin.
Hoffman, L. and Arden, M. (1983). *Joint Legal Opinion on 'True and Fair'*, London: ASC.
ICAEW (1942). Accounting principles, *The Accountant*, 107, 354.
Marris, R. (1964). *The Economic Theory of Managerial Capitalism*, London: Macmillan.
Meeks, G. (1977). *Disappointing Marriage. A study of the Gains from Merger*, Cambridge: Cambridge University Press.
Royal Mail Case (1931). Rex v. Lord Kylsant and another. 1 KB, 442.
Rutherford, B. (2007). *Financial Reporting in the UK: A History of the Accounting Standards Committee, 1969–1990*, London: Routledge.
Sandilands Report (1975). *Inflation Accounting: Report of the Inflation Accounting Committee under the Chairmanship of F. E. P. Sandilands,* Cmnd.6225, London: HMSO.
Singh, A. (1971). *Take-overs*, Cambridge: Cambridge University Press.
Skerratt, L. and Tonkin, D. (eds.) (1989). *Financial Reporting 1988–89: A Survey of UK Reporting Practice*, London: ICAEW.
Smith, T. (1992). *Accounting for Growth* (First edition), London: Century, Random House.
Solomons Report. (1989). *Guidelines for Financial Reporting*, London: ICAEW.
Stamp, E. (1969). 'Auditing the Auditors'. *The Times*. 11 September 1969.
Stamp, E. and Marley, C. (1970). *Accounting Principles and the City Code*, London: Butterworth.
Tweedie, D. and Whittington, G. (1990). Financial reporting: Current problems and their implications for systematic reform, *Accounting and Business Research*, 21, 87–102.
Watts Report (1981). *Setting Accounting Standards: Report of a Committee Chaired by T.R. Watts*, London: ASC.
Zeff, S. (Ed.). (2009). *Principles Before Standards: The ICAEW's 'N' Series of Recommendations on Accounting Principles 1942–1969*, London: ICAEW.

#### *Statutes and standard setters' publications*

Companies Act (1844). *Joint Stock Companies Act*, 7&8 Vict., c. 110.
Companies Act (1855). *Limited Liability Act*, 18&19 Vict., c. 133.
Companies Act (1948). *Companies Act*, 11&12 Geo, c.110.
Companies Act (1967). *Companies Act*, c.81.
Companies Act (1989). *Companies Act*, c.40.
ED8 (1973). *Accounting for Changes in the Purchasing Power of Money*, London: ASSC.
ED49 (1990). *Reflecting the Substance of Transactions in Assets and Liabilities*, London: ASC.
PSSAP7 (1974). *Accounting for Changes in the Purchasing Power of* Money, London: ASSC.
SSAP16 (1980). *Statement of Standard Accounting Practice No. 16, Current Cost Accounting*, London: ASC.

# 2 Getting started

## Interviewer's note

*Chapter 1 provided an* *<u>impersonal</u>* *review of publicly available information on the genesis of the new, reforming ASB – an approach repeated in the short scene-setting introductions to later chapters. But this chapter and the main part of later chapters approach the topic from a very different angle: they are unashamedly* *<u>personal</u>*. *As Chapter 1 indicated, they aim to convey what it was like for the people who embarked on a ten-year reform campaign to clarify standards and to combat misinformation being included in company accounts – to the detriment of capital market efficiency and effective corporate governance. The points of view and experiences of members of the Board are reported in their own words, and in conversation with one another. They discuss the efforts to achieve the independence normally associated with a public body detached from special interest groups at the same time as securing the expertise and buy-in of a private regulator peopled by regulatees. They reflect on the gulf between the aspirations of lawyers and those of accountants. And they illustrate the tension between, on the one hand, the short-term financial interest of some executives (and their investment bankers and even their auditors) in being economical with the truth in their accounts, and, on the other, the honesty and transparency which are prerequisites of efficient markets and of effective monitoring of managers' stewardship of complex businesses.*

*The trio of conversationalists are Allan Cook (**AVC**), David Tweedie (**DPT**), and Geoffrey Whittington (**GW**). Geoff Meeks (**GM**) poses the questions. One of the trio takes the lead in some chapters. In this chapter, it is David Tweedie.*

**GM. David, before you chaired the ASB you had been Senior Technical Partner at a top accounting firm, KPMG. What problems had the prevailing standard-setting regime presented for you in that role?**

**DPT** I think our major problem was that we didn't feel that we had a lot of backing from the standards. There was this absolute obsession from the analysts with the bottom line and the gearing ratio, and because of that the investment banks in particular were producing all sorts of schemes to try to manipulate both of them favourably for the company. Our big problem was that lawyers like Mary Arden (see, for example, her legal Opinion 1993 and Hoffman and Arden 1983) were saying that 'true and fair' is ambulatory:

DOI: 10.4324/9781003346920-2

what was true and fair yesterday isn't necessarily true and fair today, and what it consists of is the accounting standards, the law (probably the other way around knowing Mary), and accepted practice. And the trouble with accepted practice was, what did that mean? And how it came to be interpreted was, well, if a couple of the big audit firms had accepted some appalling scheme, then if you were the third one, you couldn't do anything about it: you couldn't qualify because that was the accepted practice at the time. And what would then happen is: this scheme would become the accepted base; the investment banks would make it even worse by adding bells and whistles, and then find another two auditors to accept the new version. And then suddenly we're on this downward slope which we christened the 'creeping crumple'. That was from my point of view, as a technical partner. Allan, did you have problems in industry?

**AVC** I didn't have direct experience of the creeping crumple because the primary concern at group level of both the two large multinationals for whom I worked in the 1970s and 1980s was to have high quality accounting standards that enabled them to communicate with their global investors. However, in the late 1980s, while I was chairing the ASC's Working Party on Off-Balance Sheet Finance, a man from one of my company's subsidiaries came to see me with a scheme that was being proposed to him by an investment bank. I forget the details but remember that it was a blatant attempt to disguise the real effect of the transaction. I told him that Group Finance would not accept it. He returned a week or two later with the same scheme tweaked a little. Again I said 'No go'. He was disappointed but evidently not enough, because he came back yet another time with still more tweaks that did nothing to change the essential nature of the misrepresentation. That incident showed me just how hard the banks were working to sell their schemes.

**DPT** The real problem we had as auditors was, there was huge pressure to accept the client's interpretation. People were threatening with opinion shopping, changing auditors, getting a legal opinion, and the lawyers were right in on this at that stage. I was shocked quite honestly when I came down from Edinburgh with T McL (Thomson McLintock) and we became part of KPMG. The schemes in London were quite different from the ones we had experienced in TMcL but quite frankly I thought the TMcL partners were tougher than the Peats partners. We used to call them the Mandarins and the Samurai: the Mandarins were the professionals and the Samurai were the guys who had to keep the clients sweet and get the new jobs in. And I think you were probably rewarded more by being a Samurai than you were being a Mandarin. And if you look at the individual partners, the senior partners probably had two big clients each. Well, you lose one of those and your value to the firm is questioned. So there's huge pressure not to lose a client, and that led to all sorts of things. I remember saying that what was immoral in Edinburgh was frowned upon in the Midlands and was damned good business in the City of London.

I remember vividly being confronted with an outrageous scheme, and when I saw this thing, the investment bankers said, well, two auditors have already accepted it – one was EY and the other one was Deloittes. So I phoned up Ron Paterson and Matthew Patient who were the respective technical partners. Ron said, "I think I'd better put you in touch with the audit partner", which is instant code for, "I've been over-ruled"; and the audit partner and I had a very frosty conversation. Matthew was outraged. He had heard nothing about it. The scheme had been accepted without even bringing it to him. We were faced with a scheme that had been accepted by two major audit firms. I remember going to the Senior Partners saying, "Look, we could actually for once take a high profile moral position and denounce the scheme and say we're not accepting it". This was agreed and we were working on the press release; and then one of the partners there said, "Oh, this is like the scheme I had with my client a week ago". And we said, "What do you mean 'like it'? Is it the same one?" And he goes away and checks, and he came back confirming that it was the same scheme, and I said, "Well. Did we accept it?" And he said "Yes". And several of the partners present said, "Well, that's that then". And I remember saying, "Wait a minute, we've made one mistake – let's not make any more; let's try and kill this thing". And this partner turned around to me and said, "Whose side are you on?" And I said, "Ours, whose side are you on?" And we never spoke again.

And the other aspect – I remember investment bankers, they were so cocky and there was one guy in my room with this off-balance sheet scheme going through it, and I refused to accept it; and he just looked at me and smiled and said, "You'll never stop us". I must admit that really was the incentive to stick it to them.

**AVC** As Geoff mentions in Chapter 1, the widespread use of creative accounting had prompted the publication of a number of books highlighting the abuses. One, in particular, Terry Smith's Accounting for Growth (published in 1992 but preceded by earlier papers by the author) was particularly opportune for the ASB. It included a matrix in which the accounting scams discussed in the book were listed on one axis and companies that had used them listed on the other, with one or more blobs to indicate which they had used. The chart became known as 'Blob Analysis'. I well remember one of the ASB's members, the Finance Director of a well-known company, recounting to us with a gleam in his eye how the word on the Finance Director circuit was that, if your company had eight out of the possible 12 blobs, the Chairman called you in and demanded to know what on earth was going on; however, if you had only four, he still called you in and asked "Why are we not keeping up with the competition?"

**DPT** I think it all came to a crisis when we had this major confrontation with the lawyers. ICAEW produced TR603 (1985) which was a release on Off Balance Sheet Financing and Window Dressing. And instantly there was opposition from the Law Society. They argued that substituting substance over form was dangerous and undesirable, and more importantly they considered that what was proposed was contrary to the law. So there was an absolute direct threat there. They argued that actually just giving extra information, even if the accounts were rubbish, was perfectly OK:

> it is essential to reduce to the minimum the element of subjectivity in the preparation of accounts and, accordingly, to have as much objectivity as possible, especially in relation to the basic items included in those accounts. The analysis of the legal position in relation to such items as assets and liabilities provides the best available basis for such objectivity. Such an analysis provides a clear point of reference: a subjective evaluation of the "economic" or "real" effect of the transaction does not. Such an evaluation involves not merely changing the points of reference but replacing them with vague ones whose meaning and effect is subjective and uncertain. We think therefore that the wish expressed by the Release to substitute substance for form is a dangerous and undesirable one. More importantly (since views about the philosophy of accounting differ) we consider that…what is proposed is contrary to the law.
>
> (The Law Society, 1986)

Their argument was basically that the legal position should be shown in the accounts and any deficiency in showing a true and fair view could be dealt with by note disclosure. At the time, Rosehaugh gave a vivid example of the extent of the disclosures it was possible to give – whether it was meaningful was a different question. Under an eight-page note entitled 'fixed asset investments' it dealt with 50% companies, options to purchase, interests in US partnerships, and details of their trading. It would be impossible for an outsider to understand.

How on Earth do you make adjustments to the accounts for that sort of thing?

What I felt was important was: who controls 'true and fair'? Was it the lawyers or was it the accountants? And my view is that it was us. True and fair was required by law. We had to show a true and fair view, and I didn't think the way we were doing it was right and the lawyers weren't helping. It was interesting that the FT picked up the dispute. Their editorial said (August 1987):

> The argument over off-balance sheet finance has demonstrated the frailty of the accountants' 'true and fair' concept in the face of the determined defence by the legal profession of rigid statutes and the opportunistic exploitation of artificial schemes by merchant banks.

This followed a debate between myself and John Kellas on one side and Ralph Aldwinckle on the other in Accountancy (Aldwinckle, 1987; Tweedie and Kellas, 1987, 1988).

The FT gathered what was going on. And I think my reaction was partly in my training. I had been apprenticed as a CA student to David Flint, Professor

David Flint, in Glasgow; and he is author of two papers on 'true and fair' (Flint, 1980, 1982). Having been brought up with him – you didn't have to have ethics courses – it just dripped onto you. I felt very strongly about a fair presentation. David's view was that true and fair was actually the break-away from the restrictions of the law. I used to liken it to: directors have to paint a picture of the position, and if the painting doesn't reflect what they know about the position, they've got to go back to their canvas and keep doing it until it is a proper likeness. I remember saying at the time, what you can't do is: give the outsider pots of paint, brushes, and a set of instructions, and say, go on you do it and produce the accounts. But that seemed to be what the lawyers were asking for. A do-it-yourself kit. And that, I felt, was absolutely awful and I was totally opposed to the legal position.

David's view (not surprisingly) expressed perfectly what I believed:

> Whatever may be the extent of prescription, an overriding requirement to give a 'true and fair view' is at the lowest level of its utility, a safety valve protecting users from bias, inadequacy or deficiency in the rules, a fail-safe device for the unavoidable shortcomings of prescription. However, its greater utility is in establishing an enduring conceptual standard for disclosure in accounting and reporting to ensure there is always relevant disclosure- where necessary beyond the prescription- based on independent professional judgment.
>
> (Flint, 1982)

**AVC** I would endorse that distinction between the safety valve and the positive functions of the True & Fair requirement – though I think it goes beyond disclosure.

**DPT** David was not talking simply about note disclosure – he meant presentation in the financial statements.

**AVC** The true and fair concept was often disparaged outside Europe as a kind of "Get out of Jail free" card, enabling a company to ignore any standards that it wished. The Review Panel put a stop to that in the UK. But in fact the primary requirement is positive: the first duty of directors in presenting accounts is to give a true and fair view of the state of affairs and performance of the company. That surely rules out artificial schemes designed to obfuscate rather than enlighten.

**GM That's set the scene. How were you appointed? And what were you looking for in your new Board members?**

**DPT** Well, I remember the head-hunter saying to me, "would you go and have a word with Ron Dearing[1] and tell him what you think the new ASB should do?". I had been denouncing these various schemes at conferences for two or three years so I was really quite fired up when I went in there; and it was only halfway through that discussion that I realised it was an interview for the Chairman's job, details of which are reproduced below. And, I must admit, I was surprised, as so many others were, when I was appointed

> *The Job*
>
> *Chairman, Accounting Standards Board*
>
> *Duties*
>
> *Appointed by, and within the broad policy guidance of the FRC, of which he [sic!] will be a member, this person will be responsible for the effective management of the ASB within a budget provided by the FRC. He will define and staff the organisation and effect a handover from the Accounting Standards Committee. Thereafter, he will gain acceptance of formal plans and implement agreed plans in line with policy. Tasks of the ASB will include reviewing critically present standards and practices, defining terms and standards sought, and after appropriate consultation, issue standards. He will maintain senior level contacts with all interested parties, and internationally, promoting the Board's aims and gaining feedback to ensure the standards meet the policy guidance of the FRC. He will plan, recruit and train his subordinates to achieve long-term objectives.*
>
> *The person*
>
> *Age: 45–56*
>
> *Qualifications: Qualified accountant, likely graduate.*
>
> *Experience: Must have first class reputation recognised widely as an outstanding member of the Accountancy profession and, preferably, also in the corporate sector. Likely to have spent a considerable period in the profession, tackling complex technical problems and contributing to the debate on standards and technical matters at Institute meetings and in the wider forum.*
>
> *Personality: Analytical, resourceful, diplomatic, but creative accountant, with first class communications and administrative skills. Must be intellectually very strong, with the ability to solve complex problems, but also a good planner and team leader. Must have the personality, technical competence and stature to relate well at senior level in the profession, the public and corporate arena and earn the respect of senior colleagues. Must be effective in the international arena; ability in one of the other main European languages would be an advantage. Must have the drive, determination, and stamina to achieve a demanding workload.*

Chairman because we all thought it would be a "steady as you go person" – "let's continue the work of the ASC and just move in that direction", whereas I wanted to change things.

The other full-time appointment was a technical director, and Ron asked, "have you any ideas who you want?" I knew exactly who I wanted. And I remember saying, I'd like Allan [Cook], and Ron said, "you shall have him, my boy". I remember those words vividly. He didn't ask Allan: Allan was just going to be conscripted.

**AVC** That is certainly the impression he gave me when I went to see him. Along with many others I had been interviewed by Hamish Kidd, the Head

Hunter. Some weeks after that Hamish put me in touch with David, so that by the time I saw Ron I had a pretty good idea of how David saw the work to be done. But the meeting with Ron seemed quite different from a typical final interview. He made no attempt to probe my previous experience as a means of testing my suitability for the job. And he took it for granted that I would accept.

**GW** That's an incredible change from the way things are done now. It shows how regulation has changed. In the post Nolan period you couldn't possibly appoint somebody like that – well, you could express a preference, probably in private – but officially you're supposed to advertise publicly and fill lots of forms out. And then if Allan applies, you must say, "I mustn't comment on him because I actually know something about him". That's a conflict of interest. It's interesting that regulation too has changed in similar ways – you know, the move towards the tickbox process as opposed to the essence of what you're doing: an emphasis on due process and perhaps form over substance.

**DPT** It was interesting because I think Allan and I were opposites. I recall that in the personality test that TMcL gave us, having to choose between the words 'spire' or 'foundation', I chose 'spire'. (If you look at the ASB logo, reproduced on the cover of this book, you'll notice it incorporates the spire – no accident). I always thought, and, Allan, maybe I'm wrong, that Allan would have taken 'foundation'. Would you Allan?

**AVC** I think you are right, though, like you, I had an intense desire to see UK accounting standard setting given the resources to do the sort of work I had seen at close hand in my encounters with the FASB.

**DPT** Allan is very rigorous and meticulous. No one has ever accused me of being patient: you know, I just wanted to get on with it, and Allan would make sure that I wouldn't completely expose myself. He would make sure every case was carefully built up, so he was perfect. And then came suggestions about who else to include. I wanted technical partners on board (Roger Munson (Coopers) and Graham Stacy (Price Waterhouse) were chosen). I wanted Geoff on board from the beginning. But Bryan Carsberg had been nominated, and I think Ron Dearing thought, well, there's Professor Carsberg; and my honorary title of professor which he didn't want me to use, not even Dr. He didn't want this to look too academic, but to seem practical. So Geoff became initially the Board's academic adviser.

Ron wanted the senior partner from one of the big audit firms and Elwyn Eilledge of EY joined us. And then I think the others came from the CBI, the two industrialists, Donald Main (Forte) and Michael Garner (TI Group); the analyst – Bob Bradfield from Cazenove nominated, I believe, by the Society of Investment Analysts

I think the members other than Allan and I were selected by Ron Dearing and the three Vice-chairmen: the President of the ICAEW who was also Chairman of the CCAB, the Chairman of the Stock Exchange, and the

President of the CBI. The DTI (Department of Trade and Industry) sat in on the Board as an observer – that was Sarah Brown. Sarah was very worried that I had an absolute antagonism towards lawyers (she wasn't far wrong). I remember her trying to calm me down, to get me to make peace with them. But I thought they should make peace with me.

Ron was just full of energy. And I saw that when we wanted to get started, and needed to get accommodation. Once we'd got accommodation we could get under way. Some civil servants suggested we stay at the DTI. Well, Ron was having none of this – he wanted us to be seen to be independent. I remember being at the DTI with Ron and a civil servant – the phone went – it was the estate agent saying they'd got this office in Holborn Hall, but it had got this and this and this wrong with it. The civil servant was sounding doubtful saying, before we could consider it you'd better get this fixed, you'd better get that fixed. And Ron just got up from the table, and took the phone, and said, "we'll take it". He put the phone down, and that was the end of that. We were in Holborn Hall. That was Ron: just get on with it.

That was the basis of it, getting the thing started – and the fact that the Board met on two days a month so we could really motor. (ASC only met for a morning each month.) The fact that such senior, and very busy, members of the profession were prepared to give up so much time indicated how important they felt our mission was.

We had nothing but support from board members throughout my time on the ASB. They were all committed and of extremely high calibre. The fact that the ASB could attract such talent and that their employers were willing to allow them to spend so much time with us reflects on the determination of the financial community to clean up British financial reporting. Original members were replaced with equally enthusiastic successors, namely, senior partner: Ian Brindle (Price Waterhouse); technical partners: Ken Wild (Touche Ross), Ray Hinton, and Isobel Sharp (Arthur Andersen); industrialists: John Coombe (Glaxo Welcome), David Allvey (BAT), John Buchanan (BP) and Richard Goeltz (Nat West); analyst: Huw Jones (Prudential). Like the original board members, they were determined to root out bad practice and improve British accounting, and, with the support of their firms, tackled the issues with steely determination. While we had fierce arguments, the atmosphere in our meetings was friendly, collaborative and constructive. We had great colleagues.

**GM So you'd got the people and somewhere to work. What was your personal diagnosis of the problems with the previous standard-setting regime?**

**DPT** Well, I think the Dearing Committee picked them up really well.

First, there was no conceptual framework, which meant that you had various groups working on the standards for the ASC with different ideas about accounting and therefore coming up with conflicting theories, so the standards didn't mesh too well. We were pretty keen to fix that.

That there were too many options in the standards. They stayed with us for a bit because IASC was also in that position. The old IASC used to accept the British position, the American position and one or two others; so there were several options in their standards. They started removing them, and that instantly put pressure on the British to start doing the same. Why should we be different?

There was delay. ASC members were part-timers. But the worst thing was the fact that authority was dispersed. It wasn't just the ASC. They would come up with a standard, but then all six UK and Irish accounting institutes had to agree it. So if one of them didn't agree, the whole thing ground to a halt while whatever changes had to be made got fixed.

The creeping crumple was active – the problem with the lawyers, and so on, which we couldn't stop.

The pressures I mentioned on the auditors – great pressures to accept a device, otherwise you might lose the client.

And, of course, companies were very concerned about being taken over, or taking over. So they wanted the best possible results.

So all these were there. And the ASC did not have the authority to deal with them.

**AVC** The nadir for the Profession's inability to enforce its own standards was perhaps when a British company seeking to file its accounts with the SEC was required to amend them because they had not been prepared in accordance with an accepted body of standards. The company had thought that reconciliation to US standards was sufficient but the SEC obliged it to amend the original accounts to comply with UK standards.

**GM Your predecessor standard-setters at the ASC – some very able people – had been humiliated over inflation accounting, and the investment bankers were making hay by circumventing the rules with creative accounting which was consistent with the law. Given that background, how did you aim to establish credibility for the new regime?**

**AVC** You are right, Geoff, to say that the ASC contained some very able people – the Technical Partners from four of the top accounting firms, plus Michael Renshall, its Chairman, from a fifth. What is interesting is to see how the advent of the ASB cast its shadow before it, emboldening the ASC to undertake some of its most productive work. The Dearing Report was published in November 1988 and the CCAB immediately instructed Michael Renshall to press ahead to provide its successor with as complete a body of standards and exposure drafts as it could within the, at that date unknown, time available. It responded well, finalising one standard and ten exposure drafts. And it did not shy away from tough proposals. By keeping issues alive, as in Accounting for Cash Flows or Accounting for the Substance of Transactions, the ASC pointed the way ahead and slowed or discouraged the adoption of accounting devices that were likely to be banned in the foreseeable future. The ASB benefited from that even when its own solutions differed and when hard fought battles lay ahead.

**DPT** Well, I think one of the things that we did almost instantly was to show that we were prepared to attack. We weren't going to try to get involved in some major theory, like inflation accounting, which was all-consuming. We didn't start off with a conceptual framework. Some people said you must, whatever you do, write a conceptual framework and then do the standards. Well, it took us about eight or nine years to finish the framework; so we would all have been fired long before for doing nothing. So what we did really is, we attacked what we thought was wrong. And I think that was quite popular, to be honest. What was wrong and what was deliberately misleading. Geoff, Allan and I had been discussing these issues for years.

**GW** But it is important to say that we developed an informal conceptual framework in our first Board meetings. We had inherited very similar suggested frameworks from the Solomons Guidelines (1988) and the ICAS (1988) study, Making Corporate Reports Valuable, which in turn drew on the earlier FASB and IASC frameworks. Moreover, David and I had written a paper in 1989 (published in 1990: Tweedie and Whittington (1990)) which surveyed the worst current abuses of financial accounting and identified their common characteristics which a framework would have to deal with if it were to lead to effective standards. Our informal framework was a broad consensus based on this earlier work, with the ultimate aim of achieving transparency and comparability in accounting information. Subsequently, we developed our framework (the Statement of Principles) in parallel with the standards, a good early example being FRS 3, discussed in the next chapter. Hence, the early 'quick kills', although tactically important (to make an impressive initial impact) were also part of a longer term strategy to improve financial reporting in the direction indicated by the Dearing Report.

**DPT** The three elements – bodies that are mentioned in Chapter 1 (the ASB itself, the Taskforce, and the Review Panel) really all hit the ground running.

The first blow was struck by the Emerging Issues Taskforce that Ron Dearing talked about – we didn't feel the name was desperate enough for our times, so we changed it to "Urgent". And we wanted to distinguish it from the US one which dealt with some pretty tiny issues – sometimes I didn't even understand the title of the American Taskforce's problems, never mind the proposed accounting. But we picked up three of the major issues that were causing a lot of upset.

The first, Abstract 1, aimed at the supplemental interest or premiums that people paid on convertible bonds. And what they would do is, show some low level of cash payments in the profit and loss account, knowing that at the end there was going to be a big lump sum to be paid to the bondholder. Well, we made them bring that all in so that it was accrued all the way through.

And it had been a case of "not in my backyard", let's get big profits this year, and deal (or rather let our successors deal) with the premium in the future.

The second Abstract considered restructuring costs, which companies all stuck in extraordinary items – and we'll come onto this when we deal with FRS3 in the next chapter – they put those below the so-called bottom line profit figure. And we disallowed that: we insisted that such costs should come up above the line.

And the third one – (which was outrageous – well, they're all outrageous) – was, we had this ridiculous policy in British accounting of writing off purchased goodwill to reserves. So if you bought a business for 100, including goodwill of say 60 – that goodwill disappears off to reserves. You've got assets in the balance sheet of 40. Then you sell the business for 45. So you've made a huge loss of 55, while – no, no – the accounts show a profit of 5 (45 – the sales figure less 40 net assets). And that was just unacceptable, so that got bombed out in Number 3. The loss (55) had to be shown.

The key to it all was that Ron and I went around to the Senior Partners of all the major audit firms. Ron was great at this. We told them very bluntly that we would not set up this task force unless they backed it. And by backing, they had to put somebody sufficiently senior on the Taskforce who would bind the firm: the firm would accept whatever the decision was. And they wouldn't second guess it when their representative got back to the office. There were 15 people (not only auditors) on the Task Force and to get anything through not more than two present at the meeting could be against it.[2] And what it did was, it used precedent against the investment banks. So there may have been some practice out there, but here's a new practice, accepted by everybody, and there it is. So it killed off the schemes that were already there. We started working through them, knocking them out. But it was Ron getting the audit firms lined up – otherwise, we were not even going to create the Taskforce. And that was huge.

The next thing was Polly Peck. It became an FTSE100 company in 1989. It collapsed in October 1990 (Smith, 1996). There was a huge furore about it. I remember Ron being summoned to a major television debate on the future of accounting. We'd only been going three or four months. And I was summoned to another television programme: "What are you going to do about this? Accounting's a shambles". And we were very lucky because the ASC had been working on cash flow reporting, and we grabbed their exposure draft. We could actually put out our first standard requiring a cash flow statement (FRS1 – ASB 1991) fairly quickly. The effect it had was striking – Polly Peck was a wonderful example. We were able to show that the operating profit according to Polly Peck was £120million; the funds flow statement that they had in those days showed positive funds flow of £172 million. FRS1 would have shown the cash flow from operations was minus £129 million. And what had happened is they'd increased stock, they'd increased debtors, creditors had decreased – all of which increased funds, but all decreased cash. And the company just ran out of cash. So the profits were questionable. And the cash flow statement would have shown it.

It was a bit like the old ASC when it started. It needed a quick win, and it grabbed the ICAEW's proposed recommendation on associated companies and made it SSAP1 (ASC, 1971; see Tweedie, 1981). We were very lucky we had the ASC exposure draft available, and we were fortunate in a way that Polly Peck blew up so we could demonstrate that the ASB would be improving accounting.

Well, the third leg was the Review Panel. And we've mentioned before the brilliant idea of bringing in the Review Panel. It got off to an interesting start because the Companies Act 1989 had recently required that you had to state in your accounts that you had complied with accounting standards; and I think several companies and their auditors were a bit slow in putting that on their disclosure checklist. And the next thing is the Review Panel fires off goodness knows how many letters – ferocious, you know, about the penalties which could be imposed – because the company hadn't obeyed the law. I think it caused general panic because, apart from transportation to Australia and execution, everything else was on this list. It really made people aware that they were being watched.

And then we had Trafalgar House. We picked this up in the Lex column of the FT, which said this was "British financial engineering at its finest". That set off all the alarm bells. We called in the accounts, and the Review Panel consisting of senior finance directors, auditors, lawyers, analysts, with plenty of grey hair and wrinkles, tore the company's report apart. Eventually, what Trafalgar House had as profits of over £122 million was turned into a loss of £30 million. And the main reason for that was that they had current assets which they suddenly redesignated as fixed assets and revalued them downwards so the loss went through reserves (as a revaluation) rather than going through the P&L account. And they were absolutely shot to pieces. Within a year the Chairman, Chief Executive, and auditors had all gone (Hamilton, 1993).

The press loved it, and it really set the Review Panel on its way. The interesting thing about it was, as we mentioned in the first chapter: no one queried the Panel or challenged it. Trafalgar House thought about it, and backed off. And I think it was probably because the press would have enjoyed a court case at the company's expense. It would have run for several days; they would have been slaughtered in the press, who thought this was appalling accounting anyway. And as a lawyer would say to them: you'll win on a legal technicality if you win at all; but your peers have judged your accounts not to give a true and fair view. And that is damning. And so we never had an issue over that. So that's how it worked.

So three bodies – each of them got an early win.

**GM At first sight, I would have thought the FASB regime in the US – backed by the mighty and longstanding SEC – would have**

**much more power and autonomy than your ASB. But when it came to one of the big challenges of the time, later on, making acquirers' executives accountable for the vast sums they were spending on purchased goodwill, although both FASB and ASB wanted the same outcome – incorporating amortisation – it was ASB who succeeded: you secured your standard, which carried on for several years. By contrast, "the persistent lobbying of the FASB by way of Congress succeeded in persuading the Board to reconsider" (Zeff, 2002; also Beresford, 2001): amortisation was dropped, leaving impairment alone to reflect the depletion of goodwill. How was it that your arrangements secured consent when what appeared to be a more powerful alternative failed?**

**GW** Perhaps you overestimate the independence and power of the SEC, which is subject to political influence. The FRC/ASB system had greater potential for bringing all stakeholder groups together in the common interest. Ron had a great sense of how the politics work, the law, the institutions and the interactions between them. And he designed the whole system as a sort of not public, not private body, with representation from various interest groups.

He had a very good sense of how to keep it independent and, at the same time, keep it owned by the people who were using it – which is one of the big tensions now with the Kingman Report (2018). Kingman describes the FRC as an institution from a past era, which has done its job in its time but is now irrelevant. This may describe the current FRC, with its 'add-ons' of regulating auditors, actuaries, and corporate governance, and the changed corporate structure of the FRC, but it does not describe the original Dearing structure. And what Kingman has proposed, which I think is the weakest part of his Report, is some sort of new QUANGO with wide powers and responsibilities but little stakeholder involvement. This runs the risk of becoming a body which is incapable of understanding and reconciling the various needs of stakeholders and is instead subject to political influence: possibly a bit like the SEC.

In a way, Ron's ingenious system made it much easier for the ASB to enforce things because it's based on consensus. You can see the importance of securing consensus in the current COVID-19 crisis. What is essential in a regulatory system is to get consent because you can't put a policeman behind everybody to ensure they stay 2 m away from everybody else. People have to consent to regulation in this case because they see common benefits, just as with accounting. As David's been describing, the majority with law-abiding instincts – 'the good guys' – had to see enough "in it for them" (in terms of capital market confidence etc.) to encourage them to behave properly and for the bad guys to be seen to be bad guys by comparison. The bad guys don't like that because they'd get a bad reputation, so they go along and pretend to be good guys, even though at heart they'd like to be swindling everybody because they don't like it to be out in the open: it's bad for business. Regulation by consent was a necessary principle: you got everybody on board as members of the FRC and through committee memberships and consultations. And that's something that Kingman entirely misses.

**DPT** That fits very well with what I felt too. Basically we set out seeking consent – to get the 100 Group (of finance directors) on board, the technical partners on board, and the analysts on side, with separate meetings. If we got all three of those we had a fair chance of getting the standard through. We didn't always make it, but that was the way we approached it. It was so much more difficult with IASB because that happened in every blooming country. The other aspect was that we used the press. And we didn't meet in the open (a "sunshine policy"). I find that strange now but we didn't. We debated it. I remember Bryan Carsberg arguing against Graham Stacy, and Bryan said "he who is against sunshine is against life itself". Graham just snorted and said, "sunshine gives you melanoma". Graham's argument prevailed because, unlike the future IASB, we were a mainly part-time board and the auditors especially did not feel they could condemn publicly practices used by their own clients – though they certainly did in the closed board meetings! So we never met in the open. In a way that was quite interesting because we ended up always publishing on a Thursday because that was the 'accounting day', when the major national newspapers had accounting columns in their business sections. And, of course, we gave our publication to the correspondents a couple of days in advance; we showed them why we were doing what was proposed coupled with examples of usually bad practice. They loved it, and so we got on very well with the press. And I think that was a big success too. The press were very supportive to us.

**GM You've explained that you were at odds with those executives indulging in creative accounting, and the investment bankers and lawyers advising them. Did you encounter no opposition from within the accounting profession in the early years of the ASB?**

**DPT** Well, the opposition came in 1996, shortly after I'd been re-appointed. It came out of the blue as far as we were concerned, in a paper from Ernst and Young (1996) which went around to all the major companies in the UK. This was shortly after the publication of the Exposure Draft of the Statement of Principles. And there were three essential themes to the attack. They pushed, if you like, the right buttons.

The first was that we were too academic. They said: "ASB had a rather academic agenda of its own…Accounting, traditionally the language of business, is at risk of being taken over by the rhetoric of theorists…We do not believe that the ASB should use British industry as a test bed for academic theories of accounting, and we question whether it has a mandate to do so". So it was fairly aggressive. You could understand Ron Dearing's concern about us looking academic. He obviously anticipated that something like this might happen.

The second point was that 'the ASB's vision of accounting is based on a simple economic model that involves measuring movements in a company's wealth from one year end to the next'. The paper had a rather simplistic example to say that what we really wanted to do was to measure the value of one balance sheet relative to the other, and it looked like – the way that they showed it – the profit and loss account was really just a note to the difference between two current value balance sheets. And when you think what we did in FRS3, which was already published by that time, when we really emphasised the profit and loss account, I found that very strange.

And the third issue was – and this was quite a subtle one – they said that we rejected historical cost accounting, which has been the basis of British accounts forever, and "unless the business community expresses disagreements, some version of current cost accounting will soon be with us once again". That would then light the blue touch paper: stand back! Geoff and I wrote a book on inflation accounting (Tweedie and Whittington, 1984), so we were well aware of the unpopularity of such a policy. And, interestingly enough, we got shoals of letters complaining about going back to CCA, which – Allan, you probably know better than I do – we never discussed at the Board. We even got one from Keymer and Haslam who had led the attack on the CCA exposure draft ED18, and really got CCA stopped. And I remember I wrote back to them saying we'd never discussed CCA, and it wasn't on the agenda; and I got a very gracious letter back from them, saying thanks very much: in that case, they would just stop their campaigning against us, and go and attack the European Union, or the Euro – I can't remember which.

They were all the right buttons – academic, current values, getting rid of the P&L account. And I was furious. I mean Krakatoic rather than furious. You know, I'm not very good at turning the other cheek. I'm really more of the "let's all end up blind and toothless brigade". Ron Dearing always said I'd cross a motorway for a fight. The FT phoned me up. I'd just read the document. Steam was coming out of my ears. They asked, "what do you think of it?" I came out with the view that it had all the vision of a mole and the eloquence of a whoopee cushion. And that quote went everywhere. In fact, Ron Paterson's wife even had a tie made showing a little mole with a miner's helmet with a beam of light coming out of it. But it wasn't personal. In fact, Ron and I still exchange Christmas cards. We get on well.

But I felt it was a caricature of what we were proposing. And it did cause us a lot of problems. Conference organisers loved it. They used to invite Ron Paterson, as EY's technical partner and an author of the paper, and me to keep coming back. And Ron exaggerated our position. And I created a straw man of his, and set fire to it. And I remember I used to say Ron doesn't understand that a debit equals a credit. If you have a debit, it would be either an asset or an expense. But with Ron there was a third option; and that's a whatsit. And a whatsit was an expense you didn't want to go through the profit and loss account, so you stuck it on the balance sheet. The same with credits. And even worse, I said, Ron has a concept known as a 'gleam in the eye'. And that can create a provision – if you want one. And it looks prudent in the balance sheet, but in fact it's profit manipulation. So we had great fun at these conferences rubbishing each other. And it all culminated in the AAA Conference, where I was asked to give the lunchtime speech. At this time I was still enraged with what I saw as the unfairness of Ernst and Young. And I threw in the line that if you've half a mind to join Ernst and Young, you're over-equipped. Ernst and Young in America took great exception to this, and the Conference President came along and said the Senior Partner was sending along a partner to tick me off about it. So this guy duly appeared, and he started saying how it was like a nuclear weapon going off in the national office when they had heard what I said. I was really steamed up, and I said, do you know what you guys have done to us? So I got stuck into him, and eventually I said, tell you what, get your Senior Partner to write to me with his problems – and the one in the UK – get him to write as well. I'll do a reply. Let's publish them. And Jim Leisenring of the FASB, who had been passing and was never one not to pour oil on a fire, turned to this partner and said, 'Do you get the impression, feller, this guy doesn't give a shit?'

No, it was interesting, but it was strange. I was a bit taken aback. I felt it was unfair. I didn't mind criticism, because Ron has a different view of accounting, and he's entitled to it. But I thought it was grossly overstated, and in lurid terms which did cause us a problem. The FASB was equally outraged – after all our Statement of Principles was related to their Conceptual Framework – and FASB members and staff, principally Jim Leisenring and Reed Storey, even wrote to the UK press in support of the ASB and were constantly defending our position.

**GW** It was a totally unnecessary argument because we weren't actually abolishing the profit and loss account. When we get to FRS3, we'll see that we were actually trying to enhance it. All we were trying to do was make it consistent with the balance sheet. I always used to compare that debate with the Gulliver's Travels debate between the Lilliputians where they had a war between the bigendians and the littleendians – the people who struck their boiled egg from the broad end or the narrow end: from which end did you prefer to go into the boiled egg? And the boiled egg was the accounts. We started off – like everybody did – with the profit and loss account – but we linked it to the balance sheet. If Ron Paterson was trying to defend anything, it was trying to have a totally detached balance sheet. When you talk about whatsits, surely you are accruing in the profit and loss account. The debit there is going to be an asset of some sort, not a whatsit. And asset or not is going to determine whether it's a sound entry in the profit and loss.

**AVC** Exactly. We protected the profit and loss account from manipulation by insisting that only assets and liabilities could go on the balance sheet. If a transaction did not result in an amount that met our definitions of assets and liabilities it would be either an expense or income. I do think that was the whole issue really. Our starting point was: be clear about what is an asset, what is a liability. That's almost an auditing tool, isn't it? It gives you verifiability

**GW** Yes, and deeply conservative and traditional in the way Ron kept advocating.

**AVC** Ron would make the point that, of course, we build up accounts from transactions. How do you do that? You link your expenses to the revenues that you've gained.

That sounds reasonable and it works well for the majority of transactions. But for some complex and usually very material activities, such as restructuring a line of business, it was used to justify quite subjective representations of what happened in the period. In order to get the profit and loss account to show what management felt was a fair allocation of expenses to revenues, they had to shut their eyes to the effect on the balance sheet.

**GW** I expect that what we did was transactions *and events*; and events included re-measurements. I expect that's where we differ. And they were afraid of re-measurements in the form of current cost accounting, but this was a mistaken view because traditional accounting also allows re-measurements. For example, take straightforward re-measurement– revaluation of a fixed asset which gives rise to credit for appreciation. For us, the credit would go into the STRGL (Statement of Total Recognised Gains and Losses). And critics say, "you are including this imaginary gain in the broader measure of profit. There's no transaction there; it's only an event, revaluation". I think that's where the difference was. But it's not a huge difference because, in practice, both systems allow revaluation and the corresponding credit should be disclosed. The difference is in whether the credit is included in a broad measure of profit (total recognised gains) or, as Ron Paterson would prefer, credited direct to reserves and explained in a note.

**AVC** As you say, we didn't really change the profit and loss account at all. We just added something else, and said, by the way, this is also something that you need to look at to understand what has happened in the period.

**GW** And in a sense we did it deliberately – we didn't degrade, but we de-emphasised the bottom line because we gave a lot more disaggregation – you know, continuing, discontinuing, all that stuff, and tagging the exceptional items onto particular line items. It was a much richer information set, but, of course, it was not a single number that you are going to put into a p/e ratio to value the whole company. We didn't believe in that, but I think if you'd stuck him against the wall and made him pronounce on the issue, I don't think Ron would have believed in that either. I don't think any sensible accountant would believe that you can capture the whole of performance in one number.

**GM Looking ahead, the standards you will discuss at length in this book are just a subset of those produced in your time at the ASB. Why have you chosen to highlight this particular subset?**

**GW** The first we chose – I think we all agreed on this – was FRS3, which is Reporting Financial Performance. This was a great standard from many points of view – in my view our first big standard. You know, the first, on cash flow replacing funds flow didn't have the same impact, and the other one was implementing Companies Act changes in consolidated accounts. This was our first big go at dealing with creative accounting, and it dealt with a very important problem – income smoothing basically, particularly extraordinary and exceptional items. And it got pretty wide support from the constituency for that reason. People perfectly understood why we were doing it. But in a way also it was quite a revolutionary standard in terms of the fundamental framework. We didn't have a conceptual framework at the time. We broadly adopted something that resembled the American or the International framework. But we were developing our ideas at the same time as developing new standards, and this was a very important stage because we went for this information set approach, saying that the bottom line was not the key objective of financial reporting. It was instead giving people useful information, and letting the punters do the valuation of the company, not the accountant. That was a very fundamental theoretical underpinning, as well as a practical thing for stopping creative accounting. It ticked both boxes: it dealt with an urgent issue but was also a conceptual advance. Also it got through remarkably quickly really – for a new body to do it within just over two years of starting a major change like that. It did of course stir up Ernst and Young a bit: that was one of the issues that they were grumbling about.

I think all those standards we are looking at to some extent fit those two criteria. They had a big practical impact, stopping existing, well-known malpractice. They also, though, did advance accounting in a more fundamental way. They had a good theoretical underpinning. And they stood the test of time, all of them. They had, I think, a good impact on the world. My other favourite is FRS17, which is at the other end of our time period: it appeared right at the end of the ten years. And the reason I like that particularly is that it was a very conceptual standard; it was based on our Statement of Principles (as an academic I like that); but also it addressed a really important practical problem, and it had a huge effect on the way people look at defined benefit pensions. I had to go to Scotland, to debate with the President of the Faculty of Actuaries whether FRS17 ruined defined benefit pension schemes. And I put the case – I won the debate on the vote, by the way, which surprised me – that it made people aware of an impending disaster. And it made them aware in time to at least mitigate the effects of the disaster because these schemes were in deficit, and our existing accounting wasn't showing it. Of course, FRS17 did, and it got people alarmed; but it also got them putting extra contributions into the schemes, or re-jigging the schemes, so that people didn't discover that there was nothing in the fund only when they retired. It gave them time to put things straight. So that's why I like FRS17. But I leave it to the others to talk about the other standards we chose. They all fulfil my basic criteria.

**AVC** I think all the ones we chose were chosen because they did the most to restore the quality of financial reporting. One of the most interesting was FRS5, Reporting the Substance of Transactions. I say that because for the previous five years all three of us had been involved in fighting that particular battle – the conflict between: do you represent the substance of a transaction, or do you represent its legal form? But it is interesting that we were all three involved – David fighting on the front line; David and Geoff debating those issues and writing articles about it; and I because I was involved first of all in the ICAEW's working party that started off the challenge, and then in the two Exposure Drafts of the Accounting Standards Committee. FRS5 and all the exposure drafts that preceded it depended heavily on the definitions of assets and liabilities. Similarly, our standard on Capital Instruments FRS4 depended on the definition of liabilities. And again that dependence was carried through into others of our Standards: FRS7, which dealt with the fair values on an acquisition, and later on, FRS12 on provisions. It was those tools from the Statement of Principles that transformed our ability to resolve important practical issues.

**GM That's great, thank you. David, anything to add?**

**DPT** Not really, the ones we've included that weren't mentioned were related to what Allan has just said – that's goodwill and impairment. I thought that acquisition accounting was one of the biggest scams in British accounting. It was complete manipulation and three or four standards dealt with it – the provisioning Standards, and so on. That's why they are in the group.

**GM Thinking of your work agenda, the Dearing Committee had recommended that the ASB start work on a conceptual framework. That appeared only in 1999. Does that mean you thought a conceptual framework could sit on the back burner?**

**AVC** Hardly that! You have to remember that a lot of work on concepts had already been done – pioneering work by the FASB, almost as soon as it started work in 1973; then a much slimmer version by the IASC. So there wasn't the urgency of the initial spadework on it. We had to decide how we would pitch our own statement, because the FASB's was very, very detailed and published in individual chapters. We decided that we would work on it in tandem with specific projects. Those projects were essentially testing the ideas and enabled us to come up with refinements of some of the work that had been done by others. So it was important to us and, as I think we've already illustrated, it embedded itself case by case.

**GM I think that encapsulates it, doesn't it? Any other comments on this?**

**GW** The only thing I'd add is that the gap in the FASB framework was measurement, and we did try to fill that – we had a lot of discussion of deprival value, I seem to remember – and that's one of the things that stirred up Ernst and Young. The one area where we tried to go much beyond the framework work of the FASB was in measurement.

**GM So shall we have a go at a last, personal, question? David, what were the risks for you personally in taking this big step and leaving your home in KPMG?**

**DPT** Well the risk was that I was 45, the contract was three years, and it might not work. What did I do next, especially if we failed? I'd given up a partnership with excellent financial prospects for an uncertain future.

The reason I did it was that I had found the whole reporting process demeaning. There I was, the Technical Partner of a big firm. Things were happening that I absolutely loathed and hated. The firm wasn't doing much about it. All the technical partners felt the same way. Nobody was fighting. At least, the technical partners were, but the firms weren't. So it made you very angry. My feeling was that it was setting accounting back 80 years to about 1910 the way it was going on, which was awful. And the auditors were just crumbling. It was just the chance to fix it, and this was what we should be doing. I remember when we did the Aldwinckle articles: one of the partners said, you shouldn't be writing this; some of my clients are doing these things. They shouldn't be, I retorted. That was what forced me into it.

I remember Ron Dearing – we had only been going about six months – came and said, well, that's all running, I'm off. And I said, wait a minute, Ron, I've just given up this partnership; we've got to make sure we get it through. And good old Ron – you know, he wasn't a wealthy man, and he gave up two major directorships (I think they were the NCB and ICI), just so he would have the time to deal with this. He was a lovely man to deal with. He eventually extended my term to five years and then reappointed me.

That was the risk, and Allan must have had exactly the same sort of concerns since you were coming out of Shell.

**AVC** Well, yes. Some jobs in Shell lasted forever. But I think Shell had already moved into a position where that wasn't happening anymore. But I did have a very interesting job there. It involved me in quite a lot of outside developments on accounting standards, at the ASC, the FASB, the IASC – also the OECD. I was involved in working parties and advisory groups on all of those. So I was pretty well plugged into what was going on in accounting developments – not only their importance to Shell but also for financial reporting generally at that time. But for ten years, I'd been longing to see improvements in the quality of accounting standard-setting, the resources given to it in the UK; and so, really, this was an offer one couldn't refuse.

**DPT** I remember what clinched it for me: Ron went to the Senior Partner of KPMG and asked if they could approach me to do it. And the Senior Partner called me in. And I remember during that discussion he said, "David, you've either got to do this or you've got to shut up". That made it very easy: I took the job (Figure 2.1).

*Figure 2.1* The Chairman is installed – *The Scotsman*, March 1991, by kind permission of the artist, Graham High.

## Notes

1 Ronald Ernest Dearing, Baron Dearing CB, 1930–2009, senior civil servant, Chairman and CE of the Post Office, Chair of, inter alia, the Accounting Standards Review Committee, the Financial Reporting Council, and the National Committee of Inquiry into Higher Education. His admirers report his saying "There will be problems, of course, but they will be solved"; and Lord Baker noted: 'When it came to the stage of having a chauffeur and a car, he used to drive the chauffeur home himself and pick him up again in the morning"!

2 Unless the consensus conflicted with the law, accounting standards, or the Board's policy or plans, the Board would expect it to be regarded as accepted practice in the area in question...and considered it to be part of practices forming the basis for what determines a true and fair view.

## References

### *Books and articles*

Aldwinckle, R. (1987), Off-balance sheet finance – the legal view, *Accountancy*, June, 99(1126), 19–20.

Arden, M. (1993). *Accounting Standards Board – The True and Fair Requirement, Appendix to Foreword to Accounting Standards*, London: ASB.

Beresford, D. (2001). Congress looks at accounting for business combinations, *Accounting Horizons*, 15(1), 73–86.

Dearing, R. (1988). *The Making of Accounting Standards: Report of the Review Committee Under the Chairmanship of Sir Ron Dearing CB*, London: ICAEW.

Ernst and Young. (1996). *The ASB's Framework – Time to Decide,* London: Ernst and Young.

Flint, D. (1980). The significance of the standard True and Fair View, 1980 Invitation Research Lecture, New Zealand Society of Accountants.

Flint, D. (1982). *A True and Fair View*, Edinburgh: ICAS, 1982.

Hamilton, K. (1993). The maverick analyst who went to war with the City and won. *Sunday Times*, 14 November 1993.

Hoffman, L. and Arden, M. (1983). Legal opinion obtained by Accounting Standards Committee of True and Fair View, with particular reference to the role of accounting standards (13 September 1983), https://www.frc.org.uk/frc/t-f-opinion.

ICAEW. (1985). *Off-balance Sheet Financing and Window-dressing, TR603*, London: ICAEW.

ICAS. (1988). (Ed. McMonnies P) *Making Corporate Reports Valuable*, London: Kogan Page.

Kingman Report (2018). *Independent Review of the Financial Reporting Council (FRC)*, London: HMSO.

Law Society. (1986). *Off Balance Sheet Financing and Window Dressing*, London: The Law Society.

Smith, T. (1996). *Accounting for Growth: Stripping the Camouflage from Company Accounts* (Second edition), London: Century.

Solomons, D. (1988). *Guidelines for Financial Reporting Standards,* London: ICAEW.

Tweedie, D. (1981). Standards, objectives and the corporate report, in Stamp, E. and Leach, R. (eds.) *British Accounting Standards, The First 10 Years*, Cambridge: Woodhead-Faulkner.

Tweedie, D.P. and Kellas, J. (1987). Off Balance Sheet Financing. *Accountancy*, April, 99(1124), 91–95.

Tweedie, D.P. and Kellas, J. (1988). Setting the accountants' record straight. *Accountancy*, January, 19–20.

Tweedie, D.P. and Whittington, G. (1984). *The Debate on Inflation Accounting*, Cambridge: Cambridge University Press.

Tweedie, D.P. and Whittington, G. (1990). Financial Reporting: current problems and their implications for systematic reform. *Accounting and Business Research*, 21, 87–102.

Zeff, S.A. (2002). "Political" lobbying on proposed standards: a challenge to the IASB. *Accounting Horizons*, 16(1), 43–54.

### *Standard setters' publications*

FRS1 (1991). Cash flow statements, ASB.

FRS3 (1992). Reporting financial performance, ASB.

FRS4 (1993). Capital instruments, ASB.

FRS5 (1994). Reporting the substance of transactions, ASB.

FRS12 (1998). Provisions, contingent liabilities and contingent assets, ASB.

FRS17 (2005). Retirement benefits, ASB.

SSAP1 (1971). Accounting for the Results of Associated Companies, ASC.

UITF Abstract 1 Convertible bonds-supplemental interest/premium, ASB.

UITF Abstract 2 Restructuring costs, ASB.

UITF Abstract 3 Treatment of goodwill on disposal of a business, ASB.

# 3 Reporting financial performance

## Introduction

Reporting Financial Performance was one of the first projects adopted by the ASB, in 1990, and the subject of its first exposure draft (FRED1, 1991). The project concluded with a standard, FRS3 (1992), which made radical changes to the presentation of financial statements which have become an enduring feature of financial reporting. It made an important contribution to the development of the ASB's conceptual framework (finally published as the *Statement of Principles*, 1999) by rejecting the 'bottom line' approach to measuring financial performance. Rather than focusing on a single 'bottom line' measure of income, it was based on the assumption that all sources of gain or loss are potentially relevant to financial performance, but each component will have a different weight which will change according to the circumstances and the purpose of the evaluation. Therefore, it restructured the income statement, increasing its transparency and information content by providing dis-aggregated information, and added the new primary statement, the Statement of Total Recognised Gains and Losses, known as the STRGL. The system was completed by a reconciliation of the STRGL total to movements in shareholders' funds in the balance sheet over the same period. Additional transparency was provided by a note reconciling reported profit to historical cost profit: this would improve the transparency of the effect of discretionary revaluations on inter-company comparisons.

The objective of this system was to meet both of the primary requirements of financial reporting: stewardship and decision usefulness.

Stewardship is concerned with assessing the past performance of management. This was much improved by the improved detail in the profit and loss account, disclosing the sources of income and expense, for example by separating out the contribution of newly acquired operations. Such profits should not be included in comparisons with the previous year's performance of the continuing business in assessments of the management's stewardship. The STRGL further enhanced stewardship by disclosing gains and losses (particularly losses) which might otherwise be hidden in obscure footnotes, and the reconciliation to movements in shareholders' funds provided full articulation

DOI: 10.4324/9781003346920-3

between the income statement and the balance sheet, thus ensuring that the alert reader of accounts would be able to detect any attempts to use reserve accounting to inflate reported gains by charging 'bad news' losses direct to reserves rather than to the income statement. The only example of the latter which was permitted by accounting standards when FRS3 was issued (1992) was the practice of writing off purchased goodwill direct to reserves. This substantial loophole (which appears in Table 3c) was subsequently closed by the ASB's FRS10 (1996).

Decision usefulness is concerned with the use of financial reports to decision-makers, typically investors who are making buy, hold or sell decisions. These require future-oriented information that will enable them to assess the future economic returns (often characterised as cash flows) of the business. FRS 3 sought to provide such information by its disaggregation of income, expenses, gains, and losses, each of which might be given a different weight in predicting future returns. For example, it separated out income from operations discontinued during the period: clearly these would not feature in an assessment of future returns.

FRS3 improved both decision usefulness and stewardship by clarifying the definition and reporting of exceptional and extraordinary items. Clearly, for predictive purposes, it is potentially useful to know which income or expense is exceptional (unlikely to continue at that amount) or extraordinary (outside the usual scope of the business). These disclosures were allowed by the ASC's existing standard (SSAP6, revised 1986), but the standard had been abused by creative accountants. It required exceptional items to be disclosed separately but included within the operating profit because they were a part of the outcome of normal business operations. Extraordinary items, on the other hand, were reported separately from operating profits because they were not part of the usual operations of the business. This well-intentioned distinction was, unfortunately, not sufficiently supported by tight definitions. Provisions for restructuring the business became a favoured device of creative accountants, who treated them as extraordinary, which, in a different sense, they often were: Smith (1996) gives the example of RHM Ltd. which made an 'extraordinary' provision for expected closure costs in each year from 1984 to 1991, averaging 22% of post-tax profits. The 'extraordinary' charge avoided the headline profit figure, whereas the future write-back, when the alleged 'restructuring' occurred, would reduce the costs charged to profit. In general, there was an incentive to abuse the classification system so that gains tended to appear as normal profit (as exceptional items), whereas losses were more often reported below the 'bottom line' profit as extraordinary items. FRS3 sought to remedy this: exceptional items were defined broadly to include, for example, restructuring costs, and most continued to be reported with their 'ordinary' counterpart in operating profit. Fundamental restructuring costs (of sufficient materiality to change the focus of the whole business) were to be reported separately (together with gains and losses on disposal of fixed assets and gains or losses on discontinued operations) below operating profit but before profit on ordinary activities. The definition of 'extraordinary' was tightened and narrowed to such an extent that reporting such an item would be extremely rare and would attract unusual (even extraordinary) attention from users of accounts.

The abuse of the 'extraordinary' classification made FRS3 one of the urgent projects that the ASB inherited from the ASC. Indeed, it was so urgent that it was the subject of an early pronouncement by the newly formed Urgent Issues Task Force (UITF2, 1990). However, FRS3 was much more than a 'fix' of a creative accounting problem. As indicated earlier, it represented a fundamental change in the conceptual framework which has lasted beyond the life of the ASB and the boundaries of the UK and Ireland. This will be amplified in the final section of this introduction, after an illustration of the FRS3 system.

## An illustration

The following numerical example in Table 3.1 is taken from FRS3 (1992). The multi-column format has been chosen for the profit and loss account in Table 3.1 because it shows more clearly the FRS3 dis-aggregation of acquired, continuing, and discontinued operations. The notes providing further disaggregation of expenses (as required by the Companies Act) are not shown here. The realised gains and losses displayed between Operating Profit (£51 million in 1993) and Profit on Ordinary Activities (£63 million) might previously (under SSAP6) have been classified as 'extraordinary' and therefore not included in Profit on Ordinary Activities.

The comparative figures for the prior year are restated and the details reported in a note; this was intended to improve inter-year comparisons.

The requirement to calculate earnings per share on a standard basis was also a requirement of FRS3. It was intended to improve inter-company comparison of this ratio, which was widely used by investors. Alternative calculations could be presented additionally, but with a reconciliation to the standard measure.

The example in Table 3.2 shows how the Statement of Total Recognised Gains and Losses (STRGL) adds other gains and losses (due to re-measurement of assets and liabilities) to profit for the year (£29 million, the bottom line of the Profit and Loss Account) to yield a Comprehensive Income measure ('Total Gains and Losses', £28 million). Comprehensive income is an all-inclusive measure, including all forms of recognised gain or loss to shareholders. It is therefore equal to the change in shareholders' interest between the opening and closing balance sheet, adjusted for capital transactions (distributions to shareholders, less capital contributions from shareholders, and any losses written off direct to reserve). This relationship is shown in the Reconciliation of Movements in Shareholders' Funds, reproduced in Table 3.3.

Note that the direct write-off of Goodwill to reserves (£25 million) was subsequently prohibited by FRS10 (1997). This example illustrates how a direct write-off could have insulated reported income against large expenses or losses.

*Table 3.1* Profit and loss example (from FRS3)

| | Continuing operations 1993 £mn | Acquisitions 1993 £mn | Discontinued operations 1993 £mn | Total 1993 £mn | Total 1992 As restated £mn |
|---|---|---|---|---|---|
| Turnover | 550 | 50 | 175 | 775 | 690 |
| Cost of sales | (415) | (40) | (165) | (620) | (555) |
| Gross profit | 135 | 10 | 10 | 155 | 135 |
| Net operating expenses | (85) | (4) | (25) | (114) | (83) |
| Less 1992 provision | | | 10 | 10 | |
| Operating profit | 50 | 6 | (5) | 51 | 52 |
| Profit on sale of properties | 9 | | | 9 | 6 |
| Provision for loss on operations to be discontinued | | | | | (30) |
| Loss on disposal of discontinued Operations | | | (17) | (17) | |
| Less 1992 provision | | | 20 | 20 | |
| Profit on ordinary activities before Interest | 59 | 6 | (2) | 63 | 28 |
| Interest payable | | | | (18) | (15) |
| Profit on ordinary activities before Taxation | | | | 45 | 13 |
| Tax on profit on ordinary activities | | | | (14) | (4) |

(*Continued*)

*Table 3.1* Continued

| | | |
|---|---|---|
| Profit on ordinary activities after | | |
| Taxation | 31 | 9 |
| Minority interests | (2) | (2) |
| Profit before extraordinary items | 29 | 7 |
| Extraordinary items (included only to show positioning) | – | – |
| Profit for the financial year | 29 | 7 |
| Dividends | (8) | (1) |
| Retained profit for the financial year | 21 | 6 |
| **Earnings per share** | **39p** | **10p** |
| Adjustments | Xp | Xp |
| Adjusted earnings per share | Yp | Yp |

Source: FRS3, reprinted in Wilkins (2000), p.423.

*Table 3.2* Statement of total recognised gains and losses (from FRS3)

| | 1993<br>£mn | 1992<br>As restated<br>£mn |
|---|---|---|
| Profit for the financial year | 29 | 7 |
| Unrealised surplus on revaluation of properties | 4 | 6 |
| Unrealised (loss)/gain on trade investment | (3) | 7 |
| | 30 | 20 |
| Currency translation differences on foreign currency net investments | (2) | 5 |
| Total recognised gains and losses relating to the year | 28 | 25 |
| Prior year adjustment | (10) | |
| Total gains and losses recognised since last annual report | 18 | |

Source: FRS3, reprinted in Wilkins (2000), p.424.

*Table 3.3* Reconciliation of movements in shareholders' funds (from FRS3)

| | 1993<br>£mn | 1992<br>As restated<br>£mn |
|---|---|---|
| Profit for the financial year | 29 | 7 |
| Dividends | (8) | (1) |
| | 21 | 6 |
| Other recognised gains and losses relating to the year (net) | (1) | 18 |
| New share capital subscribed | 20 | 1 |
| Goodwill written off* | (25) | |
| Net addition to shareholders' funds | 15 | 25 |
| Opening shareholders' funds (originally £375 mn before deducting prior year adjustment of £10 mn) | 365 | 340 |
| Closing shareholders' funds | 380 | 365 |

* Editor's Note: FRS 10 does not now (2000) permit goodwill to be written off directly to reserves, but it did not require prior year figures (such as 1993) to be restated.

Source: FRS3, reprinted in Wilkins (2000), p.426.

The detailed movements in reserves and the Note of Historical Cost Profits and Losses are not reproduced here.

## FRS3 in context

FRS3 was an innovative standard whose principal features have stood the test of time. However, it was a product of its time, and credit must be given to its precursors. The Statement of Gains had its origins in the earlier academic work on inflation accounting, such as Sweeney (1936), and was elaborated by Edwards and Bell (1961). It was also adopted by practical policy makers. For example, in the UK the Sandilands Committee (1975) proposed a statement of Gains which would include current cost profits and holding gains. In the US, the FASB embraced the idea of comprehensive income in its conceptual framework project (SFAC6, 1985) and this was followed in the IASC's conceptual framework (1989), as well as other influential pronouncements, such as the Solomons Report (1989) and the ICAS report, Making Corporate Reports Valuable (1988), both of which were addressed to UK standards setters. These reports all based their advocacy of comprehensive income on the 'all inclusive' view that all items of gain and loss have potential relevance in predicting the future economic returns of the entity. This was supported theoretically by the informational approach to financial reporting, pioneered by Beaver and Demski (1979) in the US, which asserts that, in a (realistic) world of imperfect and incomplete markets, such measures as the value of a whole firm or the amount of its profit are ill-defined. In such a world, the role of the accountant is not to produce 'bottom line' profit measures which capture precisely, in a single number, the total performance of a business, or measures of shareholders' funds which capture precisely the value of the share capital. Rather, the appraisal of performance and the valuation of the business are done by investors in the market, and the accountant's role is to provide them with information which they find useful. FRS3 provided improved information to meet such needs. In developing FRS3, the ASB was making conceptual assumptions which were subsequently incorporated in its conceptual framework (the Statement of Principles, 1999). Because of the urgency of dealing with the problems outlined in the previous chapters, the ASB had to develop the conceptual framework whilst working on new standards: it could not afford the luxury of completing its new framework before commencing standard-setting.

In view of this explanation of the foundations of FRS3's comprehensive income approach, it is ironic that it was attacked, particularly by supporters of the traditional 'matching' approach to income measurement, such as Ernst and Young's Ron Paterson, on the ground that it adopted a 'balance sheet' approach, emphasising the balance sheet to the detriment of the profit and loss account. The improved transparency and information content of the FRS3 system was intended to improve the utility of the profit and loss account, so it might seem odd to characterise this as a balance sheet approach. However, comprehensive income, as measured in the STRGL, did include items of gain and loss reflecting re-valuations of balance sheet items which were previously regarded as outside the scope of profit and loss. The Paterson et al. approach laid great emphasis on a measure of profit or earnings which could be used as a 'bottom line' measure for assessing the performance or value of the whole business (e.g. in calculating price/earnings ratios). It assumed that the gains and losses in the STRGL (and some that FRS3 required to be in the profit and loss account) were non-recurring and would hide underlying profitability. It therefore supported the traditional 'matching' approach to profit measurement and rejected (or was unaware of) the information approach on which FRS3 was based. Its weakness was that it was based on belief rather than empirical evidence, whereas the information approach has been supported by much empirical research in the past half century, particularly that inspired by the work of James Ohlson (1995), who developed share valuation models based on comprehensive income and its components (see Cascino et al., 2013 for an accessible survey). Beaver (1989) provides a comprehensive account of the 'accounting revolution' resulting from the information approach).

However, even Paterson and his colleagues recognised that FRS3 represented a significant forward step in financial reporting:

> FRS3 represented a radical new approach to the reporting of financial performance. Contrary to first appearances, it was much more than a mere exercise in the reformatting of the profit and loss account and introduction of additional analysis of reserve movements; it significantly changed the rules of recognition and measurement in respect of many aspects of a company's performance, including discontinued operations, extraordinary and exceptional items and provisions.
>
> (Davies et al. 1997)

FRS3 was followed by an American standard (FAS130, 1995) which adopted the same comprehensive income framework, but was less stringent in its requirements (e.g. a primary statement like the STRGL was not required), and international standards developed on similar lines. Thus, the innovative approach of FRS3 has, hitherto, stood the test of time.

## Geoffrey Whittington

***Conversation**: Cook **(AVC),** Tweedie (**DPT**), and Whittington **(GW)***
*Meeks **(GM)** asks questions; **Dog Tweedie** interrupts*

### *Aims*

**GM David, what were you trying to do with FRS3? What was the problem?**

**DPT** Our aims were threefold: to create a more forward looking income statement by separating continuing and discontinued activities; to ensure that reserve accounting by-passing the income statement would not remain hidden; and to remove the abuse of the extraordinary item which enabled charges to be omitted from the bottom line calculation. The bottom line was like a haggis: if you knew what was in it, you wouldn't touch it with a barge pole. Yet people seemed to think it was so important: both Griffiths (1986) and Smith (1996) pointed out how a few financial institutions used to run the City and determine the prices, and Ian Hay Davison (at the time Chairman of one of these institutions) is quoted as saying that every morning at 0830 the analysts got together and decided their buy/sell/hold recommendations and the key feature affecting these recommendations was earnings per share, which, of course, is based on the bottom line. So it was absolutely huge this bottom line, and what we were trying to do, I think, is become more forward-looking, so that the income statement would be more decision-useful. Any reserve accounting was now going to be brought into what is now the Statement of Total Recognised Gains and Losses (STRGL), so it wouldn't be hidden in the notes, it would be clearly visible. And, thirdly, the abuse of the extraordinary item had to be ended. And that was a huge issue because there were so many different views about extraordinary items. SSAP6 had been revised. The definition was not very different from the one we eventually used; but the interpretation of the definition varied partly due to the examples of extraordinary items given. The Midland Bank, for example, announced that in their interim accounts, they would take a huge sovereign debt loss as an extraordinary item. Nobody else did: losses on loans would normally be part of the ordinary business, hardly extraordinary. And in fact, they fell in line once all the other banks deemed the losses to be exceptional. House of Fraser took surpluses on the sale of properties and fixed asset investments into extraordinary whereas Debenhams treated them as exceptional. Who else was there? Vickers and Lonrho charged relocation costs as extraordinary, whereas the standard actually said that they had to be above the line. There was just general mayhem going on. There was a lovely example: CASE took a one-off £2 million gain on the sale of a US property as exceptional. That helped it diminish its loss. And then they brought in other things such as tax credits for the losses they expected to have. They hadn't even had them yet. And there was a lovely quote by Griffiths from The Times that said "The CASE interim profit and loss account has been constructed with all the finesse of a bulldozer. The accounting is so creative that it probably merits a grant from the Arts Council." And this was the sort of thing that was going on.

Griffiths has a wonderful tale about how this all operates. He said that it was called 'Try it on the Chairman' – the finance director goes to the chairman and says, "we've got this division that's made this huge loss", and the chairman would say "how extraordinary", so that was that answer. And then he'd go back, "we've got this other one that's made this big gain", and the chairman would say, "What an exceptional performance. Let's hope they keep it up". I used to say the definition really was, "if it's a debit, it's extraordinary and if it's a credit, it's exceptional". And the whole thing was out of control.

### *The economic rationale for the reform*

**GM Pursuing the rationale for FRS3, I wonder what view the Board was taking (explicitly or implicitly) of the Efficient Market Hypothesis which is so often quoted in financial analyses? I'm thinking of the more modest 'semi-strong' form: share prices reflect all publicly available information.**

**GW** What FRS3 was really about was giving people more information as my introduction indicates. The whole object of FRS3 was to break things down and to try and get transparency and show people what was going on rather than focusing on one single, sort of magic, number. Now that is basically consistent with the efficient markets approach, because the efficient markets approach also says that the market takes information from lots of different sources, not just from the accounts. And within the accounts, it can give different weight to different bits. And I think where the Board and I would differ from the efficient markets view is that we wouldn't consider that market efficiency was a perfect thing. But, of course, neither did a lot of followers of the efficient markets school. So what we were really trying to do was to improve the information for the market. The efficient market didn't work as well as some people of the Chicago School would have believed. If you asked the finance directors on the Board, I'm sure they would have said that analysts could be misled by certain accounting presentations, contrary to the predictions of the Efficient Markets Hypothesis. Of course, the ones done by their competitors, not the sort of thing they would do! After all, the fact that people did all this creative accounting demonstrates that they thought they could somehow fool the market.

So, we were consistent with the efficient markets hypothesis, but we weren't believers in perfect efficiency by any means. I'm sure most of the Board were really practical people and they saw the world as it operates; and they didn't believe that investors were infallible. They did believe though that we should try to create transparency, we should try and create an understanding of the way companies operate – if you like, the business model of the company is a trendy way to describe that. The aim was to put out more information, increase the information set the market has, to make it more efficient in a 'fundamental' sense, reflecting the underlying economic characteristics of the business. But also, make sure the information is reliable, transparent, comparable. That reduces search costs and makes the market more efficient in the sense that the costs of operating the market are minimised.

GM Did the Board see its role just as informing investment decisions, or did it include supporting stewardship?

**GW** I think most of the Board would have gone along – and I certainly would – with the view that stewardship matters. But we also believed that good stewardship often went hand in hand with the same information that you would need to make a sensible investment. After all, in both cases you are evaluating the firm and its management. So we wouldn't have regarded that as necessarily an inconsistent aim. There are some circumstances, though, where there is a conflict, especially resulting from that trade-off between relevance and reliability which we put in the statement of principles and stuck to, but which sadly later on got rather lost when the IASB revised its conceptual framework and went over to this view that faithful representation was the important thing. It all got a little bit abstract. But the idea of relevance and reliability most people understand; and there is a balance to be struck there, the needs of stewardship emphasising reliability more than those of the investor who is concerned with relevance to estimating future performance. Our aim was to serve both stewardship and investor needs, recognising that there might sometimes be this difficult trade-off. But when we considered stewardship in financial reporting, it was mainly the duty of directors to shareholders, which does require reliable ex post information inevitably. It doesn't necessarily require prediction – you know if they had their hands in the till, or engaged in rash take-overs leading to large asset write-offs, or were in related party contracts, that isn't necessarily predictive, except that they might do it again (if they've been caught they won't). The important thing there is that we do provide reliable information – most people require reliable information anyway, so we would have been quite happy with the idea of stewardship to shareholders.

By meeting the needs of shareholders, we hoped to meet the basic needs of other providers of finance, who will have similar concerns about the accountability of management and the ability of the entity to survive and prosper and thus meet its financial obligations. With regard to the specific needs of long-term lenders, I think that most of us would have thought, well, the bankers are supposed to be smart people and their trade is lending money, so they should be able to devise covenants that do make sense to them and serve their purpose, and we don't regard the accounts as primarily for them because they are general purpose accounts; they are not specifically for bankers or people who choose to write contracts based on them. Personally – I don't know whether the whole Board would have thought that – but I would have thought that anybody who lends money or stakes their future on a particular number in accounts, when the directors of the company have a strong influence on the way that number is presented, I think they are hazarding themselves: they need a whole array of covenants and defences, and not rely on one number in the accounts.

So I think that specific contracting requirements, such as loan covenants would have been less important to us. But the idea of more and better information is the key to the whole thing: more insight, transparency, and comparability were the things we always came back to. They should serve everybody's broad purposes, although not all of their specific contracting needs.

**DPT** I've always been very sceptical of the efficient market argument, mainly because I've been very sceptical of analysts. I found some of them complete numpties who hadn't a clue about accounting. Even before we started at the ASB I vividly remember the case of Argyll, when they took over Safeway. And they did the decent thing: they had Presto supermarkets and they decided that Safeway had a better layout so they changed all the Prestos into the Safeway style. And they charged everything above the line. And they were rewarded for that by their share price falling by almost 10%; but not only that, the entire store sector fell. The FT (26/6/87) said at the time that it had happened because of "fears of an onset of conservative accounting". And I thought, how pathetic, how absolutely pathetic! And that's exactly, of course, what FRS3 is designed to do – to stop all this nonsense. The other one I remember: when I was Chairman of the ASB, I got a phone call from the Stock Exchange, to ask whether I would confirm if we were about to abolish associated company accounting because the rumour had got out that we were going to do so, and the share prices of companies with associates were falling. And I said, "no, we had never discussed it, much as I'd have loved to have got rid of associate accounting". And then I said, 'even if we were, so what? This is a pencil entry. It's just a fictitious entry; it doesn't affect cash; it doesn't affect the value of investments; so what's the problem?' And that really shook me, the fact that this was having a noticeable effect on the market. And it was rubbish information.

**GW** An interesting example about one of the things we quoted earlier was Polly Peck. David Gwilliam and a colleague wrote an article in Accountancy in 1991 based on Polly Peck's accounts. And they showed that all the information you needed to understand Polly Peck's dire liquidity position was actually reported in the accounts. But it's mainly hidden in notes which, obviously, analysts didn't read. And that really confounds the efficient markets hypothesis, because it claims – in its most extreme form anyway – that it doesn't matter where you put the number, so long as it's there, somebody will jump on it and see it and, you know, advertise it to the world and act upon it. So even Polly Peck was not just a fault of creative accounting. It was a fault of presentation.

**AVC** I agree with what Geoff and David have said, though on stewardship I would add that materiality generally cuts in at a lower level for both relevance and reliability than it does for prediction of future performance. I think FRS3 ticks all the boxes as far as these different aspects of standard-setting are concerned. Yes, it did improve disclosure: it gave additional and also more reliable information about discontinued activities and exceptional items. I think it's important to recognise that, although the analyst had the opportunity of attending company presentations and of private meetings with the finance directors and so forth, they couldn't necessarily use any inside information. Indeed, the companies were under strict instructions not to reveal to them in private meetings anything that could move the share price. So the analysts themselves needed public information. And that's reflected actually in your first question about disclosure. It's the published information that sets the price. What the analyst gets from the private meetings is a better insight, a general understanding…

At this point **Dog Tweedie** interceded with epithets that are unprintable. He had discussed analysts many times with his sceptical master during their walks alongside the Firth of Forth and held them in the same (low) esteem as postmen.

**AVC** FRS3 severely limited the scope for what one might call idiosyncratic presentation of results. And it did improve the ability to search, by the classifications and also the clarifications it gave. You know, people could rely on knowing that the underlying judgements had been made on a proper basis. That is an important function of accounting. I remember some people would raise criticisms with us in a somewhat uninformed way. They didn't necessarily know much about the efficient market theory, but they had the feeling that, if these analysts could pick up anything anyway, then accounting wasn't necessary. All you needed was access to the transactions of the company. Some people even argued that XBRL,[1] which we now have, would do that: it would do away with the need for accounting. It doesn't, of course, because there are a lot of judgements that are fed into the financial statements and financial reporting generally. There's an interesting quote from Kenneth Boulding (1970) that we picked up from the FASB who had noted it. We cited it in the chapter on the conceptual framework that we published at the same time as our first proposals on what became FRS3. He says:

> …it is a very fundamental principle indeed that knowledge is always gained by the orderly loss of information, that is, by condensing and abstracting and indexing the great buzzing confusion of information that comes from the world around us into a form which we can appreciate and comprehend.

And that is essentially the task that we were trying to do. I would say that financial reporting goes well beyond providing the necessary information for price discovery. It does do that, but it provides a common language for discussion and analysis by many different parties about how the company has behaved.

**GW** Including the future.

**AVC** Yes.

**GW** It's interesting that the Cadbury Report and the corporate governance movement had only just got going then. I do remember at early meetings of the Board I was always of the view that the shareholders actually own the company, not the directors, and I remember our finance directors being shocked by this and thinking I was a communist because I thought that the shareholders – you know, the people – owned the company. So that view of stewardship as accountability of directors to stakeholders, particularly shareholders, was not generally accepted at that time. Even the auditors referred to the company as the client, not the shareholders, didn't they? And I think in those days that we are talking about, maybe this view that there should be a serious dialogue between directors and stakeholders was not so strong as it is now.

We do have a view now, because of the corporate governance movement, that these things should be out in the open and discussed by 'stakeholders'. If you said 'stakeholders' to our Board in 1990, I think they would have reacted to it in a rather hostile way. In fact most of the financial community were unsympathetic to it. Things have changed.

**AVC** You mentioned Cadbury, Geoff. Sir Adrian's Committee was formed in mid-1991 and published its interim report in May and final report in December 1992, seven months before our own Operating and Financial Review (the OFR). And so this really fitted in very well with the whole policy of the Financial Reporting Council in encouraging better corporate governance and accountability by boards of directors.

### *Resistance to reform*

**GM What opposition did you encounter – within the Board, and from outside – in developing the Standard? It seems to have gone through pretty fast for a reform which so changed the look of the accounts, and where you took care to consult widely and to observe due process in formulating and revising the rules.**

**DPT** Basically I think the extent of extraordinary items was a huge issue. 53% of our companies had one in the year. In America it was 9%, falling to 5%, so there was a completely different attitude to it here. And FRS3 had a very similar definition as SSAP6. But what we did, or rather didn't do, was to give examples. We said "extraordinary items are extremely rare as they relate to highly abnormal events or transactions that fall outside the normal activities of the entity and which are not expected to recur. And in view of the extreme rarity of such items, no examples are provided". Full stop. Whereas previously there were examples given. And I remember probably a month or two after FRS3 came out I was speaking at a conference, and this guy said, 'well a line item for extraordinary items is in your example Table, there must be something (it was the Companies Act that required extraordinary items to be shown). Could you give me an example?' And I said, "Certainly. If Martians were walking on Earth, it would be extraordinary, and everything else is going to be above the line and exceptional". And there were signs of Martian activity in the UK shortly after that, but the Review Panel chased them all away. But people didn't like it. I remember one of the investment houses (I can't remember which) was really upset about getting rid of extraordinary items (because, I suspect. all their models were based on profit before extraordinary items) and they put an article around with a title

I'll never forget: 'Tweedie: Descent into Chaos'. And that was because we had moved 'extraordinary' half an inch up the page into the bottom line, and they absolutely hated it.

Auditors had a terrible time with extraordinary items. Their client would look at it and say, well, you allowed him to do this, why can't I do it? So whatever was worst practice tended to spread. And we were at the stage where companies were just starting to include lots and lots of provisions in the extraordinary items. You know, I'm going to close this company down/buy another, therefore I'll provide for all this. And then when SSAP22 enabled goodwill to be set off against reserves they really went over the top with reorganisation/acquisition provisions as these were deemed by SSAP22 to be liabilities of the acquired company and no charge for these provisions ever hit the profit and loss account – an even better scam than extraordinary items! And that also really made it worse. And that's why the standards we discuss in Chapters 6 and 7 were on our list to sort them out. It was all part of a package tackling creative accounting.

So there was quite a lot of opposition. But interestingly enough some of the finance directors would turn around and say, "thank goodness you've got rid of the extraordinary item – we don't have to have these arguments any more".

One of the things that happened was that with the volatility of the bottom line, analysts had to start looking at these numbers (the components of profit) that we had given them. They couldn't just take the final number.

**AVC** Your point about analysts reminds me of the valuable intervention made by our friend, David Damant, at the time when FRS 3 was launched. David was a sometime chairman of the Institute of Investment Management and Research and played an important part in developing and representing the views of analyst societies at the European and international levels.[2] He had read philosophy at Cambridge and, though not himself an accountant, was fascinated by the conceptual issues in accounting. He bought in completely to the fundamental message of FRS 3 that the diverse factors contributing to a company's financial performance could not be reduced to a single number. At the same time, he recognised the role played by EPS in providing quick statistical information for use in daily price reporting by the financial press.

When the uproar broke over FRS 3's revised calculation of EPS (the bottom line of the profit and loss account with no exclusions), Damant authored two papers, first proposing and later specifying, a solution to meet the perceived needs of the markets. The papers argued that the word 'earnings' implied a level of profit that, other things being equal, could be expected to continue into the future. If the calculation of earnings was to be left to a company's management, it would be open to 'fudge'. However, since the information for determining a suitable definition of earnings was provided by the disclosures required in the FRS, a generally recognised analyst society could be asked to develop rules for determining 'earnings' for different types of company. The resulting number would be no substitute for a requirement on analysts to conduct their own investigation of the financial statements before arriving at an individual assessment, but it would at least be 'unfudgeable'. Moreover, it would be based on judgements by the profession that was arguably the most competent to make it, since the earnings figure was an analytical tool.

Damant interested the *Financial Times* in his proposals, which were quickly taken up as the basis for daily price reporting both by that newspaper and others. The hubbub then died down.

**DPT** Absolutely right. I had little sympathy with analysts' obsession with one number such as EPS or EBITDA (to which I used to refer as 'earnings before bad stuff') but if our good friend David hadn't intervened we would probably have received numerous requests for further EPS guidance. He let us avoid the distraction and get on with more important issues.

The area where we actually lost – I was quite disappointed about this, and Allan made sure it came into the Operating and Financial Review – I liked the idea of having the notion of revenue investment, which was basically expenditure you can turn off. And it's things like training, R&D, advertising, things like that, which can really affect the accounts if you decide that this year I'm going to miss this expenditure out, and thereby increase profit this year at the expense of future years which would have benefited from the expenditure. Drawing attention to these expenditures would have stopped another form of income manipulation.

### *Antecedents and legacy items*

**GM Had any other standard-setters already taken the approach embodied in FRS3? And did any standard setters follow you with an FRS3 equivalent?**

**AVC** No other standard-setters had actually issued a standard requiring a statement of total recognised gains and losses. The FASB in the States had been very keen on the idea of comprehensive income, which was also what underlay our version of the STRGL. And they had discussed that in detail in their equivalent of the Statement of Accounting Principles, their concept statements. So we had the ideas already there. As I say, nobody had actually issued a standard. The FASB did of course require a distinction between continuing and discontinuing operations. We toughened that, by saying 'discontinued' rather than 'discontinuing'.

But they hadn't gone so far as requiring a primary statement. They were really very interested in what we were doing. In the little group that was later called the G4+1, which was Australia, Canada, ourselves, the US, and the IASC, the plus one, as an observer, we did discuss these issues and agreed to support each other. And that led the FASB – in fact only five years later – to issue a Standard, FAS130, where they required formal reporting of comprehensive income. It's disappointing, though, that they did not require a comprehensive income statement; companies could instead incorporate the information into a reconciliation of equity. So it wasn't as tough as ours.

**GW** The G4+1 Discussion Paper which was issued in 1999, which Kathryn Cearns (from the ASB) drafted, said that in 1981 the FASB issued an exposure draft on comprehensive income, and it never got any further. I think the FASB were held up by their constituency as usual. You know, this has come up before – we tend to regard them as an all-powerful body, but in fact they are in thrall to the SEC, who in turn are heavily lobbied by politicians and their sponsors, namely big business. FASB actually were unable to make progress – they deserve great credit for originating comprehensive income as you described it – but they were unable to implement it in a precise sort of way. So they allowed a free format for the performance statement – maybe you could do it in a statement of equity reconciliation; maybe you could do it in a STRGL; or maybe you could do it as part of the profit and loss – as a lower section. And they had this entirely free format, which lost focus.

And that continued later. The IASC adopted basically the same approach in 1997, in IAS1. And IAS1 is still with us, although much revised and with a more precise presentation of the income statement which does make a clear distinction between comprehensive income (the statement of total gains) and transactions with owners (the statement of changes in equity) These improvements took place after I left the IASB (in 2006) and, at that time, I was extremely disappointed by the IASB's slow progress in improving IAS1. Even now, as far as I can make out, FRS3 was a sort of high point, and we haven't moved any further than FRS3 as far as presentation is concerned. The slow start in IAS1 was, I suspect, because of FASB's difficulties in resolving the issue.

**AVC** In the exposure draft for FAS130 they did propose doing it our way but, as Geoff said, they got pulled back by their constituency. And I wonder whether one of the consequences of that was that they were never able to resile from their position that items that appeared once in reserves then had to reappear in the profit and loss account later on…

**GW** Exactly!

**AVC** …when they were realised (what we called 'recycling') and that really angered us. We would have found it much easier to win that battle if they had had a primary statement.

**DPT** It was interesting that the IASC was almost the other way around when it was trying to do this. They liked the idea of a second performance statement because they thought it would solve a lot of problems about unrealised gains. But they could not get it through and they ended up offering a statement of changes in equity which companies could, if they wished, also show as a performance statement. It was almost the other way around from the Americans who had it as a performance statement but you could show it as changes in equity. What I thought was very significant though was in 1998 and 1999 the G4+1, in its second publication, which, remember, all these major nations signed up to, advocated the single statement, and the abolition of the extraordinary item, and we put out FRED22 in December 2000, which was going for the single statement. And it never happened. We'd left the ASB at the end of that month; but we couldn't get the single statement through in the IASB either. But in the IASB we did make it a case of: you could have a single statement, or you could have it in two bits (profit and loss and other comprehensive income) and that's where it is now.

**GM This does illustrate the issue we discussed in Chapter 2 of the relative power, or autonomy, of the different standard-setters: how easily you can implement once the expert Board members have decided on a preferred course of action? I'm surprised you had so much difficulty when you had pioneered it and got acceptance in Britain.**

**GW** Yes, there was a fundamental theoretical problem with it though. You see, comprehensive income came as an idea from the academic world – Edwards and Bell is full of comprehensive income measures and articulation of the balance sheet and profit and loss account. And there's a lot of literature on it. But I had a feeling that at the IASB we tried to over-theorise the performance statement. It is actually a format. It's just telling people what happened: unpicking it, seeing how things hang together. We got involved, and other people did as well, in exploring the various distinctions that we might use, to slice this single unitary statement into sections. And, indeed, the early IASB discussions had the same problem: they tried to say what was operating and what wasn't. And it was very difficult. It all depends on the business model. They were trying to over-define something which was very different in different companies and entities. You know, what's operating, what's capital, what do you regard as routine revenue? All those things were going to be different depending on the business model. And they got hung up on this – how to slice and dice the thing. And the importance of actually transparently showing the articulation of the profit and loss account with the balance sheet, that got lost, but to me the most important thing was to separate out the statement of changes in equity at the bottom. The statement of changes in equity deals with the bits to do with transactions with shareholders – raising new capital or returning capital in some way. And that is a different thing from performance. And the performance statement as it emerged during my period at the IASB (2001–2006) was, I'm sure, loved by finance directors because it enables people to mix up all these things in a complicated-looking table.

It really was complex and totally against the spirit of transparency which is the basis of FRS3. So I was very disappointed in this, and it was partly due to the attempt to over-define and over-theorise the sub-categories within the statement, not recognising that what we wanted was everything that added to equity, other than the transactions with equity such as new equity issued. The statement of changes in equity versus the rest of the statement is a very important distinction. And that was very muddy in the IASB's thinking at the time. And I was very disappointed in our debates. I got nowhere.

**DPT** Not just you!

**GW** But shortly after I left, the IASB made a step towards improvement, in its 2007 amendment to IAS 1. Perhaps I should have left the IASB earlier!

**DPT** FRED22 is very important too, particularly: it laid down two major things. One, we should have a single statement; and, two, there should be no recycling. And we could not sell that.

**GM Thanks. Does that cover everything on that pair of questions on antecedents and followers?**

**DPT** Just one thing. We did bring in discontinued items. That became accepted too, as a separate item, by the IASB. And you could either show an analysis of the income and expenses related to the discontinued operation on the face of the statement, or you could show it in a note

### *The Operating and Financial Review (OFR)*

**GM Allan, how did the OFR fit into your ideas underlying FRS3?**

**AVC** The OFR was the Operating and Financial Review. We developed it as a best practice statement (not a standard) at the same time as FRS3; and in fact, it was published about nine months afterwards. It does have a number of points of contact with FRS3. Particularly it requires a top-down discussion by management of their individual results and projects in the context of the business as a whole – that's the important bit. And the layered information that we had in FRS3 I think fits in very well with that. David's already mentioned that the idea of requiring disclosure of revenue investment, that is expenditure that has to be charged to the profit and loss account of the current period but is incurred because of its expected rewards in the future, failed to achieve consent in FRS3. But we did bring it in as a strong recommendation for the OFR.

**DPT** Just on that, Allan, one of the things about that was, these things could be switched off: you can delay your major maintenance for a year, or you can cut the advertising budget. Your profit goes up, but then your investment for the future is not there any more. It was another profit manipulation, only this time using costs.

**AVC** I remember in fact having come across that idea many years before, when I was with a company that did have huge expenditures on advertising and the accountant for that particular segment told me that they always knew how to meet their budget. That was the reason, of course.

Finally, the OFR did call for explanation of the other measures of earnings per share that FRS3 permitted. If you remember, there was quite an outcry that earnings per share at the level of profit attributable was not a very good guide for many companies, who wanted to have different versions of earnings per share. And in FRS3 we said, well, OK, but they've got to be reconciled. In the OFR we said, please explain why that is a better performance measure.

But I think it would be wrong to think of the OFR as just a gloss on FRS3. It had a much broader scope than FRS3. For instance it required discussion of the dynamics of the business; the effects of external events, both favourable and unfavourable; looking at trends in the market, and that sort of thing. But the motivation for the project was the same as it was for us in FRS3. It was to encourage analytical discussion by the directors of their performance and their financial position at the end of the period. At that time in the early nineties, many annual reports were essentially the work of the PR consultants. They were full of beautiful glossy pictures, of pretty young ladies who probably had no particularly important role in the business except their good looks. It might have pictures and perhaps quite a lot of narrative about the chairman's pet projects, which might be quite interesting but perhaps only a very small portion of the business as a whole. So there wasn't that analytical approach. Instead, the OFR based its approach essentially on what the American SEC had done about ten years earlier in requiring a Management Discussion and Analysis (MD&A) and were now extending also to foreign listers such as UK companies who went to the American market. The MD&A was always focused on the business as a whole, and, as I say, an analytical discussion, an even-handed treatment. They must look at the good and the bad equally.

**GW** Allan, I sympathise greatly with this, I was very keen on the idea and I supported it – but you're giving us a rather idealistic view of this. What was your impression of the way it was taken up, because my feeling is that the OFR has certainly improved the approach people take, there's no doubt about that, but still there's this huge incentive to represent things in a favourable light. And when I look at OFRs, which I do from time to time, I still find that they emphasise the good – the bad's there but in a footnote; and indeed that's true of FRS3 as well.

**AVC** There's a lot of truth in what you are saying, and we knew that it would be difficult. We never expected – certainly from the first year we didn't expect – widespread compliance with it. I think the game plan, if you like, was that we would develop the statement with finance directors, who were very helpful on that – the Hundred Group cooperated with us, and ended by joining the FRC and the Stock Exchange in commending the OFR. And so we had hoped that this would be followed in varying degrees, but the better ones would be an example to those further down. And we hoped that it might set in train a virtuous circle, that over the years would improve the quality of financial reporting. And that was consonant with the whole approach of Cadbury (1992) and the FRC at the time. It was really all that we could do. But I do agree with you that they often took the easy way out. For instance, the nearest thing they got to disclosing revenue investment was usually capital expenditure. They were happy to talk about that. They had often probably been talking about it anyway. But they presented that as their way of dealing with it. So I'm afraid, yes, without a strong regulator behind it, you wouldn't have got very much better.

**GW** Yes, and of course later on we had the business of key performance indicators. The government encouraged them and then pulled the rug from under it, I seem to remember. But I'd like to think at the end of all this that things have improved.

**AVC** Sometimes it can pay off. When I joined Shell it was just after the SEC had been publishing these proposals. And they were only proposals, but Shell took it up very seriously and regarded this as a really good opportunity for them to show that they were serious and good reporters. I feel that what we should perhaps appeal to now is the younger generation. Didn't you say, Geoff Meeks, that you recommended your students to read the OFR?

**GM** Oh, I do, yes, and they have done, especially if they were heading for a job interview with the firm in question. I've found the OFR useful if I'm coming afresh to a company. I look at the accounts, and you can get a certain amount from them alone, but they can make more sense if you have the context from the OFR. I grant you there's quite a lot of PR included. But again, I agree with Allan's point that if you get some good practice going, this might encourage the others to go beyond spin. It would be an interesting project actually to follow that through and see how far it led to top tier firms such as Shell raising their game; whether that was appreciated by users; and then whether it encouraged followers, with businesses which didn't follow being castigated or ridiculed by the press for having a shallow, PR approach to the OFR.

In a different context, we've found that good practice in voluntary disclosures – within a standardised framework – can bring rewards to individual firms, and to the efficiency of the system. We've found that, other things being equal, companies with a good record in forecasting their own earnings, and who then issue a positive earnings forecast in connection with a takeover bid, are rewarded by the market with faster completion time for the deal and a smaller premium (Amel-Zadeh and Meeks, 2019).

**GW** Analysts can make use of it as well. And they follow up with questions and prod companies. My impression is that analysts are much more sophisticated than they used to be. For the eighties, David gave us a few frank opinions about how ill-equipped they were. I think they have improved since then.

### *Unfinished business*

**GM Did you, or do you now, think there were important issues left unresolved by FRS3?**

**AVC** Geoff (W) described a moment ago in response to an earlier question how we regarded the STRGL as simply presenting all the information so that people were not blind to the fact that the business might have lost an awful lot of money. And I don't think at that stage we thought any further. But as he says, when it got to IASB then I think the Americans in particular would have wanted a more conceptual approach to it. And I keep feeling that there is in a sense a concept waiting to be discovered. But, of its nature, it's going to be a fairly general and rather abstract idea, I suspect, because inevitably, as we've seen, there are so many different things that would have to come into that sort of statement.

**GW** But you see I think that's where your Operating and Financial Review comes in, because of the way companies operate. Each company is different. We talk in standard-setting a lot about like transactions being treated in a like way. But on the other hand, every transaction is in some senses unique, and it's always in the context of the business model. And the OFR enables you – if companies cooperate with it – to understand what they are doing and why they are doing it.

**GM David, do you have any thoughts on this question?**

**DPT** I tried when I was at IASB to put forward a project which was called performance reporting, and when FASB became involved they blew it into balance sheet, cash flow, ... the whole thing became a monster. We were just trying to concentrate on the performance statement. But I remember putting a paper to them saying that the two statements fell into what you would call operating (the profit and loss account), and other comprehensive income which is more holding gains. And so you'd have pension gains, you'd have revaluation, foreign currency translation, etc. in the latter and that was how we could split it.

I think we should point out that FRS3 really made a massive impact. I remember the night we published the proposals – it must have been the exposure draft. I was at a dinner at the ICAEW. Mike Lickiss, was the President, also the Vice-Chairman of the FRC. And he announced FRS3 as being "a declaration of war on creative accounting", and made favourable comments on it. I think that's its epitaph: that's what it was about.

**GW** That's right, but what you are saying is, 'let it all hang out'. That was the whole point of it, to reconcile all the movements in the balance sheet with the profit and loss account. This is why Ron Paterson got mad about it because he thought you were adopting a balance sheet approach. But the problem even with operating versus holding gains, which was the basis of FRS3 is it's a useful classification, but when you start to dig at it theoretically, it doesn't hang together. If you don't believe me, read John Kay's (1977) review of the Sandilands Report in the *Economic Journal* – his famous gold watch example.[3] He just has the example of the manufacturer of a gold watch; and the price of gold goes up while the watch is being made. You've got the question then: what was the holding gain; what was the margin on manufacturing the watch? It's actually impossible to sustain very precisely theoretically. It's very easy to specify pragmatically. And standard-setting is about pragmatically showing people what happened.

**DPT** We left with FRED22, which was, if you like, the Mark 2 version. And that was a single statement of financial performance combining the profit and loss account and the STRGL with no recycling – that is once an item has appeared within other gains and losses, it does not appear again in the profit and loss account at a later date. That's where we would have ended up, but we never got there. We left that month. I couldn't get it through IASB either.

## Notes

1 XBRL: eXtensible Business Reporting Language, a freely available and global framework for exchanging business information.
2 In addition to his chairmanship of the IIMR, David Damant had been President of the European Federation of Financial Analysts' Societies, and, at the time of his initiative described in this chapter, was Co-Chairman of the International Co-ordinating Committee of Financial Analysts' Societies worldwide. He had been a member of the UK ASC and was involved in various representative roles at and on behalf of the IASC.
3 See Prakesh and Sunder (1979) for elaboration of these points.

## References

### *Books and articles*

Amel-Zadeh, A. and Meeks, G. (2019). Bidder earnings forecasts in mergers and acquisitions, *Journal of Corporate Finance*, 58, 373–392.

Beaver, W. (1989). *Financial Reporting: An Accounting Revolution* (Second edition), Englewood Cliffs: Prentice Hall.

Beaver, W. and Demski, J. (1974). The nature of financial accounting objectives: a summary and synthesis, *Journal of Accounting Research,* Supplement, 170–182.

Beaver, W. and Demski, J. (1979). The nature of income measurement, *The Accounting Review,* 54, 38–46.

Boulding, K.E. ((1970). *Economics as a Science,* New York: McGraw-Hill, p.2.

Cadbury, A. (1992). *Report of the Committee on the Financial Aspects of Corporate Governance*, London: Gee.

Cascino, S., Clatworthy, M., Garcia Osma, B., Gassen, J., Imam, S. and Jeanjean, T. (2013). *Professional Investors and the Decision Usefulness of Financial Reporting,* Edinburgh: Institute of Chartered Accountants of Scotland (ICAS) and European Financial Reporting Advisory Group (EFRAG).

Cearns, K. (1999). *G4+1 Position Paper: Reporting Financial Performance*, 31 December 1999, London: IASC.

Davies, M., Paterson, R. and Wilson, A. (1997). *UK GAAP* (Fifth edition), London: Ernst and Young and Macmillan.

Edwards, E. and Bell, P. (1961). *The Theory and Measurement of Business Income*, Berkeley: University of California Press.

Griffiths, I. (1986). *Creative Accounting*, London: Unwin.

Gwilliam, D. and Russell, T. (1991). Polly Peck: Where were the analysts? *Accountancy*, January 1991.

Institute of Chartered Accountants of Scotland (ICAS) (1988). *Making Corporate Reports Valuable,* Edinburgh: ICAS.

Kay, J. (1977). Inflation accounting – a review article, *Economic Journal*, 87, 300–311.

Ohlson, J. (1995). Earnings, book values and dividends in equity valuation. *Contemporary Accounting Research,* 11(2), 661–687.

Prakesh, P. and Sunder, S. (1979). Marking to market: Panacea or Pandora's Box. *Accounting Review*, 54(1), 1–12.

Sandilands Committee (1975). *Inflation Accounting: Report of the Inflation Accounting Committee under the Chairmanship of F.E.P. Sandilands,* Cmnd.6225, London: HMSO.

Smith, T. (1996). *Accounting for Growth: Stripping the Camouflage from Company Accounts* (Second edition), London: Century.

Solomons Report (1989). *Guidelines for Financial Reporting Standards: A Paper Prepared for the Research Board of the Institute of Chartered Accountants in England and Wales and addressed to the Accounting Standards Committee by David Solomons,* London: ICAEW.

Sweeney, H. (1936). *Stabilized Accounting,* New York: Harper.

### *Standard-setters' publications*

FAS130 (June 1997). *Reporting Comprehensive Income*, Financial Accounting Standards Board.

FRED1 (December 1991). *The Structure of Financial Statements – Reporting of Financial Performance*, Accounting Standards Board.

FRED22 (December 2000). *Revision of FRS 3 'Reporting Financial Performance'*, Accounting Standards Board.

FRS3 (October 1992), *Reporting Financial Performance*, Accounting Standards Board.

FRS10 (December 1997), *Goodwill and Intangible Assets.*

IAS1 *Presentation of Financial Statements* (revised 1997), International Accounting Standards Committee.

OFR *Operating and Financial Review*, Accounting Standards Board July 1993 Statement.

SFAC6 *Elements of Financial Statements,* Financial Accounting Standards Board, December 1985.

SSAP6 *Accounting for Extraordinary Items* (revised 1986), Accounting Standards Committee.

SSAP22 *Accounting for Goodwill* (revised July 1989), Accounting Standards Committee.

*Statement Principles for Financial Reporting,* Accounting Standards Board, December 1999.

STRGL Statement of Total Recognised Gains and Losses required by FRS 3.

UITF2 *Restructuring Costs*, Accounting Standards Board, October 1991.

Wilkins, R. (Ed.) (2000). *Accounting Standards, 2000–2001*, London: ICAEW.

# 4 Capital instruments

## Introduction

By the second half of the 1980s companies were experiencing difficulty in financing their expansion through acquisitions. Equity issues had become difficult and companies were reluctant to increase their reported capital gearing fearing adverse market reaction. With the increasing disapproval of off balance sheet financing schemes, investment bankers sought to assist companies by inventing products that, at least initially, protected balance sheets by maintaining low gearing ratios and flattered profit and loss accounts by avoiding a deterioration in interest cover.

Much of the incentive for new types of capital instruments was tax driven: interest on debt instruments was deductible for tax purposes, but dividends on equity instruments were not. However, if an instrument was reported as debt, the gearing (or 'leverage') ratio would be increased, in some cases to an extent that would trouble investors. Investment bankers worked to exploit the tax-accounting arbitrage possibilities, with the aim of contriving instruments that would not be counted as debt in the financial statements, but whose interest would be allowable for tax purposes. For example, the interest on convertible debt was tax-deductible, but attempts were made to report the debt as equity in the balance sheet.[1] Techniques used to achieve these effects generally relied on one or more of the following:

- anticipating future transactions that might or might not happen (*e.g. conversion of a debt instrument to equity*);
- ignoring existing commitments for future transactions *(e.g. redemption of a debt instrument at a premium)*;
- creating a series of connected transactions through subsidiaries (e.g. *to issue shares to minority shareholders that were underwritten by the group*).

The number and variety of capital instruments gradually increased. There was little uniformity in the accounting for these instruments and various arguments were advanced to justify different treatments. Accounting for capital instruments which had appeared to be uncontroversial for years was

DOI: 10.4324/9781003346920-4

suddenly called into question. Arguments about whether a capital instrument represented debt or equity, the treatment of convertible instruments, and the appropriate interest charge were commonplace.

In an attempt to deal with the bewildering array of new complex capital issues the Technical Committee of the Institute of Chartered Accountants in England and Wales published a discussion paper on the subject (TR677, Accounting for Complex Capital Issues) in November 1987. The Technical Release summed up the problems facing accountants:

"The development of agreed accounting procedures for these instruments has not kept pace with the development of the instruments themselves. The instruments are frequently legally and operationally complex and the accounting treatment adopted has sometimes been either too simplistic to reflect the benefits obtained by using the instrument, or so complex as to obscure the financial statements for a reader. The lack of published guidance in this area has contributed to difficulties in achieving consistent and appropriate accounting treatment".

TR677 was a useful start to a debate. The ASC, which had both limited resources and meeting time, did not focus on the question of capital instruments, possibly concentrating instead on the scourge of off-balance sheet financing. It was not until FRS4 was issued in December 1993 that official accounting requirements were promulgated.

Many types of capital instruments existed but instruments of particular concern were essentially of two main types (though some instruments fell into both categories and there were several variations):

1 Delayed interest: Those requiring the rate of interest to increase over time or where the interest, or a material part of it, was paid as a premium on redemption, namely:

   Stepped interest bonds;
   Deep discount bonds; and
   Convertible loan stock with premium puts.

2 Debt instruments with aspects of equity: Those with conversion rights or warrants raising questions about future events and whether these instruments should be presented as debt or share capital in the balance sheet, namely:

   Convertible preference shares;
   Convertible capital bonds;
   Synthetic convertibles (e.g. deep discount bonds with warrants attached).

## Delayed interest

The arguments over delayed interest were essentially whether companies should charge the actual cash paid in the accounting period or provide for future payments either at the commencement of the loan or as a supplement to the annual interest paid so as to provide an accrual of interest over the period of the loan. Charging the actual cash paid flattered earnings and overstated interest cover in the early years.

### Stepped interest bonds

The main feature of a stepped interest bond was that the stated rate of interest increased progressively over the period of issue. As recommended by TR677, some companies used the effective rate of interest over the period of the bond to charge the interest to the profit and loss account. Others, in particular investment trusts, simply charged the interest payable during the year. The trusts were presumably relying on the fact that the principal resistance to the use of the effective rate of interest came from the Accounting Practice Committee of the Association of Investment Trust Companies which, in its response to TR677, argued:

> For investment trusts the policy of charging the actual interest paid on a stepped interest bond reflects the economic reality that gearing inevitably takes a toll on the income account and that, at the time of the investment and in the early years, the debenture proceeds will be producing a lower initial yield; the stepped policy becomes even more realistic when the situation towards the end of the loan period is taken into consideration as it is expected that at that time a higher return will be earned. Therefore to charge only an average rate would not reflect the commercial reality.

The Committee objected that applying TR677 proposals would result in an apparent overdistribution of income in the early years and a higher than permitted level of income retention in later years.

Social housing (Housing Associations) was another sector that made significant use of stepped interest bonds. The perception was that the income from rents would rise over time so that recording only the contractual rate of interest would enable the increasing rate of interest to be offset by the increasing income. The other side of the argument was that the interest was a contractual obligation while the increase in rents was merely an expectation: it was questionable whether these should be offset.

### Deep discount bonds

Deep discount bonds carried a low nominal rate of interest but, to compensate, the ultimate redemption value greatly exceeded the cash received by the company on its issue. In its extreme form where no interest at all was payable they were known as zero coupon bonds.

Some companies charged the discount to the profit and loss account over the period of maturity of the bond but frequently companies failed to disclose the method of charging. Greycoat Group (1987), however, arguing that the discount on the bond would be met from the underlying capital growth, decided to write off the discount over the term of the bond directly against the share premium account. Balance sheet presentations also differed. Most companies showed the initial liability. Others (e.g. Thorn EMI 1987) showed the full liability ultimately due to the bondholders and included the discount in prepayments.

### *Convertible loan stock with a premium put option*

Instead of issuing convertible loan stock at a discount, some companies offered a premium on redemption of the loan. Some companies provided from the issue date for the premium which the holder would get if they put the bonds back to the company at the put date. Others either made no provision (Burton, 1988) or provided for the supplementary interest only when they thought the conversion less likely and that a cash cost might be incurred. Prior years were then restated to reflect the new accounting policy (Tesco, 1989).

## Debt instruments with aspects of equity

### *Convertible preference shares*

Like all preference shares, convertible preference shares had been reported separately from ordinary shares, as called-up share capital up to their nominal amount—which might have little, if any, significance—and the excess as 'share premium', which was also presented as part of shareholders' funds.

For taxation reasons, increasingly shares were issued by an overseas subsidiary and the proceeds lent to the UK holding company, which would benefit from the tax relief on the interest paid to its subsidiary.[2] The conversion rights were often for shares in the parent rather than the subsidiary. Some companies assumed that such shares were likely to convert to ordinary shares of the holding company and presented the balance sheet as if conversion had already taken place. The justification was that conversion was ultimately certain and therefore the minority interest should show not the proceeds of issue but the nominal value of the ordinary shares that they would obtain in the future. The difference between the two amounts would be taken to general reserves and be available for the write off of goodwill. United Biscuits' 1988 Prospectus gives a well-known example of this treatment. The proceeds of the issue of convertible preference shares by a subsidiary amounted to £110 m. The nominal value of the United Biscuits ordinary shares to be issued on conversion, and shown as minority interest, amounted to £9m. The difference of £101m was, on consolidation, to be included in unrealised reserves.[3] A similar policy of assuming the most likely outcome was also adopted by Meggitt in its 1988 annual report.

### *Convertible capital bonds*

While detailed provisions varied, convertible capital bonds were typically debt instruments on which interest was paid periodically, issued by a special purpose subsidiary incorporated outside the UK. On maturity, the bondholders were forced to convert the instruments into convertible preference shares of a group subsidiary. Prior to maturity, they could be exchanged for preference shares of a subsidiary which would be immediately exchanged for ordinary shares of the parent.

The coupon on the subsidiary's preference shares was set at such a rate that it would be uneconomical to hold on to them and, in practice, the subsidiary's shares would either be converted into the parent's ordinary shares or the bondholder would be repaid his principal by way of redemption of preference shares. The bonds and payments in respect of the shares of the subsidiary were guaranteed by the parent.

In substance, the instrument was a convertible loan stock but it was argued that, because conversion into preference shares was mandatory, the liability, in legal terms, was only contingent and therefore the accounting rules for contingencies would apply. If it were considered that the contingency was remote it was argued that the liability could be valued at zero and the instrument could be treated as if it were a convertible preference share.

In some cases, there were no redemption rights for the preference shares but instead the ordinary shares obtained in exchange for the preference shares could be placed (sold in the market) and the proceeds given to the capital bondholders. Any shortfall would be made up by the parent company.

A classic example of one variant of this type of instrument was that of the British Airways 1989 issue of convertible capital bonds where it was argued that it was highly probable that the proceeds of the issue would become part of BA's share capital in due course and, consequently, the bonds were included in the Group Balance Sheet under Capital and Reserves (see Table 4.1, derived from Tweedie and Whittington, 1990).

These bonds are convertible into equity shares. The essential feature is that there is a mechanism to prevent the issuing group being obliged to repay the bondholder except in the event of a default. The bonds will be guaranteed by the parent.

For example, such bonds were issued in October 1989 by British Airways PLC and presented between shareholders' funds and minority interests in the accounts as follows.

### *Extract from note 19*

> In October 1989 British Airways PLC raised 320 million pounds through the issue of 9.75percent Convertible Bonds 2005 by a subsidiary, British Airways Capital Ltd. The Bonds were offered by way of rights to existing ordinary shareholders of the company on the basis of four bonds of one

*Table 4.1* Convertible capital bonds: British Airways

| | | 1990 £m | 1989 £m |
|---|---|---|---|
| Capital and reserves | | | |
| | Called up share capital | 180 | 180 |
| | Reserves: | | |
| | Revaluation | 121 | 167 |
| | Other | (18) | (9) |
| | Profit and loss account | 629 | 411 |
| | | – | – |
| | | 912 | 749 |
| Convertible capital bonds | (Note 19) | 320 | 0 |
| Minority interests | | 0 | 1 |
| | | – | – |
| | | 1232 | 750 |

Source: British Airways PLC: Accounts for the year ended March 1990.

pound each for every nine British Airways PLC shares then held. The terms of the Bonds allow the holders to convert into British Airways PLC ordinary shares during the period 1993 to 2005 on the basis of one ordinary share for each 2.43 pounds of bonds held. The terms also provide that on maturity in 2005 the Company may require remaining bondholders to convert their Bonds into ordinary shares of the Company which would be sold on their behalf. If the proceeds of such sale are less than the issue price of the Bonds the Company has to fund any deficit from its own reserves.

In these circumstances, the Directors consider that it is highly probable that the proceeds of the issue of the Convertible Capital Bonds will become part of the Company's called up share capital in due course and therefore will be available to the Group on a permanent basis. Accordingly the Convertible Capital Bonds have been included in the Group balance sheet under Capital and Reserves.

### *Synthetic convertibles*

Similar to convertible loan stock was the issue of deep discount bonds with warrants attached enabling the holder to subscribe for equity shares at some future date. The treatment of warrants differed. Thorn EMI, mentioned above, credited the amount representing the consideration for the warrants to a non-distributable reserve to be transferred to share premium account as warrant holders exercised share options. City of London Properties (1986) took the whole of the proceeds of the warrants (in this case giving the right to subscribe for bonds) to the profit and loss account as an exceptional item.

In relation to financing acquisitions, therefore, these devices offered the creative accountant a range of opportunities. As compared with conventional debt, the delayed interest schemes produced higher earnings in the short run. If this earnings management resulted in a higher share price, the acquirer could benefit from more favourable terms in a subsequent acquisition financed by a share for share exchange.[4] The higher earnings in the short term would also boost interest cover – relevant to shareholders' perception of the riskiness of the business, and to a company's compliance with banks' debt covenants. Then, as compared with conventional equity, the convertible instruments would secure tax deductibility for the return paid to investors – in the form of interest, rather than dividends.

## FRS4

The problems facing the ASB involved both measurement and recognition issues. What was debt capital and what was a share? What should the appropriate finance charge for the year be? When could income be taken to the profit and loss account? Should accounting take more of a forward-looking, probabilistic view of the effect of transactions or show the formal effect of past transactions?

FRS4 was published in December 1993. It followed the publication of the Board's Discussion Paper 'Accounting for Capital Instruments' in December 1991 and an exposure draft (FRED3) a year later.

The essential features of the standard were as follows:

1 The standard used a criterion to determine whether a capital instrument represented a liability based on the definition of a liability in the Board's draft Statement of Principles:

"Liabilities are an entity's obligations to transfer economic benefits as a result of past transactions or events". A contingent liability to transfer economic benefits would be classified as a liability.

The criterion was not, however, used to determine the accounting for a company's shares (including preference shares) which had a distinct legal status in companies legislation. In all other cases, financial instruments were required to be presented in a way that reflected the obligations of the issuer. Conversion of debt was not to be anticipated and convertible debt was to be displayed separately from other liabilities.

2 Shares issued by subsidiaries would be accounted for in consolidated financial statements as liabilities if the group taken as a whole had an obligation to transfer economic benefits in connection with the shares, for example where another member of the group had given a guarantee of payments to be made in respect of the shares. In all other cases, they were to be reported as minority interests.

3 Shareholders' funds were to be displayed as being either equity or non-equity interests. The latter was to include redeemable shares (redeemable

either according to their terms, or because the holder, or any party other than the issuer, could require their redemption). Additionally, shares whose rights to receive payments were for a limited amount not calculated by reference either to profits or dividends on any particular class of equity share or, in a winding up, by reference to the company's assets or profits and such limitation had a commercial effect in practice were also to be classed as non-equity. Minority interests in subsidiaries were also to be presented distinguishing equity and non-equity interests.

4 The direct costs incurred in connection with the issue of capital instruments were to be deducted from the proceeds of the issue.

5 The finance costs associated with liabilities and non-equity shares were to be allocated to periods at a constant rate based on the carrying amount irrespective of the structure of the cash payments required by the instrument. The finance costs for a period were to be added to the carrying amount and payments deducted from it. This would result in the carrying amount for redeemable instruments equating eventually to the amount payable at the time of redemption.

6 The net proceeds from the issue of equity shares and warrants were to be taken directly to shareholders' funds. On exercise, the amount previously recognised in respect of the warrant was to be included in the net proceeds of the shares issued. Only when a warrant lapsed unexercised would the amount previously recognised in respect of the warrant be reported in the statement of total recognised gains and losses. Showing the gain in that statement rather than in the profit and loss account was consistent with the role of the statement of total recognised gains and losses as providing a summary of changes in the year in total reserves.

Introducing FRS4 at its launch the ASB Chairman summed up what was expected of the standard:

> All users of accounts should benefit from the greater clarity and certainty that will result from the publication of FRS4. We have been encouraged by the positive response to our proposals in this important and complex area, which have been adopted in many cases in advance of the publication of the standard. The number of hybrid instruments in issue is rather less now than it was a few years ago. Some of the reduction is due to economic factors, but I have no doubt that our work has removed the attraction of certain novel instruments that exploited the conventions developed for the more straightforward kinds of instruments that were used in the past.

To remove any ambiguity concerning the treatment of particular 'novel instruments', for the first time in an ASB standard, FRS4 included as part of the standard, Application Notes specifying how some of the requirements of the standard were to be applied to transactions with certain features.

The Board did not receive many Christmas cards from investment bankers for its efforts!

## David Tweedie

### *Discussion*[5]

**GM Did it work?**

**DPT** I think probably the best thing to do is to quote Andrew Lennard. Andrew was in the Technical Department at KPMG when I first went down to London and he was the person who was looking after financial instruments. And he in fact explained to me what was going on, which, I must admit, really shook me. The key issue with him was saying that, with the Statement of Principles, we've got a definition of a liability, which is an obligation; equity is held by people who are sharing in the gains and the future of the business. But they are not opposites: there is a bit in the middle. And that was the bit where the investment bankers played. And the whole idea was to have a debt instrument so that you could obtain tax relief on the interest, but in fact it was shown as equity in the financial statements thereby improving reported gearing. And a lot of the schemes were based on that. I asked Andrew, "Did it work?". I probably couldn't do better than quote what he wrote in reply:

> At a practical level FRS4 killed stone dead the industry that had flourished during my latter years with KPMG (late 1980s) of designing securities that could be reported as quasi-equity and yet have their coupon deducted for tax purposes. This was a time for the big boys, when you were summoned to explain your thinking to a team of Directors, and blokes from investment banks who looked as if their shoulders had been swollen by their Oxbridge degrees. Often these meetings took place unfeasibly early: at least once I had to leave the office to buy a new shirt and basic toiletries so that I could make an early meeting in somewhere like Leeds at 7:00 am the next day. Of course, you were always aware that if you let this one go, it would spread faster than Velveeta cheese. And perhaps the arrangement had been "blest" by a competitor. Happy Days indeed.

So this was a creeping crumple type of thing. Andrew's view was: FRS4 stopped it. I think he was right because the schemes were falling away even by the time we published. I think the Exposure Draft started scaring them off.

The effect of the standard on balance sheet gearing was, for some companies, dramatic. For example, Marshall records (see Table 4.2) that some companies provided restated gearing ratios for their previous years' financial statements in which convertible capital bonds had been classified as equity.

*Table 4.2* Restated gearing ratios of CCB issuers

| Published gearing ratios % | | | |
|---|---|---|---|
| Company | Year-end | Pre-FRS4 | Reclassified Post-FRS4 |
| Hepworth | 1990 | 41.2 | 294.7 |
| | 1991 | 33.2 | 215.3 |
| British Airways | 1990 | 61.0 | 118.0 |
| | 1991 | 107.0 | 176.0 |
| | 1992 | 118.0 | 172.0 |
| | 1993 | 189.0 | 265.0 |
| Hickson | 1990 | 33.0 | 83.6 |
| Blue Circle | 1990 | 27.6 | 41.0 |
| | 1991 | 32.9 | 47.0 |
| Boots | 1990 | 23.1 | 47.9 |
| | 1991 | 18.2 | 37.3 |
| Premier Consolidated | 1990 | −6.8 | 16.0 |
| Oilfields | 1991 | 25.6 | 72.4 |

Derived from Marshall (1995).

The increases in gearing ratios between the restated version, after FRS 4's introduction, and the original pre-FRS4 ratio are, in some cases, striking. While, prior to the publication of FRS4, convertible capital bonds had been an important source of finance, with 20 issues by 19 companies, accounting for a total value of more than £2.2 billion between 1990 and 1993, since the publication of the standard no new convertible capital bonds were issued.

It worked!

**GM So shall we move on to what resistance you met in your consultation?**

**GW** In a way, the speed with which the standard emerged shows that there wasn't huge resistance in the sense that there was later on in that area to hedge accounting and things like that. You know the trouble the IASB had with banks over hedge accounting – there was nothing of that magnitude. And I think the reason for that of course was that it was dealing with an obvious abuse within the existing model. We'll get on later perhaps to how innovative it was. There were changes in our initial position (in the 1991 Discussion Paper, followed by the 1992 Exposure Draft) of course. We were a bit timid perhaps in some respects. In particular, we initially exposed the idea that we'd require people to disclose the market value of financial instruments when it was readily available. And that was very strongly resisted by some constituents, including opposition from within the Board, I think. And you can think of reasons why market values may sometimes be unreliable, but, on the other hand, everybody knows what market values are and their limitations as well as their strengths, and it is difficult to deny their potential usefulness. So in a way we did give way on that issue, and that was probably the biggest concession we made.

We did make a few minor amendments but they were mainly technical. For instance, investment trusts complained that because of their capital structure and the way they allocated dividends to different classes of shareholders, what we were proposing would prevent them from presenting clearly the effect of these arrangements. And so we made a special concession for investment trusts. There was also comment and debate about the classification of financial instruments as long or short term. In particular, many corporates at the time had rolling paper programmes: short-term debt which was renewable and which they therefore wished to classify as long term. We allowed this only if very stringent conditions were met, surrounding the probability (or near certainty) of renewal. But the only significant thing I can think of is that retreat from current value – which, of course, was an omen of things to come. But apart from that it went through very smoothly. I have this wonderful book, which some of you may have heard of – can you see it? [He shows Ernst and Young's UK GAAP.] We were speaking rather critically of Ernst and Young in the previous chapter. In 1997, a couple of years after FRS4 had been implemented, they say (p.918): "FRS4 has been useful… in developing a framework of rules on capital instruments…The standard has created much more consistency in the classification and disclosure of companies' share and loan capital… it has proved to be one of the Board's most successful standards to date". How about that? And in some senses, their characterisation of FRS4 as a framework of rules is appropriate, because it does interpret the principles already in the Companies Act and in the Board's Statement of Principles, which was being developed at the same time as FRS4.

It was in the mainstream in some senses. Everybody agreed that there were some obvious abuses like that relating to stepped interest or the manipulation of the debt equity distinction. It was a natural topic to succeed. It was a good thing to start off. It was, if you like, an easy kill because most people agreed, whatever their persuasion on valuation and all that.

**GM Allan, you were obviously following the process through. Was that your impression too, and did your thinking change in the course of developing the standard?**

**AVC** At this distance in time I cannot easily recall. But I certainly agree with Geoff that this one went through pretty smoothly; and also that our relationship with the banks was very different from what it was in some later standards. When I looked at the notes of our meetings I noticed how much the Board was consulting, not only in this standard but also in others later on. It wasn't just the fact that it had the formal process of Discussion Paper and then a FRED (Financial Reporting Exposure Draft). On this one, we even had a later special consultation just before the end on something that we thought might be important. But throughout the development we also had consultations with the interested parties to make sure that we understood exactly what the problem was. And it was then that we could sometimes find our way to accommodate reasonable opposition while maintaining our principles.

**GM And so presumably this was building up goodwill with users at this crucial stage for the Board?**

**AVC** That's right. And it's a very good demonstration of why the accounting standard setting process needed reform – because it simply didn't have the resources to do that before. I would mention one or two other things where we met some push-back. There was opposition to our proposal to put accrued interest into the measurement of the instrument itself, rather than to carry it as an accrual. We stuck to our guns mainly on that, but in the end made a concession that if the accrued interest was payable in the following year, then that could go into accruals. And one other point where I think we took the advice of the Law Society (which we didn't always do, of course) was on the question of dealing with the share premium account. There is quite a lot in legislation about the share premium account, and the Board decided that this was a battle it really didn't need to kick off.

**GM Geoff, I wonder to what extent you thought this was an innovative standard?**

**GW** That's a good question. When I went back to FRS4 I was struck by how conventional it was in some ways. It really did accept the existing model of accounting and the existing legislation. It applied them in a sensible way. Where there were judgements to be made and scope for flexibility it tried to draw a consistent line. For instance with the distinction between debt and equity – well, it didn't quite draw a single line, it did it by a more subtle method, subdividing equity and subdividing debt so that you saw the subtleties of different securities. And equally, on stepped interest and that sort of thing it applied amortisation, which is of course anathema to the purist fair value believers. That was straightforward historical cost. It was also very sensible to do that because if you have amortisation you can understand what's going on. It gives you insight into what is the burden of the financial instruments on the firm. It may not give you the latest current value, but it tells you that interest is being accrued. It leaves a certain amount to the judgement of the user of the accounts. So I think in that sense that was one of the reasons it was successful. It didn't, like subsequent financial instrument projects, attempt to change the model and go further into what accounts could do in terms of reporting the substance of the business. It took the existing model and said, look, this is a sensible way to apply it so that people understand what's going on.

**GM Thank you. Well, that is, as it were, looking backwards. Looking forwards from the standard, how durable was it, how transferable. Was it retained at the next stage? Or did it only last a short time?**

**GW** Well, our next chapter is on FRS5, and that leads us into the more difficult financial arrangements that were happening at the time because FRS4 was concerned with individual financial instruments only. It deliberately steered clear of awkward subjects like reporting the substance of related financial transactions, dealt with subsequently by FRS5, and employee stock options, which had to be addressed later by the IASB. (Though we did issue a Discussion Paper on the issue towards the end of our time on the ASB). So it didn't solve any of those problems – it avoided them by limiting itself to a set of really important issues at the time, and dealing with creative accounting in those areas. But it drew a firm boundary. When we came to something different, we said, "stop here– over to FRS5 and later standards for the innovations".

But, having said that, the subsequent controversies and difficulties over accounting for financial instruments were due to trying to change the model, and maybe some of them went a step too far. Some of them certainly did: I remember the IASB experimenting with an incredibly complex model to try and distinguish between 'pure' debt and 'pure' equity, and draw a firm line – which was absolutely hopelessly misdirected and wasted a lot of time. It probably had to be done – going down some blind alleys is inevitable. To the extent that FRS4 stuck with things such as amortisation which fair value purists won't accept, it did actually do things that people understood, and it is still around because people haven't found a better way of doing these things. So to that extent, it preserved the best of traditional methods. Equally with the debt-equity distinction, it actually produced a disclosure approach which classified instruments in useful ways rather than pretending that it was possible to identify 'pure' debt and 'pure' equity. And I think the IASB Conceptual Framework now has come to a residual equity approach which is entirely in the spirit of FRS4.

**GM David, how did you see it later on, in the IASB? To what extent did you pick it up?**

**DPT** Well, we'd have liked to have done so. What I didn't mention about Andrew was that while he was at KPMG he was seconded to the ASB right at the beginning, and eventually he didn't go back to KPMG, he became Assistant Technical Director at ASB and later succeeded Allan as Technical Director. And because of his influence I think we knew very early on what we shouldn't do is chase the schemes – because if we did, we'd be wasting our time. If we said that if A, B, and C happen, then the accounting is X, and if instead, the investment banks created an instrument that was slightly different so that B, C, and D occur they'd say that it was not covered by the standard. So I think Andrew was pretty keen that we had principles in this, and we did. We could list the basic principles behind the standard.

First of all, we used "What is a liability?" from the Statement of Principles. And that affected issued debt, interest commitments, guarantees, etc.

And then we went on: "Don't anticipate the future': the balance sheet isn't a forecast, it's what's there now. So that killed all these "Will it convert, will it not convert? issues." At conferences, I used to explain it by the duck analogy "if it looks like a duck, walks like a duck and quacks – it's a duck. If you pay interest on it and if it can make you go belly up if you don't pay either the interest or the principal – it's a debt".

"If something isn't fully participating in a distribution, it's not equity". That's when we entered into non-equities.

"You can only take a gain when it accrues to the equity-holders", such as when warrants expire.

And "issue costs are certainly not assets" so you deduct them from the liability at the beginning and then you accrue up to the redemption amount over the period to maturity.

As Geoff said, lots of disclosures, the dates and amounts payable, redemption dates, who can redeem, what the debt can be converted into, and so on. We didn't try to deal with it the way the IASC and then the IASB did it.

When we went to the IASB we were faced with a standard already there. And it hasn't changed a lot. It had a North American influence. It was IAS32 which was developed by the old IASC in conjunction with the Canadian Institute of Chartered Accountants. The Chairmen of the working parties were American, so it tended to have very much a North American bias. And, as Geoff said, it proposed – and, in fact, it's still there – that the proceeds of instruments that have both liability and equity rights be allocated between the component parts. Now, we did not do that. We said that if it's a debt now and going to be converted it will be displayed as a debt until conversion.

So they didn't copy our way. We exposed theirs, and it was turned down by our constituents as being too subjective and too complex. I think our constituents were right. Unfortunately, internationally FRS4 did not survive. Obviously, when the UK changed to IFRS they had to take the IAS.

**Dog Tweedie** expressed his disapproval at this point. He always maintained that the ASB standards were superior to those of IASB. Some of his friends – especially the French poodle – have suggested that he was perhaps a little bit insular.

**GM Allan, in a moment I'm going to ask you about the link between FRS4 and FRS5. But first is there anything on the sequel to, or the origins of, FRS4 that you'd like to add?**

**AVC** I'd like to challenge David on that last bit about split accounting. My own impression was that split accounting – dividing a convertible stock between an equity portion and a loan portion according to the way the market valued it when it was issued – sounded like quite a good idea. But the proof of the pudding would be in the eating, and so I wonder whether split accounting has managed to survive and prove its usefulness from the time that IASB took it up.

**DPT I don't know how it's regarded but it's still in IAS32.**

**GW** Yes, but there's a distinction between split accounting and the general problem of distinguishing between debt and equity of course. I was talking about the general problem, which has a lot more to it. The split accounting issue – there is a method of splitting, but the trouble is, it's arbitrary. If you've got a loan with detachable warrants, that's easy. You've got stock, and you've got a warrant: you value them separately. You can trade one without the other. But with convertible stock, by exercising your option you have to forego your right to get the interest and payments on redemption of the loan stock. And of course, vice versa – if you decide to hold onto the loan stock because it's got an attractive return, you lose the value of the equity option, even if it's an option that would be attractive if you could exercise it with money raised elsewhere so that you'd prefer to exercise the option AND retain the benefits of the loan stock. So there's an arbitrariness. There is an inevitable jointness in this Siamese twin aspect of the convertible stock. So splitting isn't perfect; but it's a rough and ready way of doing it. I don't actually think that's the most serious issue in debt versus equity. The problem is settling what is the equity capital, the bottom line if you like, the profit figure that you are going to ultimately report to shareholders as earnings. And that is very difficult given the incredibly complicated range of instruments available. Convertibles now are almost what the Americans like to call plain vanilla instruments, simple ones. But nevertheless, the methods of splitting them into two are arbitrary. Amortisation, which we talked about earlier is an equally arbitrary allocation and was in our FRS4. So I don't think we can throw any stones at people who have been splitting convertible financial instruments. I just think that the simplicity argument that David made might be the one to go for. Accounts are so complicated these days. Business life in many ways is so complicated that if you can give people a bit of simplicity, and they know where they are, that's very welcome.

**AVC** I buy that, and I'm sure that the solution that we adopted in FRS4 was the right one for our country at that time.

**GW** Exactly, but it's a pragmatic decision in a way. You can do the split, and you tell people, this is the way we've done it. Yes, I agree. I think our arguments conceptually hinged on the future convertibility, the fact that now the reality is that what we've got is a stock and we may convert and we may not convert, but that's for the future. But I think we are on a little bit of dodgy ground there when we think about linked transactions, which are going to come up in FRS5. You know, why isn't the exercise of the option a linked transaction? In some cases, it probably would be, in the sense that the terms are fixed in such a way that you are inevitably going to exercise it. So there is a grey area there. We had to make a judgement and I think that we made the right one because we voted for straightforwardness, transparency, and simplicity, even if it doesn't give you the magic number that everybody craves, because the magic number's not there.

**GM Geoff, you mentioned FRS5, and I think that's not the first time it's come up. We had a self-denying ordinance that we wouldn't go too far into FRS5 at this stage, but, Allan, could you just give us a link to the next chapter?**

**AVC** Well, it's really interesting that, when we started, FRS5 had been one of our quick wins in David's terms. The reason was that it had already had five years of debate before the ASB was created. FRS4 started from scratch and overtook FRS5 – for some of the reasons that we have been discussing. But the issues were relatively well-known, and it was largely a matter of picking the right solutions. And we picked solutions which were in accordance with our Statement of Principles. It was a particularly exciting period because a lot of the interlocking issues were all being debated at the same time. We were developing the Statement of Principles; we were developing FRS4; we were developing FRS5. And people knew about this. They knew the issues that we were discussing, all the different standards. So some of the opposition to our proposals on FRS4 was couched in language that was taken from proposals for FRS5. They were saying, "You aren't following the substance of the arrangement". We refuted that: we explained how we were indeed doing so. But it's interesting that language was used.

We, too, used that language in FRS4. You can see some direct borrowing from issues that are more fully spelled out in FRS5. One instance occurs in the explanation of the term of a debt instrument that contains an option for early redemption. What we said was that the effect of the option should be evaluated according to the earliest date at which it could be exercised. But then we added, "unless there is no genuine commercial possibility that the option will be exercised". Those last few words are exactly what FRS5 uses. So it was very useful to have all that. We also used the concept, or the knowledge that FRS5 was coming, to avoid going down some of the more detailed paths – you know, what David would describe as "going down every rabbit hole". So, for example, we decided not to address the issue of stapled shares.[6] That was a somewhat esoteric issue. One or two companies had used these. The concept raised various problems, but it would have been a waste of time within this simple standard to go into that sort of detail. And the Board decided that people would very well be able to apply the principles of FRS5.

**GM Fine. So we've got the trailer for FRS5 now. Thank you very much.**

**DPT** Geoff, I was just going to say, in the early days of the ASB I was frequently asked at conferences, what are the major problems facing British accounting? And I used to say, there are only two problems – the profit and loss account and the balance sheet. Well there was also the statement of the source and application of funds – we abolished that with FRS1. When you look at FRS3, 4, and 5, first we tackle the profit and loss account, with all its abuses; FRS4 deals with the structure of the financing, and FRS5 deals with almost everything else – assets plus some of these issues as well, so we hit the issues that were there right from the beginning. The first standards were really anti-abuse and attacking the schemes. And that's why they are so important. The other huge issue was acquisition accounting, which we are going to deal with in the second half of the book.

**GM David, a quick one now to you, which is completely obvious to you three, but just to confirm to me: which groups of account users were you targeting? I often tend to throw my net rather wide over account users – especially when I'm trying to persuade people in my accounting classes of the wide range of potential uses for accounts; but I know you try to contain it.**

**DPT** Well, we did contain it. We used the Statement of Principles for that, and it was very clear. It says there that the key perspective is that of the informed investor – viewing financial performance and financial position to focus on cash generation and financial adaptability. That perspective is also of fundamental importance to other users because a company's profit, ability to generate cash and to meet unexpected needs and opportunities ultimately determine its capacity over the medium to long term to repay loans, meet interest payments, pay employees and suppliers, and undertake investment. So we really said investors would be our target, but the information they require is useful for everybody else. And we expanded it to say that the balance sheet shows the economic resources, which give companies the ability to generate cash, and also indicates the stewardship of those resources, which was one of our major objectives. Additionally, the information about the financial structure showed how cash flows are going to be distributed among those who have invested in the business. So FRS4 and subsequent standards were absolutely firmly targeted on the investor.

**GM Thank you.**

**Geoff, this next topic is one you and I have discussed quite a lot in the past, namely: were you in FRS4 just making the substance more obvious and transparent, or were you revealing things which were hidden and opaque and would mislead any outsider, even a skilled outsider?**

**GW** Yes, of course, that distinction is really a continuum. You can argue if you dig deep enough that in most accounts you can find out what's going on. But it's a question of how much digging you have to do. Given the time lag between the information being released and the market moving, actually where the information is and how clearly it's displayed in the accounts is rather important. I said earlier, we missed an opportunity, which I think the Americans had taken, to require disclosure of the market value of financial instruments when it was available. That would have been seriously useful disclosure, I think. And we had to step aside from that. We did require extensive disclosures, but we didn't make huge inroads into what would theoretically have been available to people if they had gone to the various company registers and other public records – looked at the legal details of charges on assets, and that sort of thing. But of course, by putting them in as notes to the accounts in disclosures we made them much more available and likely to be used by people. So, if you like, we increased the set of information that people could use, even if in theory it was probably available somewhere else. I think in that sense it definitely did improve the availability of information. And remember, people do have limits to the time they are willing to put into researching accounting information. And I think FRS4 aided that enormously.

**GM** Yes, thank you.

**AVC** On that point, Geoff, I think it's also worth remembering that accounting is a language, and it facilitates the discussion of financial issues.

It's not just what the analyst can get out of it, it's what the general public can get out of it. You know, the profits and profit components of a company are widely quoted; similarly, their capital expenditure record, their borrowing structure or cash resources. There needs to be a more general education of the public on the implications of financial information.

**GW** That's a good point, Allan. I don't normally buy into the efficient markets view of life, which says that if information is available somewhere some diligent analyst will find it and put it into the public domain. Well, maybe in the long term that's true; but the immediate effect of accounts is often important and, after all, the next set of accounts is due out in six months. So if it's going to take you six months digging away to find it, that's not a very helpful story. And we have to think about the non-professional user as well. Not everybody is, as the Americans say, price protected by the efficient market. So I'd agree with that.

**GM There's a follow-up which links to that, which is, before FRS4 was there enough disclosure in the accounts for an analyst or a bank to reverse out and see through the sleight of hand designed to reduce taxable profit or to flatter the gearing ratio?**

**AVC** I can't answer in detail but I think you raise an interesting point regarding the attitude of the banks. Although I cannot be sure without looking at the letters they sent in, which are no longer available to me, I think that the banks, when they responded to us on this, didn't take the line of their investment banking people. My guess is that, on this one, they took the line of a retail banker, both as preparer of their own accounts and as user of their customers' accounts, rather than that of an inventor of devices that could be marketed.

**GM** That's fascinating. I'd not thought of the difference between perspectives within a bank.

**AVC** I suspect that's what was behind the more collaborative arrangements that we found.

**DPT** I think basically the retail banks had been blindsided – the credit side – by their investment bankers because these guys were coming up with all these fancy schemes, and, if the auditor accepted it, you probably found that the bank accepted it as well. And therefore when we came along and said, sorry, this is not equity, it's debt, suddenly there was a massive problem with loan covenants. They usually had a reported minimum required gearing ratio within the covenant. And we had quite a lot of discussions because the first reaction was, you can't do this, you are going to blow all these covenants apart; so therefore you shouldn't issue this standard. Well, that was ridiculous, because any change in accounting was likely to affect covenants. So we had quite constructive discussions eventually with the British Banking Association (BBA), to get them to say for covenants you should base them on whatever accounting is acceptable at the time the covenant was signed (frozen GAAP). But don't require the covenant to be based on current accounting standards – they are going to change in the future and unless your covenants automatically change with them you'll have lots of breaches. The BBA issued a statement to that effect.

This was probably the high point in our relationship with the banks, it fell apart shortly after that!

## Notes

1 A further incentive was the ability at the time, under an alternative treatment permitted by SSAP22, to eliminate the whole of acquired goodwill against reserves. This treatment of goodwill and reserves is discussed below in Chapter 7: it was ruled out in FRS10. If capital instruments financing an acquisition could be deemed to increase reserves, these could be used to eliminate all or part of the goodwill, removing any effect it would otherwise have had on the pre-existing gearing.
2 Companies are assessed individually for Corporation Tax, rather than on a consolidated group basis. Hence, tax gains can be made by shifting income between companies in the group even though aggregate group income is unaffected.
3 Goodwill arising on the acquisition that the 110 million pounds was raised to finance was written off against these reserves.
4 Studies have found evidence of earnings management ahead of share for share deals, and of such earnings management boosting the acquirers' share price – for example, Botsari and Meeks (2008, 2018) for the UK. Andrade et al. (2001) report that, at least for the US at this time, share for share exchange was used to finance the majority of acquisitions.
5 In writing this chapter we are grateful for the most helpful advice of Andrew Lennard, the ASB's former Assistant Technical Director, who was responsible for drafting FRS4. Andrew eventually became Technical Director of ASB.
6 An instrument that provides full shareholder rights in different companies (normally only two) under the same management and which can only be transferred jointly. Typically, the shares would be recorded on a single share certificate. The purpose was normally tax-driven but the tax loophole was later closed, with the result that the practice fell into disuse. For more detail See Evans and Evans (2007).

## References

### *Books and articles*

Andrade, G., Mitchell. M. and Stafford, E. (2001). New evidence and perspectives on mergers, *Journal of Economic Perspectives*, 15, 103–120, https://doi.org/10.1257/jep.15.2.103.

Botsari, A. and Meeks, G. (2008). Do acquirers manage earnings ahead of a takeover bid? *Journal of Business Finance and Accounting*, 35, 633–670, https://doi.org/10.1111/j.1468-5957.2008.02091.x.

Botsari, A. and Meeks, G. (2018). Acquirers' earnings management ahead of stock for stock bids in 'hot' and 'cold' markets, *Journal of Accounting and Public Policy*, 37, 355–375, https://doi.org/10.1016/j.jaccpubpol.2018.09.007.

Ernst & Young. (n.d.). *UK GAAP*, London: Ernst and Young.

Evans, O. and Evans, W. (2007). *The Complete Real Estate Encyclopedia*, New York: McGraw-Hill.

Marshall, A. (1995). 'Demise of a Popular Hybrid'. *Corporate Finance*, August, pp.18–19.

Tweedie, D. and Whittington, G. (1990). Financial reporting: Current problems and their implications for systematic reform. *Accounting and Business Research*, 21, 87–102.

### *Publications by standard-setters*

DP (1991). *Accounting for Capital Instruments*, ASB.

FRED3 (1992). *Accounting for Capital Instruments*, ASB.

FRS1 (1991). *Cash Flow Statements*, ASB.

FRS3 (1992). *Reporting Financial Performance*, ASB.

FRS4 (1993). *Capital Instruments*, ASB.

FRS5 (1994). *Reporting the Substance of Transactions*, ASB.

FRS10 (1997). *Goodwill and Intangible Assets*, ASB.

IAS32 *Financial Instruments*, IASC/IASB.

IASB *Conceptual Framework for Financial Reporting* (revised), March 2018, London: IASB.

SSAP22 (1984). *Accounting for Goodwill*, ASC.

TR677 (1987). *Accounting for Complex Capital Issues*, ICAEW Technical Committee, November 1987, London: ICAEW.

# 5 Reporting the substance of transactions

## Background

Over the first half of the 1980s concern grew that an increasing number of companies were having recourse to legal devices that had the effect of disguising the commercial effect of a series of linked transactions. A typical example was the sale of an asset subject to a side agreement that effectively compelled its repurchase at a price that reflected the interest cost of financing the asset for the intervening period. The legal form of such a contract was a sale and repurchase. If the transfer period spanned a reporting date, the seller would be able to show reduced borrowings and perhaps a large realised gain on the asset. The commercial substance, however, was finance secured on the asset, which should therefore remain in the accounts at its historical cost, with no recognition of the latent gain but instead an interest charge for the finance. As David has described in Chapter 2, when auditors objected that such devices should be reversed in order to enable the accounts to give a true and fair view of the financial position and results for the period, they were rebuffed by the lawyers and merchant banks who had devised the schemes. These argued that only the law could provide the certainty needed when constructing or interpreting commercial arrangements.

Matters were made worse by an unfortunate comment made by the DTI following a successful prosecution of the Argyll Foods company that "it is axiomatic that any emphasis of substance over form must not be at the expense of compliance with the law". In fairness to the DTI it should be said that the comment was made at a time shortly after the[1] implementation in UK law of the EC Fourth Directive, which had introduced across all member states the statutory UK principle of the True and Fair View as the paramount objective in the preparation of company accounts. The DTI throughout the 1980s was particularly sensitive to interpretations of the True and Fair View that might be seen in Europe as abuses of that newly established objective and which might ultimately cause the objective itself to be withdrawn from EC-wide law.

DOI: 10.4324/9781003346920-5

The first formal move to reassert the primacy of substance over mere legal form was made in December 1985 when the ICAEW issued a Technical Release, TR603, entitled Off-Balance Sheet Finance and Window Dressing. The Release acknowledged that existing standards addressed aspects of the problem; in particular, SSAP17 required disclosure of window dressing arrangements and SSAP21 specified rules for recognising sale and leaseback transactions in published accounts. The Release argued, however, that there was a need for "further guidance, which should be in general terms with emphasis placed on the requirement for published accounts to give a true and fair view".

The Release had persuasive rather than authoritative status but it was buttressed by a supportive statement by the DTI, which agreed that "the substance of a transaction was a relevant consideration in considering how appropriately to reflect [the information necessary to give a true and fair view]". Finally, the Release called for coordinated action by the ASC and the APC and suggested that, even before then, consideration might have to be given to the implications of the Release in the context of the Guide to Professional Ethics.

## The ASC's response

The ASC immediately took up the challenge, producing over the next four and a half years two exposure drafts, ED42 issued March 1988 entitled Accounting for special purpose transactions, and ED49 Reflecting the substance of transactions in assets and liabilities, which was issued in May 1990. ED42 followed the suggestion in TR603 by remaining at a fairly general level of prescription. However, in response to comments received, every subsequent proposal, both by the ASC and later by the ASB, provided greater detail of application to certain types of transactions.

The tension between the need to prescribe at a general level and the need for clear application guidance arose from a number of different factors.

- A standard would necessarily rely on principles if it were to be proof against a new twist in every fresh scheme proposed.
- But principles applied to all transactions. Care would have to be taken to avoid disrupting perfectly acceptable existing practices.
- Certain existing practices would need to be analysed to determine whether some transactions of that class required on-balance sheet treatment while others did not. The analysis would have to be sufficiently clear to provide effective guidance to those faced with similar circumstances in other trades.
- Innovative financial transactions were not automatically to be regarded as devious, despite the difficulties of formulating appropriate requirements for their accounting treatment.

ED 49 sought to resolve the tensions described above by developing a series of "application notes" each explaining how its principles should be applied in a particular type of transaction. The subjects covered were:

- Consignment stock – a common arrangement in, for example, the motor trade under which a manufacturer supplies stock to a dealer while retaining certain rights over it or the price to be paid.
- Sale and repurchase agreements – arrangements under which assets are sold by one party to another on terms that provide for the seller to re-acquire them in certain circumstances.
- Debt factoring – a widespread practice under which a business could transfer all or part of its trade debtors to a factor in order to obtain finance, sales ledger administration or sometimes, cover for bad debts.
- Securitisations – arrangements under which a specific block of assets (e.g. a portfolio of household mortgages) is transferred by one party, the "originator" to a special purpose vehicle, the "issuer", which finances the purchase by issuing loan notes carrying different degrees of risk. The first slice of risk is normally either borne by the originator or covered by insurance at the originator's expense. Once the arrangement is set up, neither the vehicle nor the loan note holders have recourse against any other assets of the originator. The vehicle is designed not to fall within the Companies Act definition of a subsidiary of the originator.
- Loan transfers – arrangements under which a lender transfers specific loans or parts of them to another party, the "transferee", either for an immediate cash payment or for a series of payments over the terms of the loans.

The same application notes, though much developed and better analysed, were carried forward in FRED4 and FRS5.

## The approach of FRS5

For FRS5, as for all the exposure drafts from ED42 onwards, the starting point in determining the substance of transactions lay in identifying the assets and liabilities that arose from those transactions. For this purpose, initially the "essential characteristics of assets and liabilities" were described in terms used by the FASB or IASC but for FRED4 the ASB was able to use the definitions from its own draft Statement of Principles:

> **Assets**
> Rights or other access to future economic benefits controlled by an entity as a result of past transactions or events.
>
> **Liabilities**
> An entity's obligations to transfer economic benefits as a result of past transactions or events.

Another feature common to all the exposure drafts and FRS5 was the requirement that a vehicle that was effectively controlled by the reporting entity, though not qualifying as a subsidiary in terms of the Companies Act, should be included in the group accounts of that entity. In FRS5 such vehicles were called "quasi-subsidiaries".[2]

FRS5 stated that in identifying a quasi-subsidiary regard should be had to who in practice directed the financial and operating policies of the vehicle or could prevent others from enjoying the benefits arising from the vehicle's net assets. When those policies were predetermined, the party with control was the one that gained the benefits arising from the net assets and was exposed to the risks inherent in them.

In identifying whether transactions had created new assets and liabilities or changed existing ones, FRS5 enunciated two key principles:

- A group or series of transactions that achieve or is designed to achieve an overall commercial effect should be viewed as a whole.
- All of a transaction's aspects and implications should be identified and greater weight given to those likely to have a commercial effect in practice. This principle was particularly relevant to analysing the effect of options.

The standard specified rules for recognising and derecognising assets and liabilities but went on to address "special cases" where there had been a significant change in an asset, though not enough to justify derecognising it completely. These cases involved a transfer to others of:

- only part of the item in question;
- all of the item for only part of its life; or
- all of the item for all of its life but leaving the transferor with some significant right to benefits or exposure to risk.

The detail of this requirement reflected the extent to which the standard had to deal with transactions that sliced and diced the benefits and risks normally attached to assets and liabilities in order to transfer them to parties more interested in accepting certain of those benefits and risks.

## Securitisations

By far the most difficult issue faced by the ASB in producing FRS5 was the treatment of securitisations. Views were strongly divided both among the Board's constituents and within the Board itself. Some argued that a balance sheet should display the full resources of the business and, separately, the finance that supported them. Secured loans, project finance, and other forms of ring fencing had not been regarded as justifying netting the finance against the asset so as to present only the net asset. Similarly, even when a parent had not guaranteed the loans of a subsidiary, it was still required to present them separately in its consolidated accounts.

Against this it was argued that separate presentation of securitised assets and liabilities would fail to reflect the nature of the arrangement, in which, for example, the loan notes issued by the vehicle would typically have a higher credit rating than that of the originator.They were secured, not against the originator's assets, but solely against those of the vehicle, with not even a contingent claim on the resources of the originator. Furthermore, it was claimed, it was more important for the balance sheet to show the exposure of the entity to credit loss than to show resources from which it retained a flow of future profits (for example through retention of mortgage servicing rights) but which were not available to other creditors.

The Board inclined to the former view and in October 1991 issued Bulletin 15 on this single issue, proposing a requirement for separate presentation of securitised assets and their supporting liabilities on the balance sheet. After reviewing the responses and following an intensive search for a solution that met the practical needs of the industry while remaining compatible with its own principles, the Board devised a new form of "linked presentation", under which the finance was deducted from the gross securitised assets on the face of the originator's balance sheet.

## Profit and loss account

While remaining essentially focused on the balance sheet, FRS5 addressed profit and loss recognition at a number of points. It echoed the requirement in SSAP18 Accounting for Contingencies that, where the amount of any gain or loss on a series of transactions is uncertain, full provision should be made for any probable loss but recognition of a gain should be deferred to the extent that it is in doubt. In analysing securitisations, it clarified that profit recognised on the transfer of a portfolio should be restricted to the difference between the non-returnable proceeds and the amount at which the portfolio was previously held. Any further profit flowing to the transferor should be recognised only as it occurs. And, in dealing with linked presentations, it specified that only the net income or expense need normally be reported in the profit and loss account, with the gross components in the notes.

## Offset

Having introduced into UK accounting standards, through FRS5, definitions of assets and liabilities, the Board took the opportunity to specify the conditions under which debit and credit balances should be offset, on the grounds that they formed a single asset or liability. The debit and credit balances must be in the same or a freely convertible currency and the reporting entity must have the ability to enforce net settlement, that is, to receive payment of the amount due to it at or before the time it settles its debt to the other party.

Unlike the FASB, the Board did not require that the reporting entity intend to settle net, since this was regarded as a matter of administrative convenience with no implications for the rights and obligations of the parties.

## Conclusion

By April 1994, when FRS5 was eventually issued, the issues it tackled had been debated, both within and outside the formal standard setting process, over some ten years. The initial focus had been on halting practices that were widely regarded as abuses. In this, the project was largely successful, even from an early stage. ED42 in March 1988 put those who devised the more blatant schemes on notice that the days for such manipulation were numbered. Schemes were put on hold pending issue of a definitive standard, leading some commentators to quip that the project should remain indefinitely at the exposure draft stage. The precise terms of a standard, they said, would be quickly circumvented, whereas the uncertainty surrounding an exposure draft left scheme designers unwilling to draft proposals whose accounting representation could be reversed in the near future.

As the project progressed, two factors mentioned above in the second section of this resumé increased the complexity of the task. First was the need to avoid the trap of "mission creep". To rewrite the principles of accounting might be a fair objective for a Conceptual Framework, or "Statement of Principles" in the ASB's terminology, but it was not a suitable brief for an accounting standard. The ASB picked its way through this minefield through extensive consultation and significant elaboration of the standard, particularly in the Application Notes, to clarify precisely where it was introducing change.

The second complicating factor was dealing with the challenge posed by innovative transactions involving highly complex structures, which in many cases continued to evolve, even as the Board attempted to determine its position on the examples first presented to it. Eventual success in this area owed much to the perseverance and intellectual energy of the staff member leading the project, Sandra Thompson. Her ability to identify the issues raised by every twist and turn of the evidence or of the Board's own thinking and respond rapidly with a clear set of options for Board decisions kept the project on course and delivered a standard consistent with the Board's Principles, while also largely acceptable to all sides of the Board's constituency.

## Allan Cook

### *Discussion*

**GM What were the forces that led to FRS5?**

**DPT** I think the main ones were the schemes that were around in the mid-eighties, especially the type of devices used by Burnett and Hallamshire.

This was a company that was one of the glamour stocks of the markets about five years earlier, and it ended up with losses even bigger than Westland Helicopter, which was the big issue of the time. It raised huge questions of accounting which were mentioned by the *Financial Times* reporting on the rescue of Burnett and Hallamshire; and it was a cautionary tale about businesses expanding too fast and just really going completely over the top. At the meeting where they had to rescue the company, there was a rueful banker who said Burnett and Hallamshire had taken off balance sheet financing to a new art. I think people were quite shocked by the scale of it.

There was heavy recourse to off balance sheet financing by the company. It was the biggest opencast mining contractor to the National Coal Board. It had coal mines in Pennsylvania, South Africa, lignite reserves in Northern Ireland, property in California, investments in Terra del Fuego, construction business in Iraq; and at one stage in 1981, it was buying a company a month. And in the FT report on it the Chairman was quoted as saying to his staff, 'Have we bought anything else this morning?' So it was almost a daily occurrence.

And then it all went belly up. The year-long coal strike wrecked the UK business. The Iran-Iraq War hit the construction contracts in Iraq. There were profits of 11.8 million pounds taken on a property joint venture in California. But the joint venture was on the basis that, having sold half of it to this other party, the other party could pull out if planning permission wasn't given. So there was almost 12 million pounds profit shown although no cash had yet changed hands in the deal, and then it all had to be reversed when in fact they didn't get planning permission – which led one of the shareholders at that meeting…

**Dog Tweedie** intervened noisily at this point. He had not been alive at the time of the Burnett and Hallamshire scandal. But the master of his great grandfather had been one of those shareholders. And Dog Tweedie vividly remembered his great grandfather calling together all his great grandpuppies – including Dog Tweedie – shortly before his death, to tell them the sorry tale of Burnett and Hallamshire and exhort them always to lead their masters clear of accounting skullduggery. [Interviewer's note: This is reported to be why Sir David, Dog Tweedie's master, ended up a regulator rather than a (much wealthier) investment banker.]

**DPT** … to ask very interesting questions, such as: when is a profit not a profit? Having taken this gain in a previous year, it had all to be written back. There were all sorts of hidden off balance sheet problems. Six speculative ventures in California incurred borrowings of about 28 million pounds hidden under a general contingent liability for "guarantees amounting to £41.23 million in respect of certain contracts and undertakings entered in the ordinary course of business". In Pennsylvania, they had to pay the vendors of a coal company royalties of $7.5 million every year whether or not they mined coal, and they didn't! In South Africa, one of their subsidiaries had an onerous contract with a shipping company and to prevent the company's collapse Burnett and Hallamshire had to buy the ship involved, which they did on hire purchase. So the whole thing was really a complete mess. And looking at Tonkin and Skerratt, Financial Reporting 1986–1987 – it says that in the accounts of 31 March 1984, the group showed net assets of 108 million pounds and an innocent-looking contingent liability note. A year later the accounts of 31 March 1985 show net liabilities of 4 million, reveal a myriad off balance sheet ventures and show two balance sheets at the year end, one of which follows the substance of transactions, and one which adopts the legal form. And in the accounts the directors themselves stated:

> In the opinion of the directors the balance sheet of the group prepared in accordance with Schedule 4 does not provide sufficient information to give a true and fair view. Accordingly an adjusted group balance sheet has been drawn up to show the substance of the group's liabilities and obligations [and it mentions various companies]. The group balance sheet at 31 March 1985 must be read in conjunction with the adjusted group balance sheet set out above, and the notes.

So it was actually emphasising that last bit: you've got to read the other balance sheet alongside – you might say 'the legal one'.

So what was the main issue? They had to write off 116 million pounds during the year in which they were rescued. And I think it really started showing up the problems. The Companies Act really didn't have enough bite in it. It only required you to show a company as a subsidiary if:

you were a member of it and controlled the composition of its board of directors; or

you held more than half in nominal value of its equity share capital

And, of course, people just waltzed past it – which was quite easily done. For example,

- i You could have less than 50% of the shares, but you could have an option to buy the others. Then you just controlled it because the option was hanging like the Sword of Damocles;
- ii You might have no shares but you might have provided all the finance, which you could pull out if the directors didn't do what you wanted;
- iii You could have an equal number of directors with, say, a merchant bank as the other 50% shareholder; but your directors had two votes each and the bank had one. So you didn't control the composition, you just controlled the board;
- iv You had the golden share, and maybe gave 100% of the equity shares to somebody else but they had no powers – it was all controlled by the Memorandum and Articles or by the golden share, which channelled all the benefits to you.

So these were the things that the Companies Act did not take into account. It was just really not fit for purpose in the end. And, you know, I think the reaction around the financial community was pretty strong. You've got Griffiths (1986) – who said:

> There's been a steady increase in the number of schemes which are not visible even to the most highly trained eye. This is the most sinister aspect of creative accountancy, and stems from what has been called "off balance sheet financing". This involves 'schemes which, rather than manipulate existing figures, actually exclude them altogether from the financial statements. It's impossible to detect them, even from a detailed analysis of the small print in the notes.

Really there were two points being made – he went on to say:

> The problem for the accountancy profession is that it has condoned, and in some cases quite properly encouraged, an element of creative accounting by its corporate clientele. For it to turn round suddenly and say that off balance sheet finance is the unacceptable face of creativity may leave it with some awkward questions to answer about the acceptability of tactics and techniques which have been permitted in earlier accounting periods. The crucial question is: where should the line be drawn?

Rather sadly in a way – the Financial Reporting chapter I quoted earlier ends up by talking about Burnett and Hallamshire. It says:

> This one example alone demonstrates the inadequacy of the position propounded by the Law Society and the relevance of the Institute Technical Release (TR603), but it is the lawyers' position that now prevails in practice and will continue to do so until either the accounting profession regains control of its own territory or a series of financial disasters exposes our deficiencies and perhaps imposes unwelcome regulation over us...meanwhile billions of pounds are being invested in off balance sheet schemes.

So that's the background to it, and that's why we got involved very early on with the problem. I thought I would just talk freely about the shortcomings of the consolidation requirements and the off balance sheet subsidiaries, but there were other schemes – and Allan mentioned one earlier which was a very common one I met in practice – the whisky sale. I used to say to my students: "Whatever you do, don't drink a one year old whisky; because if you do you lose the bouquet and flavour; but more importantly you lose your power of speech". And it was done very easily. What the distillery would do was, since they had to hold the stuff for five years before blending it, the whisky would be sold to a bank with an option to repurchase it; and the bank would have an option to put it back. And the terms were identical. The call option was to pay back the bank at the purchase price and interest at normal lending rates up to the time of the repurchase. And the whisky never left the distillery; the distillery paid the interest quarterly. And they would claim – the lawyers would tell them – it was a sale. And it was just a loan secured on stock. That was a classic.

So all these things were happening at the same time. And that shows you the real problems faced by the ASC and the profession in general. I used to say that the balance sheet was an optional extra. There was so much missing, it was hardly worth showing what was left. On the right side (assets) there was nothing left, and on the left side (funds) there was nothing right. It was just a complete shambles.

That's my latest rant over.

**GM Thank you, David. Anyone want to say anything more on that question before we move on? I think Allan's going to pick up on the relations with TR603 and the rest.**

**GW** The only thing I'd add is that David gave a most lurid and prominent example. There was a huge variety of these things, you know. There were five application notes to the standard, and these were illustrative rather than comprehensive. That tells you the variety of issues. The fundamental problem was the way markets developed in the 1980s, particularly the growth of financial engineering and the role of investment banks. I was quite amused that it was a banker who complained about Burnett and Hallamshire because no doubt it was another banker who devised the scheme you couldn't see through. So it was a whole business climate, and that's why the standard – although the application notes were vital for showing you how you applied principles to circumstances – the standard had to be a principles standard. And it had to cover things that hadn't happened yet. It had to apply to all financial engineering of that sort, asserting substance over form, which was the essence of TR603, I think.

**AVC** I was interested in the example that David quoted about royalties that had to be paid whether you were extracting anything or not. And that's an obvious case where the legal form may say 'royalties' and that's something to be recognised in the future. But the substance is: you have to pay them whether anything is extracted or not. You've got a future liability there already. You are stuck with it. And it was those sorts of issues which needed at that time to be brought out very clearly.

**GW** 'Substance' is a very vague word. That's why the application notes were extremely important because you could argue that in the situation David was describing when things hadn't gone wrong the substance was that they made profits. If you took a fair value approach and looked at the future and did the valuation on that basis, you had made a fair value gain. We had that long IASB project on insurance with discussion about when you took the profit: when the insurance policy was issued, or do you spread your gains over the lifetime, or wait till the thing is completed? So I think it's important to say that substance is a difficult concept to pin down. And the whole standard shows the difficulty of that, of actually doing principled accounting. You can assert a principle and if people are scoundrels they will immediately weasel their way around it. So you've got to have examples to show how to apply the principle, and that's where FRS5 scored, and indeed ED49 before it, because that's where the application notes originated.

**GM Allan, were you going to tell us about the development of the foundations of FRS5 in TR603 and the subsequent ASC Exposure Drafts?**

**AVC** You note from what David was saying there that the Burnett and Hallamshire financial accounts were for March 1985, and it was in 1985 that the Technical Committee of the ICAEW decided it was time that there was something official – or semi-official – said. You have to remember that the individual Institutes of Accountants had passed over the standard-setting responsibility to the Accounting Standards Committee, the ASC. So the Technical Committee had to pick its way rather carefully so as not to imply that they were trying to steal a march on the ASC. The worst result would have been if they had tried to do that and it had been like a firework that had failed to go off. In fact that rather suited the Technical Committee's purpose because it wouldn't have been possible to have elaborated detailed guidance – as you can see from the time it took to produce FRS5.

In the short term, something was needed. So instead the Committee did stay at a pretty high level of generality, but it was quite subtle in the way that it did it. First of all, it moved away a little bit from the term 'substance' – although it used the word, it took its stand firmly on the legal requirement to show a true and fair view. And it spelt out the various steps to be taken if following the normal rules did not achieve that. You had to provide additional information to enable a true and fair view to be obtained by the reader. And that might require putting more things into the balance sheet, or profit and loss account. Or it might be sufficient just to give disclosure. Those were the two options – it called the first one an accounting solution (nowadays we would say 'recognition'), and the second one disclosure. But it pressed if possible for an accounting solution. It recommended at the end of its short statement that the ASC should work to produce a standard identifying the type of schemes that they were talking about and requiring good presentation for them.

**GW** Allan, who was the author, or who were the authors of TR603? Because I was on the Technical Committee at the time, and **we** certainly didn't write it. I seem to remember you coming along with drafts of it and we commented on it. Is that right?

**AVC** I think it is right. I was asked by Ken Wild, Technical Committee chairman, to lead a sub-committee on this, and I said, "Why me? I don't know anything about this". And he said, "Well, we think you should". I think I now understand why. The other members of the committee apart from Geoff and myself were probably already committed, or at least their firms were. And they might have felt conflicted. Or they might just have encountered trouble back home when they came to talk about it.

**GW** So you did draft it, Allan.

**AVC** At least, I worked with a team that did – I may well have done the scribing, but I think that a lot of the really useful information came from others, especially John Kellas, David's partner at KPMG, who came up with the important principle that where something is just a return, where a repurchase price is effectively just the original selling price plus interest for the period, then it's not a sale at all, it's just a loan.

**DPT** I should point out, Allan, that John was at Thomson McLintock at the time and not KPMG.

**AVC** I beg his pardon. The Scottish conscience was already informing us. Another of his key principles was that one should look at the commercial rationale behind things. If you couldn't see why both parties would have entered into an arrangement, there was something fishy about it. That kind of idea has really emigrated from FRS5 into all sorts of other things now that we'll come across later in our conversation.

I said that TR603 was subtle, and the final subtlety was it not only suggested the ASC should do something. It also suggested that the APC (the Auditing Practices Committee) should enquire into cases where substance had apparently not been reflected. And it went further, and it said that perhaps there should also be consideration of "whether there are any implications resulting from this Technical Release in the context of the Guide to Professional Ethics". And that was quite cunning because those ethical principles applied not only to auditors but also to directors that were members of the Institute. And the thought of having an ethics committee pronounce against you would not have been particularly welcome to anybody. I don't remember whether there were any such cases, but it was certainly not an empty threat.

So the next move was taken by the ASC. TR603 was published in December 1985 and the ASC immediately set up a working party. Again it was natural that John and I, together with others associated with TR603, were put into the working party. I continued to learn quite a lot about these various schemes, but also about many other perfectly ordinary practices that had to be distinguished from the devious ones. And I began to realise how difficult and complicated the problem would be.

Well, initially, the first Exposure Draft produced in March 1988, ED42, was called Accounting for Special Purpose Transactions. That shows you the line that was being taken: we are not trying to capture ordinary transactions, we are trying to capture those that are out to do something rather special. And that stayed at a fairly high level of generality. There were no application notes, but it did enunciate the principles. However, the responses we received on that indicated that further guidance was needed. And that led eventually to ED49, with its five application notes.

But in this period I began to find out, as I said, how some of these arrangements were made. And I remember in particular speaking at a conference where a fellow presenter came from Salomon Bros. You can imagine what he was proposing. He gave a very good defence of securitisation. And it was my first detailed encounter, I think, with that. He backed it up – I forget whether it was given to everybody, but certainly I got a copy of the prospectus for what we would now call a plain vanilla securitisation, one of the fairly innocent types. And it was evident from that document that intensive due diligence had been done by the originating bank. Securitisation was essentially an arrangement whereby a bank moved a portfolio of its mortgages into a vehicle, which issued loan notes to finance the purchase. But there was a lot of detail there about where those mortgages had come from, the type of households that had entered into them, and so the loan note holders would understand exactly what were the risks of that portfolio.

It seemed to me at that time that that was a useful financial innovation.

**DPT** I remember being present at a London conference a year after the global financial crisis when the CEO of a major British bank praised the great financial innovations of the previous decades. Paul Volcker snorted that "the only good financial innovation of the last 25 years was the Automatic Teller Machine!"

**AVC** It was not a devious scheme at all. The banks had their reasons for wanting to do this, which we can go into later, but it was a sensible financial arrangement. It enabled each level of loan note holders to take up different levels of risk, depending on their appetite for risk. And that served the general purposes of the market, as well as the desires of the originator. So I was won over perhaps. I did form a strong impression at that stage that securitisation was something that we would have to allow in some form. But the problem was: in what form? Because they were changing all the time, and particularly later.

**GW** But surely the issue is not whether securitisations are a good idea or not, because of course they are a means of financing, and may provide cheaper financing to people in some circumstances. But the problem is: how do you report it? Does the thing remain, as the quote from Griffiths said, does it remain obscure so that even a skilled observer can't tell what's going on? I mean that's to do with the reporting, not the deal. Nobody is arguing people who do securitisations are crooks. Maybe if they do it for the purpose of deceiving their investors and shareholders you might think they are crooks. But if they just do it to raise money, and they tell everybody what they are doing, that's fine. But they weren't telling everybody what they were doing. And they were opposing you. And we'll discuss why it took four more years after ED49 for the ASB to come up with FRS5. It was because people did want the other advantage, which was a less worthy one – they wanted to improve their reported gearing ratios, make people feel they weren't so burdened with debt and interest as they actually were.

**AVC** Yes and no. The banks faced the problem of capital adequacy controls. There was a limit to how much they could borrow. Therefore a bank that had got good access to mortgages could make a business out of taking in portfolios of mortgages, continuing to administer them, and then shipping them off its balance sheet to the vehicle…

**GW** Yes, and it's not a good thing if it's designed to circumvent the capital adequacy requirements.

**AVC** As you've just said – the issue was how should these arrangements be reported. I accept that the problem wasn't that the proponents of these schemes were crooks. It was that they wanted to say these things were no longer on their balance sheet. And that, of course, raised the hackles of the accountants. I nearly said the purists, but it goes to the fundamentals of accounts that subsidiaries are included in the consolidation. And ED42, as later ED49, was using the idea of a quasi-subsidiary to describe certain off balance sheet schemes, and it was pretty obvious that these securitisation vehicles were indeed quasi-subsidiaries. So that raised all sorts of difficult issues which really hit home when the ASB took over from the ASC.

**GM Thank you. Geoff, I wonder if you could fill us in on the link between FRS5, the DTI and the 7th Directive?**

**GW** The 7th Directive altered the definition of subsidiaries and was implemented in the 1989 Companies Act. And, of course, that to some extent helped with the problem of off balance sheet financing, because it moved the basis for consolidation from ownership to control. As David described earlier, it was possible to manipulate ownership so that you nominally didn't own the thing, but nevertheless, you controlled it, and it was all for your benefit – just by structuring the terms of the shares, the management, and who appointed the directors. So that did alter things in the ASB's favour, as it were, towards making FRS5 have less to do.

But of course it didn't remove the need to deal with quasi-subsidiaries, which were not subsidiaries under the Companies Act still. It was possible to structure such vehicles in such a way that they did not have to be consolidated. And that's what FRS5 dealt with.

At the same time, of course, while that was going on, the ASB was being formed; the Dearing Committee and then the ASB. And that in a sense was a product of the 1980s and the cowboy financial engineering that had gone on. It was the general dissatisfaction with accounting – in fact, accounting became a worthy item for news in the press. They don't seem to have accounting correspondents anymore. The Times used to have a regular weekly column by Robert Bruce. Everybody was fascinated by it.

So the Dearing Committee was sitting in 1988. The ASB was set up a year or so later. And that, of course was what led to FRS5. But the ASB took over, as we've seen, the work of the ASC. The problem with the ASC was not its technical competence or its capacity to deal with the problems by crafting standards. It was enforcement. The ASC had lost a lot of authority in the inflation accounting debate when there was a wholesale rebellion against ASC's proposals. The Institutes, who had legitimised the ASC through the CCAB, no longer felt confident to claim authority to say what a true and fair view was, or what generally accepted accounting principles were. It just didn't wash anymore. An ASC pronouncement which was widely rejected in practice could not be described realistically as 'generally accepted'.

So there was always that fear in the ASC that it would happen again. And the finance community was a sufficient lobby, I think, to make the ASC frightened. They weren't frightened to produce ED49, which was very good, because they knew that they weren't going to have to turn it into a standard: they were handing over to the ASB by then. That's what the ASB did inherit – a rich heritage from the ASC. But it was a poisoned chalice potentially.

**AVC** I'd just add there that I think there was an interesting change of attitude about the importance of control as a basis of consolidation. The 7th Directive had a number of different ways of implementation that were open to the member states. At the beginning of the 1980s I do remember that there was an effort – of which I was part, I'm now ashamed to admit – to say to the DTI: "Look, you must try to restrict some of these rather Germanic ideas of purposive control. We must stick to tight legalistic definitions. Otherwise, anything might be control". Then, obviously as a result of the sort of events that David has been describing, we all began to change our minds.

Certainly, as soon as I got involved in preparing TR603 I was lobbying hard for a broader concept of control. DTI officials were sympathetic and introduced into what became the 1989 Companies Act language that considerably enlarged the previous understanding of control. For example, in addition to the earlier criteria for defining a parent based on majority voting rights or appointment rights over a majority of the board of directors, the Act included: the right to exercise a dominant influence under the other company's Memorandum and Articles; and even, holding a participating interest and actually exercising a dominant influence. Another criterion for identifying a parent was that it held a participating interest in a company and was managed on a unified basis with that company. A parent would also be recognised if it was a shareholder in another company and under an agreement with other shareholders controlled alone a majority of the voting rights in that company.

**GM Why did FRS5 take so long? We were saying in the last chapter how quickly FRS4 went through, and FRS5 is the other extreme, isn't it? You've given us half the answer already, haven't you, because you've talked about the genesis of FRS5; but is there anything you would add?**

**AVC** I think I would say that it wasn't only securitisation, although that was the principal factor, that caused the problem. One of the points I've just been making is that the prior drafts – TR603, followed by ED42, then ED49 – all advanced to greater degrees of specificity, but at the same time expanded the scope of the principles, as can be seen from their titles: so ED42 – Special Purpose Transactions and ED49 – Reflecting the Substance of Transactions in Assets and Liabilities still tied the subject quite firmly to off balance sheet finance. But when we moved to FRS5 the Board was taking a much broader view of its principles (We were developing our Statement of

Principles at the same time, of course) and you can see that from the title: Reporting the Substance of Transactions. That's pretty well all embracing. That did lead us into some difficulties because all sorts of areas that we never intended to be dealing with here suddenly popped up. And, David, I think you have a good story about British Aerospace, don't you, on that one?

**DPT** Well I remember we were just about to publish FRED4 when suddenly the finance director of British Aerospace, realised that they had sold most of their aircraft on the basis that they would buy them back at the end of their life. And, of course, 'sale and repurchase' almost would have nullified the sale. So we would have taken out most of British Aerospace's profits by knocking out all their sales. I remember the CFO, who had been consulted about our proposals, coming in with a purple face and knotted veins. It was a real pain because we had to consider pulling the publication. Eventually, to avoid delaying the project for months, we decided to publish the exposure draft as already written and told BAe to comment on it emphasising their problem which we would examine with them before issuing a final standard.

**AVC** That all flowed from the fact that we'd introduced recognition and derecognition as general principles. So not only British Aerospace and its buyback at the end of useful life, but earnouts on sales of businesses, indeed any kind of warranties would have postponed recognition of the original sale. The draft standard could also have affected the reporting of derivatives, which we had never really begun to think about very seriously, by implying that both sides should be grossed up. That would have completely transformed balance sheets, utterly swamping them. All sorts of things like that. So we developed a series of tests for what we called 'partial derecognition'. And you find that now in the Standard, which sets out how you should deal with circumstances where you might dispose of an asset for part of its life, or all of its life but only part of the asset. We've mentioned some of that in the Introduction to this chapter.

Another thing that caused us problems right at the end was that we thought that if we were dealing with derecognition this was the moment to talk about offset. So we did set out some – to my mind – very sensible offset rules. But those also caused a certain amount of anxiety among the particular industries or areas that felt that they were suddenly having to re-do all their accounting. We got requests for delayed implementation or complete exemption. We refused complete exemption but we did give delayed implementation to one or two industries.

**GW** I think what this shows, Allan, is that we were – the Board – having to deal with the constituency and, of course, the objections that they raised. That's why I said the ASC did a lot for us, but in a sense they did the easy bit: they didn't have to implement it. Most of the basic ideas were in ED49. The way I'd put it is: we were actually the innovators in implementing for the first time. But we didn't have quite the powers that we'd have liked. Our powers under the Companies Act were quite ambiguous, and so were the remedies against companies that didn't conform with the standards. Ultimately, it was the court that would have to apply them. And I don't think the FRC would have been very keen on going to court. I remember they'd put most of their cash into a big reserve to fight a case. But if the merchant banks and so on had wanted to take us on and had refused to implement FRS5, and they had ended up in court, they'd have had huge resources. And there was no guarantee that it would have gone our way.

Yet it was really a flagship standard; we wanted it to get through to establish the ASB's authority. So – as I put it earlier in one of our emails, we were not actually walking on water –a powerful, messianic, new Board with new powers, telling people what to do and sorting out the world – instead we were actually walking on very thin ice. We needed to tread very carefully, get everybody on board so that all the nightmares that standard-setting had suffered under the inflation accounting debate – that sort of thing – didn't emerge in relation to off balance sheet financing. So ultimately the delay was the constituency's fault, not ours!

**AVC** Well, I would pay tribute here to Sandra Thompson (first of all Sandra Webb – she got married in the middle of one of the most difficult parts of the Standard), who was extraordinarily good at finding out all the nooks and crannies of the problems. And we pursued those with the various parties. As I said, it was securitisation that was the real problem. The first thing that the Board did was to discuss the responses to ED49. And by the middle of August 1991, they were beginning to line up with their views. David arranged a presentation by two of his former colleagues which set out the case for treating securitisation as somewhat different from a normal consolidation problem. One of those colleagues was a banking partner, and the other was a senior technical partner. And from different angles, they both were making the same point – among other things the point that the credit rating of the vehicle, applicable to the loan notes it issued, was often better[3] than the originating bank's credit rating. And that showed the difficulty – it showed how different it was from a normal kind of subsidiary, where a parent might have guaranteed the loans of its subsidiary. Here it didn't need to guarantee anything. It needed to take the first level of risk, but nothing more.

To my surprise, the Board was unpersuaded by those arguments. I think I was the only member who didn't vote for a hard line to be taken in a subsequent announcement of the Board's intentions on how securitisations should be reflected on the balance sheet – what was called Bulletin 15. (We didn't call it an Exposure Draft because it addressed only a single issue.) The Board said that securitised assets should remain on the originator's balance sheet and the finance supporting the loan notes should appear among the liabilities on the other side. In other words, treat the vehicle as any subsidiary – as a quasi-subsidiary – so that it goes on both sides of the balance sheet.

The responses that we got lined up exactly how you would expect. All the technical partners, or most of them, agreed with that hard line. All the banks and the banking partners were on the other side. The Board dived into this and discussed all sorts of different ways of resolving the conundrum, including the idea of net presentation, where the asset would be shown under some sort of asset category (some suggested right at the bottom of the balance sheet), but the finance deducted immediately from it. This is what we subsequently called "linked presentation". Some Board members' positions shifted from the uniform, hard line of Bulletin 15, with the consequence that the debate aligned broadly along the two sides of the divide described in the introduction to the chapter. In some ways that was no bad thing because it meant that all aspects of the problem were thoroughly explored.

By the time we'd got to April 1992 Sandra produced a paper which was effectively reading the Riot Act to the Board. It said you've now had six discussions since Bulletin 15 (of course, we'd already had plenty of discussions leading up to Bulletin 15); and it's now vital that we do something because all this is holding up the rest of the Board agenda. That moved things forward a little, but what particularly concentrated minds was that the following month the Counsel who had been advising us on what we could do with some of our more innovative standards said that, if an originator securitised a hundred's worth of assets – retaining only ten, as a liability for the first slice – he couldn't see that there was a remaining liability of a hundred. And that gave a pretty good indication of what a court would find if that sort of issue came up. Now it's interesting because it wasn't the first suggestion that the liability should be netted, but it did give a strong push towards the netting solution; and from then on we worked to develop conditions for a linked presentation. We hedged around that part of the standard very carefully to make sure that there really was no possibility of any further risk coming back for the whole period of the contract.

It's probably the only standard that is conditional on five 'whatsoevers' – no possibility whatsoever five times over in the standard – when describing how secure the originator should be from any possibility of loss on the hundred. With that, the linked presentation was able to cut the Gordian knot of securitisation in a way that I think worked rather well. I personally was very satisfied with it, though some members of the Board were less so, I think. At one stage we had explored the possibility of making exceptions on a pragmatic basis, but that proved to be a fool's errand really because it was impossible to draw the line. Should it be just banks, because they were subject to capital adequacy requirements, other institutions that did banking-type transactions, or every one of five other types of financial businesses that were subject to official regulation of some kind? And where should it stop? There were at least two major originators of household mortgages that were not regulated at all. The netting solution with linked presentation seemed to me and, I think, most of the Board to be an elegant solution to a difficult problem.

**GM Very good. Thank you.**

**Geoff, you had been talking about 'thin ice'. Do you wish to pursue that?**

**GW** Well, what Allan's been saying indicates how responsive the Board had to be to the community, and it is obvious that these issues are very complex and raise difficult accounting problems. Navigating between them was quite difficult, but, in addition, navigating between principles and detailed rules is very difficult. Dealing with the details always leads you towards rules, that's the problem. Allan's just praised the netting approach – sorry, the linked presentation approach – and that really was a compromise, you've got to face it. You can say, well, no line in accounting is dead clear and so this is on the borderline and could be resolved one way or the other. But it was a compromise between what some members of the Board wanted and what some of the constituency wanted. Ernst and Young are a good example – Ernst and Young's commentary. Ron Paterson and Alister Wilson, principal authors of this book [*UK GAAP* (Davies et al., 1997) waved at the camera] say that they think the linking approach ought to have been 'strangled at birth'. And they say that it breaks the basic Companies Act rule – if it is a rule – that liabilities should be on one side of the balance sheet and assets should be on the other side. And if you want to question net presentation, you could say, well, with subsidiaries we insist that they report gross, even when there is no comeback to the holding company. Holding companies don't have to pay the liabilities of subsidiaries unless they specifically guarantee them, but the parent does have to report all of the subsidiary company's liabilities in the consolidated balance sheet. So, you know, it is an arguable thing. FRS5 does have compromises.

I don't go along with Ernst and Young all the way, of course. They complain that the whole standard is far too detailed in the applications, and they think the whole thing should be revisited in five years' time or something. But the point of it is that it was a complex area, and it was a complex standard; and we were drawn into these complexities by doing the application notes. We did our best, and it was a robust standard at the end. And I think the problem went away. But I think it was the principle that drove its success. It was the principle that you've got to go for substance over form. And if you don't do that, then you'll probably find your reporting of a deal banned after the event if not before it. And in that sense, it was a successful standard, and it was a really honest attempt to introduce principles into accounting, and actually explain what those principles implied. Explaining what they implied was a nightmare. And obviously, the constituents put up quite a battle, as Allan described.

**GM But it did work in terms of closing down the worst of the schemes, is that right?**

**GW** Oh yes, it did. After all, it's a very pedantic, accountant's issue. Do you show the asset less the liability and the net amount on one side, the assets side, of the balance sheet; or do you show the asset on one side and the liability on the other side, with a note saying, by the way, these two are linked?

**GM Sure. I was thinking more broadly, though, considering the whole thrust of the Standard. You look back on it as a success?**

**GW** Oh, definitely. I think the intellectual success, if you like, goes with Allan, if you spare his blushes. And the other people who drafted TR603.

They started us on the right lines – with the principle of substance over form, and the ASC carried it forward very well with ED42 and ED49. And ED49 pioneered the application notes. They started them. It was all done at that stage. But the ASB's job was, as I say, this walking on thin ice. It was actually getting the constituency to accept this, and they kept coming up, as Allan related, with new deals and "what about this?" "What if this happens, and that happens?" It led us into some of the things Ernst and Young criticised us for – unfairly in a way. If we had done it without the application notes, Ernst and Young would have been saying this is airy fairy stuff, it isn't specific enough. It's very easy to be a critic of these things. No, I think it was a very good standard in the end; it did seem to deal with the problems. We didn't in those days do a formal review of standards like people do now.

**GM David and Allan, would you agree with Geoff on that?**

**DPT** Yes, I would.

**AVC** I think it was effective. It certainly killed off the bespoke schemes. And linked presentation was welcomed by the banks. They actually lobbied for it to be retained at the moment when we moved to international standards.

**DPT** I remember being in South Africa and they were very interested in FRS5. This was just after we'd issued it; and they were thinking of bringing it in South Africa – they had exactly the same sort of issues.

**AVC** It was well ahead of its time. The FASB had a series of different standards and interpretations at that time, which were certainly inadequate. About two years later they produced their first comprehensive standard on this, in which they did refer to the FRS5 solution and considered the linked presentation, eventually deciding against it. But the FASB's approach was based on control of components of an original asset. That led them into detailed analysis of the legal effects of such minutiae as the limited special powers of the Federal Deposit Insurance Corporation to repudiate certain contracts. We would have felt that that kind of detail distracted attention from the key questions.

You had to ask, who was getting the benefit? Who was bearing the risk? And that to the FASB at that time was anathema because the issue had been presented in earlier standards in terms of the balance of risks and rewards. The FASB argued that it was impracticable to require different kinds of risks and rewards to be evaluated against each other. FRS5, by contrast, listed key identifiers of risk and reward that would tip the balance one way or the other. That approach worked very well in dealing with the Private Finance Initiative (PFI) a few years later.

**GM What about the government? Obviously this impinged on them in a number of ways. What response did you get from the different arms of government?**

**AVC** I don't remember them specifically responding as such. But I know that HMRC staff were very interested in the development of the standard. I went to a number of seminars where these issues were discussed. And you can see the results in some of the modern developments in taxation. The idea of looking to see if the parties get only a lender's return. That's led to the thin capitalisation rules. And the general anti-abuse rule is a straightforward application of FRS5. So I think FRS5 principles did take root and develop there. And at that time the Revenue was very pleased that our standards were becoming more specific because tax rules don't always go into the finest level of detail. They like to be able to draw on accounting standards or generally accepted accounting practice. So this was very helpful to them.

**DPT** Interestingly enough, there were other people who did like it – I was looking at Griffiths' book – he said in his chapter on off balance sheet financing (excuse the self-promotion!):

> The excellent pioneering work carried out by Professor David Tweedie, of accountants KMG Thomson McLintock, on which this chapter draws heavily, has prompted swift action, and his concern has also been echoed by the regulatory authorities such as the Bank of England. The upshot of Professor Tweedie's prompting should be that off-balance-sheet financing is relegated to the same shady category as the now discredited window-dressing, which was perhaps the forefather of the current schemes. (p.174)

So I think the Central Bank was genuinely concerned about what was going on with the banks.

**GM And what about the Treasury? They were developing adventurous financial transactions, such as PFI that Allan mentioned, weren't they, at this time?**

**DPT** At the time of FRS5 we'd just got the new Blair government and they wanted to accelerate things like building hospitals, roads, and so on. They didn't have the money to pay for them, so they set up this Private Finance Initiative (PFI). And the idea would be that the operator would design, build, finance, and operate a property, and would be paid over a period. And the question was, whose property was it? We weren't interested in services because they often did services like catering in hospitals, things like that. We weren't interested in that at all. It was just: whose hospital/road/prison etc is it? And we had to do this from scratch.

The Treasury was pretty hostile. They wanted all this off the government's balance sheet as it would affect the Public Sector Borrowing and all they wanted to do was record the payment when it was made each month or whenever it was. And we had to devise these rules which basically considered: who gets the benefits? Where does demand risk lie? If in fact your motorway isn't used very much, does the Government have to pay anyway, or does the operator get less money? And obviously if the government has to pay regardless, it's their motorway. And if, on the other hand, the operator relies on revenues from third parties to cover its property costs it is evidence that the property is an asset of the operator – things like that And even: who makes the key decisions about the property – who designed it? Who says what it's going to look like, how is it going to be operated? Again, if it's the government making these decisions, it sounds like it's their hospital or whatever it is.

Well, they did not like this at all, and we had some pretty blistering arguments about it. Interestingly enough, after I went to the IASB I had exactly the same argument with the Spanish Government. They were up to their eyeballs in PFI, and their government didn't like the rules either. At ASB we told the Treasury you've got liabilities; and you've given guarantees; and you've got to show them on the balance sheet. So the Treasury was not pleased at all, and that led to the sixth application note in September 1998. And I've got a lovely cartoon of Gordon Brown, then Chancellor of the Exchequer, being pretty cross with me – reproduced below – and they had us in a swordfight. But the Treasury accepted it (Figure 5.1).

The DTI liked it too.

**GW** It's amusing though that the government loved applying standards to other people, but PFI is off balance sheet financing by government, there's no doubt about it. You pay for your motorway with alleged private money, but you have to service it, just as if it's your own debt; but it doesn't go into that magic number of the public sector borrowing requirement. So they massaged

*Figure 5.1* Brown vs. Tweedie – Chancellor and ASB Chairman at odds over accounting for the Private Finance Initiative, by kind permission of the artist, Simon Farr.

it just like companies were massaging gearing ratios. It's the old 1984 war cry of "Do it to the others!"

**GM I think Allan mentioned FASB and the difference of approach in the States. It was a bit after these deliberations, but what would have been the implication of this for Enron, if Enron had been operating in your jurisdiction? Would it have changed things very much?**

**AVC** It's very dangerous to opine on what would have happened in another country with all the different structures and so on that they have there. But I can say that I was approached to see whether the NatWest 4 could have used the argument that in the UK we had a standard that was weaker than American standards, and therefore they should be able to plead this in their favour in the court case in America. But it was pretty obvious to me, and I said it immediately to the legal team that approached me, that there was no way that they could have argued that with regard to FRS5.

I do think actually that the fact that FRS5 was so clearly based on principle, rather than detail – it did have application notes, but the principles were really upfront in the Standard – I think if there had been a standard like that in the US it would have been a bit more difficult for the auditors to have hidden behind the forest of individual rules. I think they would have had to shoulder their responsibilities at a much earlier stage.

**GM Well, that's FASB. What about IASB, David?**

**DPT** Just before we go onto that – Enron, I think, was such a classic off balance sheet issue – when you looked at Enron you saw their operating revenues in 1998 were $31 billion. They had jumped to $40 billion by the next year – a colossal jump and by 2000 they had gone up to $101 billion – can you believe it? It was farcical what they were doing in boosting sales and hiding liabilities. I found, surprisingly, a quotation which says:

> The readers of CFO Magazine were being told that in 1998, as US wholesale electricity prices spiked upwards, Enron used a special purpose vehicle to buy generating capacity close to New York City. Enron's CFO, Andrew Fastow, told the magazine: 'We accessed $1.5 billion in capital, but expanded the Enron balance sheet by only $65million.'[4] The magazine seemed to approve, awarding Fastow its 1999 CFO Excellence Award for Capital Structure Management.

**GW** He was very transparent, wasn't he?

**DPT** Yes – he obviously thought it was very clever! Well, turning to the international standard setter, IASC had been following the general trend of moving towards control, and the 7th Directive, to which the IASC was obviously paying a lot of attention, the Directive was based on control, but it said in most cases, legal control takes the form of the holding of a majority of voting rights. Member States could also require consolidated accounts to be prepared in other cases where a parent company has only a minority shareholding but exercises de facto control. They could provide for exemption from this obligation. So it was pretty vague. The Companies Act 1989 tightened that up, and that was so with the IASC as well, because in June 1988 it issued IAS 27, and it was pretty successful. It was based on control, again taking the same sort of idea as Allan's mentioned that FRS5 did, of who gets the benefits? It was moving off the risks to who takes the benefits. But unfortunately the Interpretations Committee of IASC issued SIC12 some ten years later, and it placed greater emphasis for special purpose vehicles on risks and rewards, so there were two systems running and inevitably games were played. And the IASB had to bring out IFRS10 and actually get rid of the confusing SIC12. And IFRS10 is based, as is FRS5, on who gets the benefits. So it was very similar. People were all moving in the same direction at the same time.[5]

We were pleased with FRS5 when it was published but we were not naive. We realised that the merchant banks would soon start looking for loopholes. So in the press release, we stated:

> "We are determined to see that the objective of the FRS is fulfilled. The Standard has deliberately been constructed on general principles rather than as a series of detailed rules, so that it will be applicable to new schemes as they develop. If new schemes should nevertheless be developed to circumvent its provisions, we will refer them to the Urgent Issues Task Force, or, if necessary, we will revise the FRS itself." In other words "don't try it on!"

## Notes

1 The issue was whether a planned acquisition could be anticipated in accounts published before its completion. TR603 was not suggesting that it should, but the DTI comment went further by implying that substance (or the True and Fair view) could not override detailed statutory provisions, whereas the ability of the True and Fair view to override was itself part of statute.
2 The legal justification for this treatment was strengthened by the 1989 Companies Act, which changed the basis for consolidation from reliance primarily on ownership to requirements based on control.
3 It would be better because a large first slice was either borne elsewhere or insured.
4 We have been unable to trace the precise publication date.
5 SIC12 (1998) and IAS27 (1988 and 2008) were replaced by IFRS 10 in May 2011.

## References

### *Books and articles*

Argyll Foods case and DTI statement, *Accountancy* (August 1981, p.19 and February 1982, p.11). London: *ICAEW.*

Griffiths, I. (1986). *Creative Accounting.* London: Unwin.

Davies, M. Paterson R. and Wilson, A. (5th edition 1997, p.976) *UK GAAP,* London: Ernst & Young and Macmillan Reference Ltd.

Tonkin, D. and Skerratt, L. (eds.) (1987). *Financial Reporting 1986–87: A Survey of UK Reporting Practices*, London: ICAEW.

### *Publications by standard-setters*

*Amendment to FRS5* (September 1998) *'Reporting the Substance of Transactions': Private Finance Initiative and Similar Contracts*: ASB Publications.

Bulletin 15 (October 1991). ASB Publications.

Companies Act (1989). (Consolidated into Companies Act 1985). *Companies Act c.40.*

ED42 (1988). *Accounting for Special Purpose Transactions*, ASC.

ED49 (1990). *Reflecting the Substance of Transactions in Assets and Liabilities*, ASC

FRED4 (1993). *Reporting the Substance of Transactions*, ASB.

FRS5 (1994). *Reporting the Substance of Transactions*, ASB.

*Seventh Council Directive 83/349/EEC* of 13 June 1983 based on the Article 54 (3) (g) of the Treaty on Consolidated Accounts.

SIC 12 (1998) *Consolidation Special Purpose Entities.*

IAS27 (1988 and 2008). *Consolidated Financial Statements and Accounting for Investments in Subsidiaries*, IASB.

IFRS10 (2011). *Consolidated Financial Statements*, IASB.

SSAP17 (1980). *Accounting for Post Balance Sheet Events*, ASC.

SSAP18 (1980). *Accounting for Contingencies*, ASC.

SSAP21 (1984). *Accounting for Leases and Hire Purchase Contracts*, ASC.

TR603 (1985). *Off Balance Sheet Financing and Window Dressing*, ICAEW.

# 6 Accounting for mergers and acquisitions

## The problems in 1990

### Interviewer's note

*Terry Smith's famous book on creative accounting quotes with relish a comment by David Tweedie: Acquisition accounting is 'The Black Hole of British Accounting'. This, writes Smith (1996), is "Because UK GAAP allowed a heaven-sent opportunity to an acquisitive company to cook the books" (2nd ed., p.27). And the Black Hole had been growing fast in the years leading up to the creation of the ASB: Smith reports that the annual value of UK public company M&A in 1989 was equivalent to about 20% of GDP, and 17 times its value in 1980. A single year, 1986, saw two mega takeovers (Hanson/Imperial and Guinness/Distillers) at around 2.5 billion pounds each.*

*Chapter 2 discusses some of the institutional changes associated with this – Big Bang, the arrival of the US investment banks in London, … Acquisitions had become a very significant source of fees for the banks and were very actively promoted by the banks. They did not wait passively for potential acquirers to help with deals they had identified: Kynaston (2001) reports that in one of the banks' corporate finance departments "from 1979 there was a systematic policy of targeting companies that could potentially be persuaded into launching a takeover bid" (p.605). And they wanted the deals to be completed so that they could collect the large 'success' fees which followed and the income from arranging funding for the deals. A rash of creative accounting schemes were devised by the banks to flatter the reported performance of the merging businesses and increase the incentives for executives to embark on bids.*

*There had been criticism of some of these accounting practices of predator companies by defending companies, which alleged that some predators had taken advantage of the flexibility in accounting standards to make their financial performance look better. Concerns had been raised by, among others, Government ministers and officials and the Confederation of British Industry (CBI).*

*In response, during the 1990s the ASB issued no fewer than five Standards relating to different aspects of accounting for M&A: FRS6, Acquisitions and Mergers; FRS7, Fair Values in Acquisition Accounting; FRS10, Goodwill and Intangible Assets; FRS11 Impairment of Fixed Assets and Goodwill; and FRS12 Provisions, Contingent Liabilities and Contingent Assets. In what follows we diverge from the standard-by-standard approach of most other chapters, and bring together this battery of*

DOI: 10.4324/9781003346920-6

*standards as a programme in which abuses are tackled on various related fronts. In this chapter we outline the challenges faced by the Board; and in the next how the Board responded to those challenges.*

*A recurrent challenge in accounting for business combinations is how to deal with the discrepancy between the purchase consideration and the book value of the target's net assets. One reason this discrepancy is often highly material is that the pre-bid stock market value of the target is typically around 50% higher than the book value of its assets (Penman and Reggiani, 2014). Another is that the bidder has typically to pay a premium of around 25% of pre bid market value to secure control (Amel-Zadeh et al., 2016). These are only averages and can vary greatly between companies and over the stock market cycle. Occasionally, the buyer pays less than book value. In one major deal at the end of the 1990s, Vodafone/Mannesmann, the acquirer paid 101 billion pounds to buy net assets with a collective book value of 18 billion. As this chapter explains, the rules in force in 1990 would have allowed Vodafone to record the acquisition at 101 billion, or at 18 billion, or at various other valuations – with different implications for reported profits in the year of combination and afterwards.*

*In explaining the challenges the conversation below refers to Table 6.1 and Appendix Table A6.1. The Appendix Table shows the accounting entries for a representative combination with six of the main accounting schemes permitted in the UK in 1990. From that Table the outcomes for reported profit and equity are collected in Table 6.1, to illustrate how the reported values of these two key bottom line numbers, from the profit and loss account and balance sheet, would differ according to the accounting choice.*

**GM David, Why did you call accounting for M&A 'The Black Hole of British Accounting'?**

**DPT** As a Technical Partner, I think accounting for business combinations was what worried us the most because basically companies could choose their profits. And that was done for various reasons – one to put themselves in a

*Table 6.1* Reported profits and equity in the year following the same combination under different accounting methods

| | | | |
|---|---|---|---|
| 1 | Merger accounting | 265 | 805 |
| 2 | Acquisition accounting, goodwill shown as asset | 251 | 931 |
| 3 | Acquisition accounting, goodwill written off | 260 | 850 |
| 4 | Acquisition accounting, goodwill shown as asset, reorganisation provision (RP), stock write down (SWD), RP then reversed | 368 | 1,048 |
| 5 | Acquisition accounting, goodwill written off, reorganisation provision (RP), stock write down (SWD), RP then reversed | 390 | 850 |
| 6 | Merger accounting with reorganisation provision | 165 | 705 |

Note: Detailed workings are provided in Appendix Table A6.1.

better position for a takeover, or – on the other hand – to defend against one. Of course, if you can get the profits going up in the right direction, that can lead to higher remuneration if it's based on earnings per share and so on. So there were a lot of incentives to play games here. And the problem was, there were so many ways you could do it – it was like a thousand flowers blooming, only many of them turned out to be weeds. And we had the same problem as we mentioned very early on in our discussions – that if an auditor accepted a scheme and then another one accepted it, the next minute everybody was doing it. And then we went onto another trick, and so on. So there was just a series of schemes which we'll come on to discuss. The extant accounting standards didn't help – both SSAP22 dealing with goodwill and SSAP23 setting out the requirements for business combinations allowed a choice between treatments. This plus the tricks made the auditor's life impossible.

**Merger vs acquisition accounting**

**DPT** The overriding issue was: there were two main methods of accounting for business combinations: merger accounting and acquisition accounting. That had always been the case, though in fact a tax case in 1980 just about stopped merger accounting – (Shearer (Inspector of Taxes) v Bercain Limited) – and the government had to put through some very simple rules to allow all who had merger accounted before to continue doing that, and to allow companies not to report a share premium by showing the acquiring company's shares at nominal value rather than at their fair value when the combination took place. Very simple rules, but that led to the ASC bringing in SSAP23, which set out the precise rules for merger accounting. If the rules were not met, acquisition accounting had to be used. The intention was to limit merger accounting though in practice companies could virtually choose the treatment they wanted.

The incentives were pretty high to select the method that suited their purposes. The advantage of merger accounting was that you kept the target's balance sheet numbers whereas with acquisition accounting you reflected the typically much higher price paid for the target and showed the fair value of the assets purchased (the cost to the acquirer – so the depreciation was usually going to be less with merger accounting as the target's existing book values were used). With merger accounting, you had no goodwill, so there was no obligation to do anything about it. Profit of the combined entity showed a higher number in the year of combination because the full year's profits of both companies were shown, whereas under acquisition accounting the acquirer included the acquiree's profit only from the time of acquisition.

**GW** The omission of pre-acquisition profits arises because the acquisition approach regards them as having been 'bought' by the acquirer not 'earned'. The merger approach regards the transaction as a pooling, not an acquisition so the joint profits for the full year have been 'earned" by the merged parties. In the appendix, the balance sheets for year one show profits in the year of acquisition at 80 for the acquirer and 160 for the company taken over. So, as the business combination took place on the last day of the financial year of both companies, under acquisition accounting the combined group profit would be 80 whereas for merger accounting it would be 240. Furthermore, under merger accounting, the pre-merger profits of both companies were generally available for distribution. So there was a lot of incentive to do merger accounting but the ASC's SSAP23 brought in rules that stopped many of these schemes – at least, initially.

**DPT** Basically what SSAP23 did was to require that to qualify for merger accounting a share offer (not a cash offer) had to be made to the holders of all the target's equity shares and the holders of all voting shares which were not already held by the acquirer. As a result, the acquirer had to end up with at least 90% of all the target's equity shares (taking each class separately) and the shares carrying at least 90% of the votes. And, prior to the offer the acquirer couldn't hold 20% or more of all the equity shares, again of each class, nor could it have more than 20% of the votes. Finally, not less than 90% of the fair value of the consideration had to be in the form of share capital.

So these were the rules, and it was assumed then that would stop a lot of phoney mergers. But even under the rules merger accounting was still an option – or rather it was not long before people found ways around the rules to make the choice. You can see from the Table why this mattered. Considering examples 1 and 2 in our example, profit was 14 higher under merger accounting, equity 126 higher under acquisition accounting – with essentially the same transaction.

**GM** You reported in Tweedie and Whittington (2020) that in the BP/Amoco acquisition BP's finance director, John Buchanan (a member of the Accounting Standards Board) told the press that it had the advantage of qualifying for merger accounting. Li (2007) estimates that, had the combination instead been reported as an acquisition, the amalgamation's reported earnings would have been reduced by percentages ranging from 8% to 37% in subsequent years.

## Means of achieving merger accounting

**DPT** The ASC's SSAP23 had already imposed various requirements we mentioned earlier to restrict the use of merger accounting. But the investment bankers had developed ways around them. The key requirement was that resources should not leave the combined organisation and you had to offer equity shares. And, of course, it turned out sometimes that the shareholders of the acquired company didn't want your rotten shares, they wanted money. And then you had this business of OK, we'll give you shares but we'll place them for you in the market, and you get the money that way – a scheme known as vendor placing. Or they would go for something slightly different: the acquirer would place the shares with its own shareholders, in essence, a rights issue (vendor rights) and then the acquired company's shareholders would get the money that way. Another method was, just before the acquisition took place, the about-to-be-acquired company would issue preference shares to its shareholders replacing its equity, and the acquirer bought the preference shares for cash because they weren't equity.

So there were all these schemes: you could do merger accounting if you wanted to, and even the 20% limit – you couldn't have more than 20% of each class of equity shares before you started – was no obstacle. If the acquirer had 25% it just phoned up its friendly merchant bank and sold it 6% and then bought them back once the rest of the acquiree's shares had been purchased (bed and breakfast holdings).

You could do what you liked. Do you want big profits this year? We can do merger accounting. A rising trend of profits? We can do acquisition accounting. Do you want a really big rise in profits? (As we discuss later) we can create reorganisation provisions and provide for future losses and then credit them to profit later as we won't need these provisions; we can write down your stock and have a huge margin when it is sold. You are going to get a bonus on this next year out of this world. Anything you like. That's what made the black hole. This was the whole problem we were facing. Do you want acquisition accounting? Do you want merger accounting? We can deal with it, sir.

And the other option, of course, was that under acquisition accounting there were two policies to deal with goodwill. Either you could amortise it (example 2 in the Table), by showing it as an asset in the balance sheet; or you could write it off against reserves – the treatment encouraged by SSAP22 (example 3 in the Table). Write off gave you profit higher by 9 than amortisation, and equity lower by 81.

**GW** I think the whole point about the numerical examples you have is that the preferred method all depends on the company's situation. I mean, this is a specific example you are looking at; you could create examples where the values are different, and so are the relative advantages of the different accounting treatments. The really egregious thing about merger and acquisition accounting as it was in those days was that you had huge choice, and you could suit the method to fit the company. It wasn't so much that you had one set of rules that you could bend; you had a whole array of alternative rules from which to select to suit your purpose. You didn't necessarily have to bend them really; you just chose the rule to fit the situation. I think that's the real point of it all. There was such variety of treatment, and the flexibility that was available both to select merger accounting and within acquisition accounting – the treatment of goodwill, for instance.

**AVC** One of the principles for merger accounting that was enunciated in SSAP23 – certainly I remember it being discussed at the ASC – was that no assets left the company in making this 'merger', which of course was a disguised acquisition. They didn't pay for it other than by shares. So you could preserve the fiction that it was just two companies coming together. But if the first company was a shark, the second one was often a minnow, and it was not really two sharks sharing the same pool. It was the shark acquiring the minnow and not giving it very much of its own business in return for taking over the entire business of minnow. And this was made possible essentially through the strength of the share price of what we will call the shark – which we're not allowed to call the acquirer. And, of course, as mentioned above, even though no cash left the business, there were ways found to ensure that the shareholders of the acquired company got cash if they wanted it.

## The flexibility of acquisition accounting

**GM What were the features of acquisition accounting that gave scope for this flexibility?**

### *Reorganisation provisions and future losses*

**GW** One of the great flexibilities with acquisition accounting was associated with the fair valuing of assets and liabilities on acquisition. That's the key to it. When you decide what's the nature of the beast and opt for acquisition accounting, you've basically got to calculate the net assets of the acquired company at fair value and then compare that with the consideration you've paid. The thing has to balance, of course, because we're all accountants! So we create goodwill to balance the balance sheet. The way in which provisioning for future losses, and other aspects of the fair valuing process on acquisition, affected goodwill (the residual item) is illustrated in Table 6.2, extracted from appendix 3 of SSAP22.

Fair values are subjective, particularly those relating to provisions. And provisions for reorganisation became a regular feature of acquisition accounting. They were really anticipating future expenditure – the ASB put this right eventually (as we explain in the appendix to the next chapter). But that provision for reorganisation (see notes c and h above) enabled companies effectively to create what the Americans call a 'cookie jar' – this provision which was then fed back to profit over future years. And creating the provision itself was not a charge on profits, because it arose out of the fair-valuing on acquisition, and goodwill (115), the balancing item, could be manipulated to reduce or avoid its impact on future reported profits. For example, it was normally written off to reserves, and even if the goodwill had to be amortised, the period chosen was likely to be well in excess of the period immediately following the acquisition, over which the provision was used up. So the provision came from nowhere as far as the profit and loss account was concerned. But its reversal was credited to the profit and loss account in later years, boosting post-acquisition profits.

I have this quotation from Ernst & Young (1997), our assiduous critics, in their *UK GAAP* – on page 320 of their 1997 edition there is this tactful but critical description of reorganisation provisions and how they were used or sometimes abused. And it's interesting in showing the professional firm balancing its professional instincts against the fact that it doesn't want to lose

*Table 6.2* Example of fair value adjustments (adapted from Appendix 3 of Standard Accounting Practice 22)

*Purchase consideration*

100,000 shares at mid-market price of 3.06 pounds on day of transaction:

Total 306,000 pounds, giving rise to goodwill of 115,000 pounds

| Thousand pounds | Book value | Revaluation | Provisions for trading losses | Other provisions | Acc'ting policy alignment | Other major items | Fair value to group |
|---|---|---|---|---|---|---|---|
| Fixed assets | | | | | | | |
| Intangible | | | | | | [f] 80 | 80 |
| Tangible | 160 | [a] 20 | | | | | 180 |
| Investments | 20 | [b] 5 | | | | | 25 |
| Current assets | | | | | | | |
| Stock | 40 | | [c] −4 | [d] −5 | [e] −2 | | 29 |
| Debtors | 35 | | | | | | 35 |
| Investments | 10 | | | | | | 10 |
| Cash at bank | 12 | | | | | | 12 |
| Total assets | **277** | 25 | −4 | −5 | −2 | 80 | **371** |
| Liabilities | | | | | | | |
| *Provisions* | | | | | | | |
| Pensions | 30 | | | | | | 30 |
| Taxation | 45 | | | | | [g] 10 | 55 |
| Other | 10 | | [c] 8 | [h] 15 | | | 33 |
| *Creditors* | | | | | | | |
| Debenture | 2 | | | | | | 2 |
| Bank loans | 15 | | | | | | 15 |

(*Continued*)

*Table 6.2* Continued

*Purchase consideration*

| | | | | | | | |
|---|---|---|---|---|---|---|---|
| Trade creditors | 30 | | | | | | 30 |
| Other creditors | 10 | | | | | | 10 |
| Accruals | 5 | | | | | | 5 |
| Total liabilities | **147** | | 8 | 15 | | 10 | **180** |
| Net assets | **130** | 25 | −12 | −20 | −2 | 70 | **191** |
| Goodwill | | | | | | | 115 |
| Purchase consideration | | | | | | | **306** |

Notes

a Increase in value of freehold properties since last revaluation.
b Increase in value of shares of USM investment since purchase.
c Losses expected to be incurred prior to closing down a division.
d Write-down following reassessment of realisable value of stock which is more than one year old.
e Change of stock valuation from weighted average cost to FIFO which is used by the group.
f Recognition of intangibles – relating to publishing titles and brands acquired.
g Adjustment to deferred tax arising from the incorporation of fair values.
h Provision for reorganisation expenses.

too many clients, so it's got to be nice about them. What it says about the reorganisation provisions is:

> In practice, this has been one of the areas of fair value accounting which prior to FRS7' (which was the ASB's solution to the problem) 'had given rise to a great deal of controversy and alleged abuse. The ability to provide for costs of reorganization programmes without having to charge these costs in the profit and loss account is a very attractive opportunity, and one which has understandably tempted some companies to be enthusiastic in their estimation of these provisions.

If there were insufficient reserves against which to write off goodwill so that there was a possible future goodwill amortisation charge, the reorganisation provision could be offset, in some cases, in the process of calculating fair values of the acquired company, illustrated in Table 6.2, by optimistic assessments of the fair values of non-depreciating assets, such as real property (and intangibles) (notes a and f above).

So, in Table 6.1, example 4 shows the effect of reporting goodwill and including a reorganisation provision and write-down of inventory (discussed later). Example 5 has the same provision and write-down but also immediate write off of goodwill. Example 5 has the highest profit of the six methods. Example 4 has the second highest profits and the highest equity.

Something that needs to be said about that is: example 6 in the Table does show that you don't get this advantage out of merger accounting because you have in that arrangement to charge the creation of the provision to profit. In the case employed in the Table, this scheme gives the lowest profit of all six – less than half that of examples 4 or 5.

Reorganisation provisions were, of course, addressed in FRS3 (discussed in Chapter 3), which restricted them to circumstances in which future reorganisation expenses were existing obligations rather than future hopes or intentions, and required clearer presentation in an enhanced profit and loss account, as well as greater disclosure. But FRS3 was dealing with expenses charged to the profit and loss account. It would have been beyond its scope to have strayed into acquisition accounting – which was where the most serious problems arose.

**DPT** Absolutely right. One of the things that concerned us earlier was the extraordinary item (discussed in Chapter 3), and exceptionals. Prior to FRS3, most of these reorganisation provisions used to go through as extraordinary items, so companies weren't that fussed about them as they didn't affect the sacred 'bottom line'. But once they started doing acquisition accounting it was much better, as far as the accounting results manipulation was concerned, not to try to put the provision through this year's profit and loss account as extraordinary, but to stick it into these acquisition provisions with no effect whatsoever on the profit and loss account. And such provisions almost vanished from extraordinary items, even before the extraordinary item was itself virtually banished under FRS3.

**GW** Another thing about it is that, of course, profit manipulation does run out in the end. The best thing about accounting is that things come back down to earth. Ashes to ashes; zero to zero. Eventually, even though you've got it from nowhere, your reorganisation provision runs out. And then, of course, you have a challenge because your profits are going suddenly not to benefit from this subsidy. But, of course, with serial acquirers, this doesn't necessarily happen, because new acquisitions can replenish the provision. There's an incentive there to go on acquiring other companies. I don't know whether you've thought about it but one of the big incentives for the merger boom at the time – and the acceleration of it – was that people were almost drunk with these things – these adjustments made on acquisition, not just the reorganisation provision, but certainly those provisions. If you kept topping it up when making new acquisitions you could go on forever showing a nice steady stream of reported profits.

**GM** Yes, Terry Smith (1992) gives an interesting example of doing just that, doesn't he, with Coloroll, who over four years took over 13 companies. In their last year (1988/1989) they took 52 million from the reorganisation provision, the lion's share of their reported profit of 56 million. So they'd only made 4 million without the subsidy from the provision, from the 'cookie jar'. Of course, the next year they went bust, so everyone suddenly saw what was going on. But they had done just what you describe.

**DPT** The FT told me that three or four of our multinational conglomerates had three or four years' profits tucked away in these provisions, just to drop into profit any time they wanted. And they could just do what they liked. And it looked very conservative: there's this big provision sitting in the balance sheet. It was a scam, the worst scam we had – apparent balance sheet prudence coupled with outrageous income statement manipulation.

**AVC** The funny thing is that a lot of the debate at that time was about banks and their secret reserves, and here were ordinary bricks and mortar companies doing exactly the same thing in broad daylight.

**DPT** I can tell you, Allan, in the technical departments of the audit firms it was a pretty big issue of discussion.

**GW** I once had reason to study the accounts of bus companies that went in for serial acquisition. A number of companies were doing this in the late eighties when the industry was consolidating. Some were really high on provisioning for future reorganisation costs. I mean, how on earth do you get guaranteed profit growth out of the bus market? They were buying clapped out bus companies in a market that was not expanding. And what some would do was to revalue the acquired bus garages and related real property. These were always in the town centre – very valuable for resale and redevelopment. And they don't have to service buses overnight in the centre. They can take them off to a yard in the countryside somewhere where some country garage is willing to do the maintenance very cheaply, and they leave the buses out in the open.

So they revalue the bus garage to fair value – reflecting their genuine assessment of its redevelopment potential – and this has the effect of reducing the balancing number, goodwill. At the same time, a provision for the reorganisation is made, thus increasing goodwill. The two adjustments largely offset each other. Subsequently, the reorganisation provision is fed back into post-acquisition profits.

The overall result is that the revaluation of the bus garage on acquisition is used to boost post-acquisition profits. The companies concerned would argue that the provision forming part of the cost of acquisition might reflect genuine 'one-off' costs of reorganising the acquired businesses, but the simple lay person looking at the accounts might question the apparent enhancement of profit. So, if you like, the bus driver's wages for the next few years might seem to be offset by the revaluation of the bus garage on acquisition – very simple. And, of course, they kept acquiring new companies all the time in their heyday, so they were able to continue this and to show continuous growth of operating profit. But the bubble did eventually burst because there was not an unlimited supply of suitable take-over prospects.

**AVC** I think one point relevant to such takeover battles is, how unfair this was on the defender, the target. The target may have, perhaps for years, had to deal with the problems that it knew it had, but it just couldn't take the hit of charging costs of the needed reorganisation against profit and reducing its reserves, and perhaps cutting its dividends in order to do the necessary things. Along comes the acquirer, the shark, who can do everything and still increase earnings per share. They always promise to increase earnings per share, knowing that they can achieve that through accounting sleight of hand despite relatively poor results of operations. Unlike the poor target, the acquirer can simply anticipate the reorganisation costs by creating an acquisition provision and bypass the profit and loss account altogether. That helped it, as you have explained in your book,[1] Geoff, helped it to win.

**GM** Yes – I'd not thought of that asymmetry. All the accounting cards are in the hand of the acquirer, all these options we've described for getting an artificial boost to earnings.

**AVC** And the target has to put out its own profit forecast. It can't compete.

**DPT** One of the things that upset us as technical partners was the inability to say, "that's not a proper liability", because the acquirer had the option to record invented liabilities. The acquirer could include estimated reorganisation costs into this acquisition liability. What was equally bad was that it could also add estimated future operating losses of the acquiree into the liability. Try auditing that number!

### *Inventory write downs*

**DPT** Furthermore, in addition to these dubious 'liabilities', the acquirer could also reduce the fair value of the target company's assets, such as inventory, by arguing that it was obsolete or so excessively large that to be sold the price would have to be cut. These adjustments enabled the acquirer to manufacture any profit figure it wanted.

The deflating of assets was a major problem. And one of the worst occurred during the Distillers takeover where Guinness wrote down all these stocks – I don't know how much they wrote down the whisky stocks – to next to nothing if I remember correctly (I'd have given them a fiver for the whisky!). And they made massive profits: there was almost no cost of sales involved. It was outrageous. Financial reporting was out of control, some provisions were genuine charges or write downs. But most of the time they weren't genuine. The acquirer would say, "whoops, we got this provision wrong, so we're going to write it back to profit", even though it had never been charged to profit in the first place. With phoney asset write downs, the profit appeared the minute the inventory was sold.

**GM** Ron Paterson, whom we mentioned earlier, your counterpart senior technical partner at EY, reported (1988) that Guinness wrote down Distillers' stock when they took them over by 344 million pounds – a handy addition to the cookie jar.

## The treatment of goodwill

**DPT** The other thing we should mention: writing off goodwill to reserves to avoid future amortisation had its problems. While SSAP22 stated that the write-off to reserves did not imply an equivalent loss of value but was simply an accounting adjustment, companies started to get worried because they found situations occurring where the markets began to be concerned about net worth. While the write-off may not have been a loss in value it was often interpreted that way.

**GM** Yes, Ken Wild (1987), a senior technical partner at Touche Ross, illustrated the potential materiality of the choice under acquisition accounting between amortising and writing off goodwill: in 1985 Saatchi and Saatchi wrote off 177 million pounds of goodwill, leaving only 73 million as total capital and reserves.

**DPT** It became a real issue for companies. The larger the acquisition provisions – mentioned by Geoff earlier – that the company had, the larger the goodwill write-off would become and the more damage would be done to the gearing ratio. Some borrowing requirements were linked to gearing and loan covenants had to be renegotiated, usually on the basis of interest cover rather than balance sheet ratios. Large groups with minuscule equity found they were constantly having to seek their shareholders' approval for proposed acquisitions or disposals since these breached a Stock Exchange size test based on equity. Writing off goodwill to the retained profits reserve reduced distributable profits. This began to force companies to use the amortisation option especially when the goodwill write off virtually eliminated their reserves.

There were, however, other ways to reduce the impact of writing off goodwill – by reducing the size of goodwill itself. Techniques involved, as Geoff has already noted, the optimistic assessment of fair values of the acquiree's fixed assets or the revaluing of fixed assets purchased many years ago (Grand Metropolitan's goodwill write off of £332.9 m in 1988 more or less equalled the surplus arising on revaluation of properties of £332.6 m).

Other companies decided to solve the goodwill problem by calling it something else. Rowntree in its unsuccessful defence against a takeover had argued that its balance sheet did not give an indication of the company's true worth as so many of its brands were not shown. This spurred acquisitive companies to begin to identify intangibles such as the acquiree's brands (thereby reducing the goodwill figure), which they would then argue had almost indefinite lives and therefore didn't need to be depreciated.

On the reserves issue, the usual treatment was to write off goodwill against retained profits but because of the effect on distributable profits other reserves began to be chosen. The DTI did not like companies writing off goodwill against the revaluation reserve and before the ASB was formed it had already issued a consultative document indicating that, in the Department's view, goodwill may not legally be written off against the revaluation reserve. Companies, however, were by now seeking approval for the cancellation of their share premium accounts to create a reserve against which they could write off goodwill. (The use of the share premium account was restricted in law, being used to write off expenses or discounts on the issue of shares or debentures or providing for premiums payable on redemption of debentures.) Some companies did not bother with such refinements – they simply created a special negative reserve called goodwill write-off reserve. So they didn't bother writing off to any reserves, they just put a minus figure in reserves – the 'dangling debit'!

**AVC** A pseudo asset.

**DPT** And they played other games. In the income statement, they would amortise goodwill but then showed a "profit before goodwill write-off" and then "profit after goodwill write-off"' – to try to confuse people. Others amortised goodwill over two years – that was the Marley Group while Beecham chose a 40 year period. It was a complete mess.

**GW** It's interesting that all the discussion we've just had has been to do with acquisition accounting, although the great focus has often been on the choice between merger and acquisition accounting. Acquisition accounting is the one that has been preserved, with merger accounting being the 'wicked' practice that has been banned. It may not be a very good method of accounting in terms of representing the facts, but at least it's consistent; and it doesn't have the flexibility in it that acquisition accounting does.

## Understanding of investors

**GM How far do you think the stock market saw through these shenanigans? Do you think they were ever taken in, or do you think the analysts were actually readjusting their assessments and were**

**reversing out these changes? Was it possible in all cases to reverse out these devices?**

**AVC** There was a lot of emphasis in discussion at the time that the cash flow statement was very important, and of course we used that, we acknowledged that ourselves. But analysts were, I think, using cash flow as a way of cutting through this chimera of accounting.

**DPT** Well, you must remember, of course, until FRS1 they didn't have a cash flow statement. They had the sources and application of funds, which didn't really show these issues. And in the case of Coloroll, clearly they didn't pick it up.

**AVC** If they were smart enough, they could see that cash was bleeding away, despite stable or increasing profits, even if they could not always identify the precise reasons.

**DPT** When Coloroll collapsed it was a shock. As you said, Geoff, almost all the profits came from the reorganisation provisions being brought back.

**GM I suppose with the reorganisation provisions, some of them would be more legitimate than others, but an outsider wouldn't be able to figure that out, would they? I mean, at one extreme, a provision for next year's losses is opaque – hard for an outsider to interpret. But at the other extreme, an acquirer might have committed to costly redundancies, and this could be transparent.**

**GW** With the accounting standards as they emerged it became much easier because we did try to define precisely what was eligible and what wasn't – basically you had to have a liability. Something had to have happened now, and you should ignore things you've not committed to yet. I think that was the core of it, wasn't it, David? And when that was required, there was much greater clarity. We're talking here about around 1990 or so, before the ASB sorted things out, and then there wasn't clarity. Of course, we'll come onto the standard on provisions, contingencies, and so on in the next chapter. But before the ASB standards there wasn't the clarity about recognition basically – the point of recognition, that was the key to it. And of course, the other piece of discretion is not in making the provision in the first place, it's when you write it back in the profit and loss account. And again, managers can always tell you a very plausible story about why they are doing what they are doing if they want to, and it's just very difficult for the auditor to check.

**DPT** It was almost impossible for the auditor. Companies would come up with figures for next year's losses. How do you say they are wrong? And how does an analyst know what next year's losses are going to be? It was hopeless.

## The international position

**AVC** I would make one point about the differences of approach across countries. You've talked about the disadvantages of acquisition accounting because it forces you to recognise the very large numbers for goodwill and for uplifting the assets to fair values. And the Americans dealt with that in two ways.

One was that they allowed amortisation up to 40 years; and the other was that merger accounting was much more easily available there than it would have been under SSAP23. In the UK we took refuge in the fact that we could write off goodwill to reserves. And, interestingly if you look at Table 6.1 you see how close that comes to the effects of merger accounting. Merger accounting ends up with profit of 265 and equity of 805 in the first example. But if you compare that with the third example, of acquisition accounting with goodwill written off, profit is only slightly lower – from the depreciation on the revalued fixed assets; and again, equity shows only the difference in the now restated assets. So that was the UK's way of getting out of this.

**GM** So they are both getting to the same destination by different routes.

**AVC** That's right. Indeed, every country has had some method of achieving that, except the rather brave Australians. I'm thinking of a talk I gave in Australia where I pointed out that they were the only ones that insisted, first of all on banning merger accounting, and secondly on a relatively short period for the amortisation of goodwill, and no write-off to reserves. Or at least that's what they were proposing at the time. This observation went down a bomb with the Group of One Hundred over there (the Finance Directors), who were sponsoring the conference; but I think I blotted my copybook forever with Warren McGregor and the Australian Accounting Research Foundation (AARF).

In relation to supplying information to investors there's an interesting contrast between the approach we took in the UK in those days and the approach that was taken in America. I attended one meeting of the ASC where Martin Gibbs, the Senior Analyst at Phillips and Drew, said, we analysts don't think goodwill has any meaning at all, and amortisation of goodwill even less. So the first thing we do is, we just set it off against reserves. And that argument carried quite a lot of weight with his ASC colleagues and may well have led to SSAP22 declaring that to be the preferred method of dealing with goodwill.

**DPT** That's interesting. So the genesis of the preferred method of dealing with goodwill in SSAP22 stemmed from the user community?

**AVC** I always thought so. Now the Americans – with their insistence at that time that goodwill, if it appeared, should be amortised, were taking exactly the opposite view. Yet in their philosophy of accounting they say that what you should be doing in accounting is providing information for investors to assist them in making decisions, whereas what they were essentially doing, by saying it's got to be amortised, was exercising stewardship, which was our argument rather than theirs.

**GW** It's a different strand in American accounting. If you look at American accounting, it's incredibly conservative in many respects. Steve Zeff is always strong on this issue (e.g. Zeff, 2013). Take, for instance, revaluations: American professional accountants think we are real cowboys for allowing revaluations of property. But the American profession is incredibly conservative partly because their businessmen are such cowboys and lobbyists and benders of rules. It's the academic stream in the US that is more innovative: FASB has a strong academic stream in it and they wrote a high-minded conceptual framework, and that says financial reporting should be "forward-looking, predicting future cash flows" and all that stuff. But I don't think many American businessmen really believe that. They are more concerned with having the ability to report results that will maximise their bonuses or the value of their stock options.

**GM** I think that comparison is very revealing. And I hope we can pick up on it again in the next chapter and compare the ASB standards with what came out of FASB in the end after all the lobbying they faced. First they were going for a very similar arrangement to yours, and then they backed down under lobbying pressure.

**GW** That debate that they had in America illustrates the point I just made in that business lobbied very heavily against the FASB proposals and stopped them. And FASB reached that compromise on the impairment tests. Actually it's scandalous really the way that they implemented it. And of course they planted that on the IASB as well. We've all suffered from that.

## Note

1 Meeks and Meeks (2022).

## References

### *Books and articles*

Amel-Zadeh, A., Meeks, G. and Meeks, J.G. (2016). Historical perspectives on accounting for M&A, *Accounting and Business Research*, 46(5), 501–524.

Ernst and Young. (1997). *UK GAAP*, London: Ernst and Young.

Kynaston, D. (2001). *The City of London, Volume 4: A Club No More, 1945–2000*, London: Chatto and Windus.

Li, K. (2007). Goodwill, Ph.D. dissertation, University of Cambridge.

Meeks, G. and Meeks, J.G. (2022). *The Merger Mystery: Why Spend Ever More on Mergers When So Many Fail?* Cambridge: Open Book Publishers.

Paterson, R. (1988). Fair value accounting following an acquisition, in Tonkin, D. and Skerratt, L.(eds.) *Financial Reporting 1990–91: A Survey of UK Reporting Practice*, London: ICAEW.

Penman, S. and Reggiani, F. (2014). The value trap: value buys risky growth, working paper, Columbia Business School, https://www.gsb.columbia.edu.

Smith, T. (1992). *Accounting for Growth: Stripping the Camouflage from Company Accounts* (First edition), London: Century Business.

Smith, T. (1996). *Accounting for Growth: Stripping the Camouflage from Company Accounts* (Second edition), London: Random House.

Tweedie, D. and Whittington, G. (2020). Developing new accounting standards for M&A: a standard-setters' perspective, in Amel-Zadeh, A. and Meeks, G. (eds.) *Accounting for M&A: Uses and Abuses of Accounting in Monitoring and Promoting M&A*, Abingdon and New York: Routledge.

Wild, K. (1987). Merger accounting and goodwill, in Tonkin, D., and Skerratt, L., eds., *Financial Reporting 1986–87: A survey of UK Reporting Practice*, London: ICAEW.

Zeff, S. (2013). The objectives of financial reporting: A historical survey and analysis, *Accounting and Business Research*, 43(4), 262–327.

***Publications by standard-setters***

SSAP22 (1984). Accounting for goodwill, ASC.

SSAP23 (1985). Accounting for acquisitions and mergers, ASC.

FRS1 (1991). Cash flow statements, ASB.

FRS3 (1992). Reporting financial performance, ASB.

FRS6 (1994). Acquisitions and mergers, ASB.

FRS7 (1994). Fair values in acquisition accounting, ASB.

FRS10 (1997). Goodwill and intangible assets, ASB.

FRS11 (1998). Impairment of fixed assets and goodwill, ASB.

FRS12 (1998). Provisions, contingent liabilities and contingent assets, ASB.

# Appendix

*Table A6.1* Examples of impact of M&A on financial statements under different accounting methods

*Assumptions*

1 Acquisition/merger on last day of year 1

2 Balance sheets at time of acquisition

| | Acquirer | Target |
|---|---|---|
| Ordinary share capital | 200 | 100 |
| Retained profits | 80 | 160 |
| Total | **280** | **260** |
| Fixed assets | 150 | 100 |
| Inventory | 130 | 160 |
| Total | **280** | **260** |

3 Acquirer offers 200 shares to purchase target

4 Price of acquirer's shares is twice their nominal value

5 With sales at the same price and mark-up, inventory turns over once per annum

6 Mark-up on inventory = 100%; all sales are for cash

7 Fair value of Target's fixed assets on acquisition/merger = 150

8 Depreciation/amortisation rate for fixed assets and goodwill = 10%

9 Cost of reorganisation (where applicable) = 100

10 Acquirer and Target have each been trading for one year

**I. Merger accounting**

Consolidation of Acquirer and Target under merger rules

| | Acquirer | Target | Adjustm't | Consolidated |
|---|---|---|---|---|
| Year 1 on merger | | | | |
| Balance sheet | | | | |
| Ordinary share capital | 400 | 100 | −100 | 400 |
| Retained profits* | 80 | 160 | −100 | 140 |
| | **480** | **260** | | **540** |

| | | | | | |
|---|---|---|---|---|---|
| Fixed assets | 150 | 100 | | 250 | |
| Investment in target | 200 | | −200 | | |
| Inventory | 130 | 160 | | 290 | |
| | **480** | **260** | | **540** | |
| Year 2 | | | | | |
| Profit and loss | | | | | |
| Sales | | | | 580 | (100% mark-up) |
| Cost of sales | | | | −290 | |
| | | | | 290 | |
| Depreciation | | | | −25 | (10% of 250 fixed assets) |
| **Profit** | | | | **265** | |
| Balance sheet | | | | | |
| Ordinary share capital | | | | 400 | |
| Retained profit | | | | 405 | (140+265) |
| | | | | **805** | |
| Fixed assets | | | | 225 | (250−25) |
| Inventory | | | | 290 | |
| Cash | | | | 290 | |
| | | | | **805** | |

* Effectively 100 of Target's reserves are capitalised, reducing the amount available to the new group for distribution

(*Continued*)

*Table A6.1* Continued

**2. Acquisition accounting with goodwill shown as asset**
Consolidation of Acquirer and Target under acquisition rules

| | Acquirer | Target | Adjustment | Consolidated |
|---|---|---|---|---|
| Year 1 | | | | |
| Balance sheet | | | | |
| Ordinary share capital | 400 | 100 | −100 | 400 |
| Share premium | 200 | | | 200 |
| Retained profits | 80 | 160 | −160 | 80 |
| | **680** | 260 | | **680** |
| Fixed assets | 150 | 100 | 50 | 300 |
| Goodwill | | | 90 | 90 |
| Investment in Target | 400 | | −400 | 0 |
| Inventory | 130 | 160 | | 290 |
| | **680** | 260 | | **680** |

Note the share premium, and the revaluation of Target's assets to 310, goodwill (400−310) – none of which appears under merger accounting rules. A further point to note is the reduction in the group's retained profits from 140 under the merger rules to 80 under the acquisition rules.

| | Consolidated |
|---|---|
| Year 2 | |
| Profit and loss | |
| Sales | 580 |
| Cost of sales | −290 |
| | 290 |
| Fixed asset depreciation | −30 |
| Goodwill amortisation | −9 |
| **Profit** | **251** |

| | | |
|---|---|---|
| Balance sheet | | |
| Ordinary share capital | 400 | |
| Share premium | 200 | |
| Retained profits | 331 | (80+251) |
| | **931** | |
| Fixed assets | 270 | |
| Goodwill | 81 | (90−9) |
| Inventory | 290 | |
| Cash | 290 | |
| | **931** | |
| **3. Acquisition accounting: goodwill written off to reserves** | | |
| Year 1 | | |
| Balance sheet | | |
| Ordinary share capital | 400 | |
| Share premium | 200 | |
| Retained profit | 80 | |
| Goodwill write-off reserve | −90 | |
| | **590** | |
| Fixed assets | 300 | |
| Inventory | 290 | |
| | **590** | |
| Year 2 | | |
| Profit and loss | | |
| Sales | 580 | |
| Cost of sales | −290 | |
| | 290 | |
| Depreciation of fixed assets | −30 | |
| **Profit** | **260** | |

(*Continued*)

*Table A6.1* Continued

| | | |
|---|---|---|
| Balance sheet | | |
| Ordinary share capital | 400 | |
| Share premium | 200 | |
| Goodwill write-off reserve | −90 | |
| Retained profit | 340 | (80+260) |
| | **850** | |
| Fixed assets | 270 | |
| Inventory | 290 | |
| Cash | 290 | |
| | **850** | |
| **4. Acquisition accounting; goodwill shown as asset; reorganisation provision of 100; stock write-down of 30** | | |
| Year 1 | | |
| Balance sheet | | |
| Ordinary share capital | 400 | |
| Share premium | 200 | |
| Retained profit | 80 | |
| | **680** | |
| Fixed assets | 300 | |
| Goodwill | 220 | (90+130) |
| Inventory | 260 | (290−30) |
| Provision | −100 | |
| | **680** | |
| Year 2 | | |
| Reorganisation provisions unnecessary – written back | | |
| Inventory sold at normal price | | |
| Profit and loss | | |
| Sales | 580 | |

| | | |
|---|---|---|
| Cost of sales | −260 | (30 lower because of year 1 write down) |
| | 320 | |
| Depreciation of fixed assets | −30 | |
| Amortisation of goodwill | −22 | |
| Provision written back | 100 | |
| **Profit** | **368** | |
| Balance sheet | | |
| Ordinary share capital | 400 | |
| Share premium | 200 | |
| Retained profit | 448 | (80+368) |
| | **1,048** | |
| Fixed assets | 270 | |
| Goodwill | 198 | (220−22) |
| Inventory | 290 | |
| Cash | 290 | |
| | **1,048** | |

**5. Acquisition accounting: goodwill written off, reorganisation provision of 100; stock write-down of 30**

| | |
|---|---|
| Year 1 | |
| Balance sheet | |
| Ordinary share capital | 400 |
| Share premium | 200 |
| Goodwill write-off reserve | −220 |
| Retained profit | 80 |
| | **460** |
| Fixed assets | 300 |
| Inventory | 260 |
| Provision | −100 |
| | **460** |

*(Continued)*

*Table A6.1* Continued

| | | |
|---|---|---|
| Year 2 | | |
| Profit and loss | | |
| Reorganisation provisions unnecessary – written back | | |
| Inventory sold at normal price | | |
| Sales | 580 | |
| Cost of sales | 260 | |
| | 320 | |
| Depreciation of fixed assets | −30 | |
| Provision written back | 100 | |
| **Profit** | **390** | |
| Balance sheet | | |
| Ordinary share capital | 400 | |
| Share premium | 200 | |
| Goodwill write-off reserve | −220 | |
| Retained profits | 470 | (80+390) |
| | **850** | |
| Fixed assets | 270 | |
| Inventory | 290 | |
| Cash | 290 | |
| | **850** | |

**6. Merger accounting with reorganisation provision**

If on merger, reorganisation provisions were made, they would have to be charged to the profit and loss account, either before close of play in year 1 (assuming the merger took place slightly earlier), or in year 2. The example below assumes the provision was made at the beginning of year 2.

Note: if the provision was later deemed unnecessary it would be credited to profit in later years. Under acquisition accounting, the provision would not have been charged to the profit and loss account.

| | | |
|---|---|---|
| Year 2 | | |
| Profit and loss | | |
| Sales | 580 | |
| Cost of sales | −290 | |
| | 290 | |
| Depreciation | −25 | |
| Reorganisation provision | −100 | |
| **Profit** | **165** | |
| Balance sheet | | |
| Ordinary share capital | 400 | |
| Retained profit | 305 | (140+165) |
| | **705** | |
| Fixed assets | 225 | |
| Inventory | 290 | |
| Cash | 290 | |
| Provision | −100 | |
| | **705** | |

# 7 Accounting for mergers and acquisitions

## Dealing with the problems

*The previous chapter describes the considerable task facing the ASB as it sought to bring order to the numerous options open to acquisitive companies to adopt whatever accounting policies would reflect their post-acquisition results and financial position in the most attractive light. A table summarising the principal options and the FRSs that dealt with them is given in the Appendix to this chapter.*

*The ASB's game plan was to begin with principles already familiar to its public. FRS6 Acquisitions and Mergers and FRS7 Fair Values in Acquisition Accounting, published together in September 1994, each built on the existing foundations of a late ASC exposure draft. FRS7 had the additional advantage of drawing on the definition of a liability published six months previously in FRS5, which enabled it to go beyond the equivalent work of the ASC. However, although the main lines of a solution were already clear, the FRS7 project attracted the most hostile criticism from preparers of accounts of any of the ASB's proposals.*

*More difficult conceptual and practical issues lay in the path of building consensus on the appropriate treatment of goodwill and its practical application. FRS10 Goodwill and Intangible Assets was published in December 1997, after extensive consultation including the ASB's first and only public hearing, and was followed seven months later by FRS11 Impairment of Fixed Assets and Goodwill, after field-testing of its requirements with a number of companies.*

*Finally, FRS12 Provisions, Contingent Liabilities, and Contingent Assets were published in September 1998 to apply the principles enunciated in FRS7 to all reorganisations, whether or not related to an acquisition. An interesting aspect of this standard is that it was developed jointly with the IASC and has no differences of substance from the international standard in its common requirements.*

### Allan Cook

#### *Discussion*

*Merger v acquisition accounting*

**GM In the last chapter you spoke about the ability of companies to choose almost at will whether to use merger or acquisition**

DOI: 10.4324/9781003346920-7

**accounting. What was the objective of the ASB in tackling the problem and what principle guided the Board in FRS6?**

**GW** We were guided by our Statement of Principles, which we had got by then. But essentially it was an issue of comparability – in particular we didn't like the idea that like situations would be reported in a different way at the discretion of the preparer of accounts. Acquisition accounting and merger accounting were almost free options with potential for manipulation. That was the core of the matter. The thing that was sometimes overlooked, though, was there was a good deal of disclosure attached to FRS6; and the enhanced disclosures gave a great deal of transparency that wasn't there before about the make-up of performance, particularly profit – but the composition of profits, not just the aggregate profits, both before and after the merger, or combination. So there was a deal more disclosure and information made available as well.

But the core of FRS6 was this critical choice between merger accounting and acquisition accounting, and tightening up, particularly of the conditions that had been proposed by the ASC in their work.

**DPT** I think one of the key things was that this was to be a real uniting of interests – a merger, a partnership if you like. It wasn't just to be a mechanical arrangement.

**GW** Yes, one thing that came out of our deliberations was an important understanding that mergers do still exist. We accepted that. What we didn't accept was that anything could be called a merger if you wanted the benefit of merger accounting. And later work by standard-setters, particularly in the US, followed by the IASB, led to the view that the prime thing had to be uniformity. So everybody had to do acquisition accounting; therefore everything was to be regarded as an acquisition. We took a different view: let's look at deals. At the extreme you can see what a merger looks like. But you put tight conditions around that and say it's a relatively rare activity. Although, since the standard some very big combinations have done merger accounting. They are rather large, some of these pooling of interest arrangements.

**DPT** One thing I should maybe mention is that IAS22 allowed both. It did say that, where you had the same set of circumstances, you weren't intended to have a choice but it didn't stop you. IFRS3 banned merger accounting. It said that a merger of equals was so rare that it was virtually non-existent. Many people agreed with that; others said that, even if it was allowed it would be too difficult to form a boundary, and the IASB accepted that, unfortunately. But the other thing I thought was very interesting was that the IASB decided, even if it could determine a boundary, what it shouldn't do is to adopt the carry-over method using the existing carrying values of assets and liabilities of both parties. They said that the fresh start method (which instead involved fair valuing the assets and liabilities), which both Geoff and I have argued for some time, would be a far better method. So they did acknowledge that, but they just said the boundary was too difficult and moved on.

**AVC** I was quite keen on the fresh start method. When I was at IASC I had tried to push that one, but, as merely the Secretary, I had no vote; I was merely able to propose things. But they didn't buy that.

Personally, my own industrial experience was in two enterprises which essentially were mergers. It was before the days of arguments over this. Unilever and Shell always behaved as merged companies.

**GW** Yes, there have subsequently been mergers of a similar type – big companies. My bible, Ernst and Young, tells me that among the post FRS6 mergers were not only BP/AMOCO (1998), of course, which was controversial, but also Glaxo/SmithKline (2000). And I had forgotten that, actually, GlaxoSmithKline was the coming together of two really genuinely independent companies. They were of similar size and, viewed from the shareholders' perspective, it was not the same as an acquisition. There are big companies around like that which were formed by a merger process.

**DPT** I should tell you a story about the SmithKline one. John Coombe was one of our board members – he was FD of Glaxo – and it was quite clear that he was working towards merger accounting. And we drafted a spoof UITF pronouncement and sent it round to his office. It abolished merger accounting with instant effect. Goodwill had to be amortised. And the only clue that it was a spoof was that it had to be amortised over the expected term of office of the finance director.

**GW** Which was usually quite short, actually.

**DPT** We had to phone his PA beforehand to make sure that he didn't call the merger off. Another story about merger accounting arose when IASC was debating the issue. A Canadian partner in Coopers said he'd never ever seen a combination that wasn't an acquisition. And this was just at the same time as they'd merged with Price Waterhouse. And they had said that was a merger of equals. I remember saying, "Well, could you tell us all then who was the dominant partner in PwC?".

Silence.

**GW** I had forgotten that actually. It means that we had two ASB Board members who were actually finance directors of companies that did major mergers after the standard came out: John Buchanan at BP, where I think he just sneaked over the line with AMOCO and the 40% rule, and John Coombe of course at Glaxo.

**GM If we go back to arrangements before the ASB was formed, SSAP23 clearly wasn't working. Did the ASC attempt to improve it?**

**AVC** As we explained in Chapter 6, the focus of the ASC's work on M&A during the first half of the eighties was essentially an effort to preserve merger accounting after a tax case which decided that it was illegal. That all got settled, partly through legislation, and partly through the accounting standard SSAP23, by 1985. But it didn't take long for all the problems that we've been discussing in the last chapter to emerge. And by the end of that decade, the ASC was seriously concerned. The level of its concern is shown by significant disclosures added to the acquisition accounting standard, which they first proposed in 1988 and issued as a revised standard in July 1989. The new disclosures identified all the tricks in acquisition accounting, enabling an informed user to see what was going on. They didn't address the merger v acquisition distinction of SSAP23, but they demonstrated the concern of the ASC to take urgent action in this area. It is just as well it did, because our own standard, FRS6, only came into effect some six years later.

Interestingly, the ASC's initiative was led by a working party which was chaired by Roger Munson, who, of course, subsequently joined our Board, though he had retired by the time that we finalised the standards. Roger's working party went on to produce ED47 and ED48, which dealt both with mergers and acquisitions and with goodwill. So the ASC had really got its teeth into this thing by the end of the decade. But it knew that it was going to have to shut down its operations and hand over to the ASB – which may well have hardened the proposals that it put into these Exposure Drafts.

*Means of achieving merger accounting*

**AVC** In the Exposure Draft on mergers and acquisitions the ASC set out the key principles, the key criteria that would determine whether something was a merger or not. And these formed essentially the basis for the ASB's exposure draft, FRED6, starting with the point that neither side should see itself either as acquirer or acquiree. That replaced the key principle of SSAP23 beforehand, which had been that no resources should leave the company. That earlier principle was designed to ensure that mergers should result from an exchange of shares rather than from payment by the acquirer to shareholders of the acquiree. However, as a stand-alone principle, that requirement merely invited the merchant banks to find ways of enabling the shareholders of the acquired company to get cash: vendor placings, vendor rights, as well as deals that allowed an acquirer to park shares acquired through earlier purchases with a friendly bank and receive them back in the form of a share for share exchange.

Essentially the ASC had identified the problems, and ASB then took them over and produced the standard relatively quickly.

The proposals on the distinction between merger and acquisition were received quite well by the public; so I think that getting FRS6 out was not a great problem for us. The problem arose when we tried to get into the much more contentious issues of determining fair values on an acquisition.

**DPT** I think it would be quite useful to remind ourselves of the five criteria which had to be met to enable merger accounting to be used as they appeared in FRS6.

Basically, the first one was: no party is portrayed as either the acquirer or the acquiree, either by its own board or that of the other party.

Second, all parties participated in establishing the structure, choosing the management, location, etc.

Third, relative sizes weren't to be too disparate. I think the presumption was that nobody was to be more than 50% larger than each of the other parties to the combination.

The fourth one was that the consideration required equity to be paid to each party, obviously through equity shares.

And fifth, no shareholder retained any material interest in only part of the business. So these were the five criteria, shrunk from the six that were proposed by the ASC – they were essentially the same, but tightened.

**GM Any other comments on those issues?**

**GW** Just that, if I were being critical – which I'm not!

**GM** No, never!

**GW**. I would say that we set out to do principles-based standards, and actually ED48, the original draft by the ASC, was very principles-based. But the only trouble is that principles alone wouldn't have worked because they would require good will and terribly honest – perhaps self-sacrificing – appraisal by people, by preparers, to implement it. And the unfortunate finance director would, say, be faced with an ambitious chief executive who wanted to get good figures out of this deal. And they would find it very difficult to implement the pure principle-based description of what you treated as a merger or an acquisition. So ED48 and FRS6 had to put what really are rules there, such as the 60:40 rebuttable presumption, which is what was used to justify the AMOCO merger. It's a purely arbitrary number; it had no scientific basis at all. So we have to confess that in order to make the omelette, we had to break a few eggs. But adding some precise rules worked in practice, which is the ultimate test of a standard.

**DPT** Just for the avoidance of doubt, in Geoff's comment, 'good will' is two words!

**GW** Yes, and there wasn't enough of that about, although there was lots of the other sort of 'goodwill'.

**GM Last question on this topic: Did FRS6 manage to stop the various means such as vendor placings, vendor rights, bed and breakfast deals, etc. used by the merchant banks to achieve merger accounting?**

**DPT** We were pretty tough on this one. First of all, we defined equity much tighter than in the Companies Act. We used the FRS4 definition, and that meant that some of the shares that in our terms were non-equity didn't count anymore towards the merger. Secondly, we said that, in determining whether the extent to which consideration for the deal had been in the form of equity, account had to be taken of any side arrangements that enabled those receiving equity shares to dispose of them for cash. And that killed the vendor placings and the vendor rights issues. That was done quite deliberately. A further device that we really attacked was the bed and breakfast deals whereby, if you had acquired an interest in a target company in either of the two previous years, and you'd used non-equity consideration, that was taken into account when you were trying to look at how much you had actually paid in terms of equity. That stopped the prospective bidder building up a holding through cash purchases, selling it to a merchant bank, then buying it back for equity shares at the time of the formal offer. So bed and breakfast died.

**AVC** I confirm that all those ideas were in ED48. At ASB we were able to make them stick.

## *The flexibility of acquisition accounting*

*'The acquirer's perspective'*

**GM Accounting standards at the time, both in the UK and internationally, required fair values to be assessed from the 'acquirer's perspective'.**

**You did not use that expression. Did you think it had no meaning?**

**AVC** Actually, I can remember when I was Secretary of IASC being prompted to include that little phrase in the original version of their standard on business combinations. And it seemed innocent enough – a bit unspecific – but it was at least consistent with the idea of 'value in use', which was the concept under which the value to a business through using an asset was often more than it could get from selling it.

**DPT** So all these problems are due to you, Allan, are they?

**AVC** That's right. I blessed it, accepting it from older and wiser colleagues, an international board of eminent accountants, who said, of course, you must include the 'acquirer's perspective'. But the words 'acquirer's perspective' soon became code for acquirer's intentions, and that's another matter altogether, which justified all the things that FRS7 was trying to put right. That standard said very firmly, it is events, not intentions for future actions that increase or decrease an entity's assets or liabilities. So, instead of that vague phrase, which meant whatever the acquirer wanted it to mean, it insisted on assets and liabilities, which had been defined by now in FRS5 as resulting from a past event that creates rights or obligations.

And it said two things – one about recognition, that in looking at fair values you only recognised those assets or liabilities that existed at the date of acquisition. And, second, you measured them at conditions that also existed at the time of acquisition. That essentially is the way in which we replaced the phrase 'the acquirer's perspective'.

**DPT** I think what Allan's just said – they were the two key principles, and this was very much a principles-based standard. It had two very short sentences which Allan has just described. And everything was based on those two sentences.

The other thing, Allan, I don't know if you wanted to extend that, what it really meant: it actually specifically banned 'intention' after that, and any changes or events after the acquisition date were out, any provisions for future losses or reorganisations incurred as a result of the acquisition were also not allowed. So it was very clear: bang, bang, bang – these were out.

When dealing with the acquirer's perspective, we had a bit of a problem. Contingent assets, for example, depended on conditions at the year end, which might well be affected by the acquisition. Therefore we recognised some assets that, had the acquisition not taken place, wouldn't have been recognised – certainly that went for tax losses. FRS7 specifically said that you could take tax losses of the acquired company into account if they were going to be recoverable as a result of the acquisition – a contingent asset which had now crystallised.

The thing that I think people missed in this – Geoff will be dealing with this in the next chapter – we actually got rid of the SSAP24 pension figure which spread surpluses and deficits over the working lives of the employees. Now under FRS7, on acquisition, you had to measure the surplus or deficit in the pension fund of the acquired company using the same principles as applied to other financial assets or liabilities and conditions existing at the acquisition date. That caused quite a stir. I think they probably didn't realise what was coming in the future.

**GW** That's a good point. It shows that FRS7 was a principles-based standard, based on our framework. But it showed where the framework led in terms of pensions, quite strikingly. You know it really was an application of FRS17, the way we dealt with pensions on acquisition, even though FRS17 didn't exist then. It's surprising in a way that people didn't object to that more.

**AVC** Companies accepted the FRS7 recognition basis for the pension liability on the occasion of an acquisition because they were familiar with the idea that transfer values (applied when a group of employees were moved from one scheme to another) were always calculated at the conditions that existed at that point in time. In their eyes, that was a different issue from accounting for the ongoing cost of providing for pensions, with all its uncertainties.

*Reorganisation provisions and future losses*

**GM Providing for future losses and reorganisations was long-established practice. Before launching a bid an acquirer would assess the changes that would need to be made and take them into account in determining the price it was prepared to pay. Many would say that was prudent management, which enabled people to see the total investment on which a return had to be made.**

**How did you answer them?**

**GW** Well, basically we said, quite rightly I think, that we were looking at the state of the acquisition at the time of acquisition, not the way it was going to be. There were these arguments – Donald Main's dissenting view, for instance – that the finance director and others involved in an acquisition would be looking at the prospects for what they were going to do with the business. And they'd assess the assets and the liabilities according to that. And therefore they might anticipate losses on such things. But, of course, you don't do that when you make an ordinary investment in a firm. If you set up a new plant, you invest in it at what it cost – you record it in the balance sheet at what it cost – you don't record it at what you think it might be worth ultimately in terms of net present value. And specifically in the case of fixed assets, the standard said that normally you'd expect depreciated replacement cost to represent the value of fixed assets – factories and such things.

That's a thing we might come back to later in relation to fair value. But what we were interested in was what was acquired at the time it was acquired, not the gleam in the acquirer's eye, which so often – as your research had already shown, Geoff, considerably before then (Meeks, 1977) – came to grief. These gleams don't turn into a shining light, they flicker away and disappear. So we were looking at the state of the business at the time it was acquired and of course, in the case of provisions for future losses, there's the question of commitment – our framework made that very clear, that you don't recognise a liability until there is a commitment. If you can get out of it, it's not a liability. And things that haven't happened yet, that are prospects, they aren't liabilities at the moment. And there are things that can be escaped by good management: you are not committed to future losses. You may think that difficulties lie ahead, but you don't know the outcome until they have actually happened. And accounts, if they are prudent and all the other things that our critics would have wanted, they don't show things that haven't yet happened. They show the state of the business at that point in time. The balance sheet has a date on it.

**AVC** I must admit, I had a flicker of sympathy for the arguments of the business community, having sat there over some years and looked at things like cash flow forecasts for capital investments and so on. Within business, people are trying to manage future cash flows. And then they come up against the rigours of financial accounting, which says, that's all very well, but those are not assets and liabilities, (with all the arguments that you've just put forward). And so there is sometimes a feeling in business that they are being made to stand on their heads to tell their story, rather than actually tell it as they have understood it, the rationale for their own business decisions. That's understandable but we had to take a stand against it nevertheless, because, as you say, you can only start from where you are now. Accounts don't pretend to tell you the whole of the future. They tell you where you are now, and look at each period in those terms. And that was the essence of the conflict, the point where you couldn't get a proper meeting of minds. The same problem occurred many times over in the unhappiness over the pension proposals later on: that business was trying to manage cash flows, and the accountants were trying to say, "Where are we now?"

**DPT** I remember the project manager on this standard saying to me, 'You can't do that' – which meant that you can't stop acquisition provisioning because we've always done it this way. And I remember saying, 'Just watch'. SSAP22, which was in force at the time, allowed future losses, it allowed reorganisation expenses although ASC later put out an amendment which said "Disclose these losses and expenses", so it was more visible now. They then issued ED53, which proposed disallowing future losses, but still allowing reorganisation provisions provided there was a clear plan. And then we came in and bombed the whole lot out, announcing our intentions, with a Discussion Paper. We argued it was consistent with the Statement of Principles; it was consistent with FRS3's information set approach; and otherwise, as Geoff has said, we'd have arbitrary cut-off lines trying to fix this.

**GM What sort of reaction to this issue did you get when you published your proposals?**

**DPT** We had quite a lot of opposition from industry on that one, as Geoff again has mentioned. Support from the users – the institutional investors, the analysts. And eventually we got substantial support from the accounting firms and Institutes. And industry gradually came round – I suppose they saw the way the pendulum was going anyway. But we still had opposition; and Donald, I thought, did a pretty good dissenting view summarising the position, as Geoff has said. But it was a revolutionary standard: we actually changed the mindset.

I should probably add that the IASC's Standard didn't quite follow us. We'll probably come onto FRS12 and IAS37, which were pretty well identical. But the IASC was also about to base the business combinations standard, which was IAS22, on our provisioning proposals. And I got the UK's view pushed through, and we had the votes in the IASC meeting and then I had to leave the meeting having established that we had a majority to do what we did in FRS7. In my absence the Dutch and the Swiss, who were very much industrialists, managed to change it and had a paragraph put in that said, you could provide for reorganisations, etc. for three months after the acquisition and they would become part of liabilities at the acquisition date. And that became IAS22. Steve Zeff, in his book on the IASC, commented that I was absolutely outraged when I heard and I gave them Hell at the next meeting for it (Camfferman and Zeff, 2007, p.389). But it was too late: it had gone through. So there was opposition all the way.

### *Inventory write-downs*

**GM In Chapter 6 you cited the enormous write down of Distiller's stocks when that company was acquired by Guinness. Would not the auditors have been able to challenge that, even on the basis of the accounting standards of that time?**

**DPT** This was an appalling situation because it was instant profit. You think, why didn't the auditors do something? Industry would come up with some plausible tale about there being a glut of whisky or something – that they couldn't possibly sell it, they'd have to slash the price – all this sort of thing. And the auditors – I often used to say in speeches at the time that the only difference between an auditor and an airport luggage trolley was that the airport luggage trolley had an independent mind of its own. And this was an era where you had the situation of companies challenging their auditors by opinion-shopping (approaching other auditing firms for their view on an issue – with the implied threat of changing the incumbent auditor), of getting legal opinions, etc. And so there was huge pressure, and the auditors caved, quite bluntly: they just didn't deal with it. So what the ASB had to do was to bring in a disclosure that drew attention to any unusual margin on the sale of acquired inventory either on the face of the profit and loss account as an exceptional item or by way of a note. We couldn't say you couldn't write down stock because clearly people did have different views about its value. But we did make them show the profit, and that was the embarrassment factor. Now if we'd had that requirement at the time of the Guinness takeover of Distillers, that would have hugely embarrassed them. And I think they would have been rubbished in the Lex column and elsewhere. But it wasn't there at that stage. We did require a re-examination of the fair values of the stock if exceptional profits seemed to be earned and if necessary the values were to be adjusted with a corresponding adjustment to goodwill.

There were other anti-avoidance requirements. For example, if provisions for future costs were made by an acquired entity shortly before the acquisition they were not allowed to be shown as a liability unless the acquiree was demonstrably committed to the expenditure. If obligations were incurred by the acquired entity as a result of the influence of the acquirer, it would be necessary to consider whether control of the acquired entity had transferred at an earlier date. So any provisions made within 12 months prior to the acquisition had to be disclosed. So there was a lot of, if you like, embarrassment features in the standard.

### *Fixed assets*

**GM What constraints, if any, did FRS7 put on unrealistically high estimates of the fair value of fixed assets (e.g. the bus garage discussed in Chapter 6)?**

**DPT** Well, basically for fixed assets we used value to the business. Mainly it was going to be market value; but, if not, it would be then on the basis of estimated replacement cost or value in use (or recoverable amount I should say) – not taking account of acquirer's intentions. The trouble is it was very difficult sometimes to get a value if you had an unusual asset. It was alright if it was one that was frequently traded. But if you had a unique asset, how did you value that in the absence of a reliable market value? So, despite our guidance, there remained some scope for flexibility, especially if the fixed asset was a brand or similar intangible.

## *The treatment of goodwill*

**GM Why was the treatment of goodwill so contentious – were there different views on what goodwill was?**

**AVC** It certainly was contentious. I think there were two special reasons for that. First of all, it had had significant effects on financial statements, and these were growing because the size of goodwill in relation to an acquirer's net worth was getting larger and larger mainly as a result of the increased use of reorganisation provisions on acquisition. Secondly, it was a conceptual conundrum. So it was easy for people to argue on a purely self-interest basis for whichever treatment would suit their own needs. And, unfortunately, because it was a conceptual conundrum, the Framework – our Statement of Principles – didn't really give a self-evidently right answer. It contrasts in that respect with the fair values issue, where the Framework gave a very clear answer, and we were able to build and fight on that – just as well, because we had a really tough battle on fair values.

The conceptual problem is illustrated, I think, by the fact that goodwill is the only asset in the balance sheet that is defined – not merely measured, it's defined – by its cost. That seems to conflict with the Statement of Principles. It's a difference, a difference between what you pay and the assets that you can identify. ASB said it was a bridge between the identifiable assets in the consolidated accounts and the total investment that appears in the parent's accounts. And I think that was quite a good way of explaining to people. Unfortunately, it worked in the UK, where we have parents' accounts. It didn't work abroad, it didn't work in the US, where they don't know about parents' accounts. They regard the parent's accounts as the consolidated accounts.

ASB went on to say it's a bit of an accounting anomaly. It's a huge accounting anomaly because internally generated goodwill is not capitalised. So, if you capitalise only the purchased goodwill, you have an inconsistency. The expenditures that create internally generated goodwill are just charged to income as incurred. So some people would argue that you should therefore write off purchased goodwill immediately to reserves, to maintain consistency with internally generated goodwill. The trouble is that that doesn't reflect a potentially significant part of the investment that has been paid out. So management isn't held accountable for the return on that investment. If you accept that, then the alternative is to capitalise, and that immediately raises the question: do you amortise as well? There's no problem if the investment clearly loses its value. If you've acquired something in order to run it down and just get the cash flows, then that's fine. You can obviously amortise that. But what if it retains its value? Some say you should amortise anyway because – if you think about the purchase decision – the really distant cash flows have little effect on the value that you attach to your investment. It's the nearer cash flows that have the greatest effect, so you should amortise over that period, of the nearer cash flows. However, to sustain that argument you must distinguish between the cash flows that are deemed to flow from the original investment and those that emerge year by year as new cash flows appear over the horizon to replace those already recognised. The advocates for amortisation in such a case claim that the new cash flows derive, not from the original investment, but from the internally generated goodwill that inevitably replaces it as time flows on.

That's a somewhat abstract argument, not one that particularly appealed to business. Moreover, it's inconsistent with the way we treat non-depreciable assets such as land. We can maintain that in the balance sheet on the basis that, as each year's cash flows get used up, another future year emerges to take its place, so it does maintain its value. Similarly, for certain kinds of assets that are valued on what's called the renewals basis, it's argued that the expenditure on renewals maintains the value, and you don't have to depreciate. The goodwill argument is very much like that. The expenditure needed to maintain the value of your purchased goodwill is already there in those periods subsequent to the acquisition. So if you insist on amortising you get double-counting of the charge. That appears to be unfair. So the argument then shifts to the practical issue of testing for impairment. And that's the point at which the ASB chose to attack this problem.

**GW** Actually, I take a slightly different angle on that. When I re-read FRS10 I must say I thought we were a bit extreme with this business about goodwill being an asset but not an asset. You know it was a bit like the Bishop of Woolwich talking about God: "I don't know where he is, but he's somewhere". And, in fact, the problem of goodwill is essentially an aggregation problem and the perspective that comes from that.

In other words, if I look at it from the point of view of the acquiring company and I look in the company's own accounts, I see an investment there that costs money; part of it is goodwill. In the parent company accounts, the investment is simply the cost of some shares that I bought.

If I look at it as a consolidated deal, I look at it from a group perspective. Then, of course, I've got to try and identify all the assets I acquired and consolidate them in the group. And goodwill is a residual which includes the rather nebulous bit that's left on the end, including measurement errors from other assets. Of course, that's one of the problems. But it is in a sense an asset, as the name goodwill suggests. It's the premium paid to reach the going concern value of the business you've acquired. It's a very fleeting thing, a thing of the moment when you acquired it, and it can disappear very quickly – which is why we have the initial impairment test in the standard. It can disappear particularly quickly if the information was wrong when you acquired the company. It does seem to me that goodwill is at the extreme of being an asset and not being an asset. It's not separable from the rest of the business, therefore we have difficulty in recognising it as a separate asset of the business. And equally it doesn't meet the other requirements for recognition very easily. It isn't easily measurable usually. It doesn't have a ready market price. It's not objectively observable. So I just think goodwill is an extreme case of something that's marginally an asset and extremely difficult to pin down.

But it wasn't the conceptual problem, of course, that created all the controversy. It was the fact that goodwill was the balancing item in many of the creative accounting deals involved with acquisitions. In the case of provisioning for future losses, for instance, if I provide more for future losses the initial impact of it is to increase goodwill. I create this nebulous asset on the other side of the balance sheet, and it was very easy to manipulate because it was such a difficult asset to pin down. For example, it was easy to argue against amortisation charges. And that was the source of the controversy. People were doing very well out of goodwill in terms of making their post-merger performance look very good, and they didn't want to lose that ability.

**AVC** I have to agree with that, Geoff, I think we're both arguing the same thing.

**GW** I said different angle, I'm not disagreeing with you. I'm just looking at it from a slightly different point of view. You know, I think that the controversy was driven by creative accounting rather than any conceptual difficulty. The difficulty that arose in dealing with it was, of course, that we wanted to get something that was conceptually sound. And things that are conceptually sound do lead to consistency and become more difficult for people to manipulate if they can be found.

**GM How did the ASC deal with the issue?**

**AVC** The ASC looked at all these arguments and it's interesting to see some of the positions taken by the people who subsequently became board members on the ASB. Graham Stacy, for instance, saying you shouldn't be amortising, you should write off the goodwill. He even thought a dangling debit might be the answer, which was subsequently espoused not so much by him as by Ray Hinton, who came in at a later stage.

The ASC stated clearly that it did not consider goodwill had an indefinite life. In determining the useful life over which goodwill should be amortised, it pursued two lines of argument. First, it pointed out that at the time of the acquisition, the benefits expected to arise from the acquisition would be evaluated so that, the more distant in time a benefit was expected, the more it would be discounted in making the decision to acquire and at what price. It added that the matching concept required that the costs incurred in making the acquisition, including the cost of purchased goodwill, should be matched against the benefits expected when that cost was set; moreover, the effects of subsequent expenditure or other circumstances affecting the company after the date of acquisition should not be taken into account. Secondly, it listed five types of real world factors that might be expected to be taken into account at the time the acquisition decision was made. These had to be disclosed if an amortisation period of more than 20 years was chosen. Despite all this, the exposure draft permitted amortisation over up to 40 years. I can't help feeling that that was because that was what the US did at the time, and there would have been too much opposition to have insisted on a shorter period. They had to say that it was over useful life, but they also said that there should be a review for impairment – that the directors should look annually at it for impairment. What they didn't do was go into the kind of detailed impairment tests that we adopted.

**DPT** Geoff – I was looking through some of my old speeches. I have very few of them left. One was on goodwill which I gave in November '95, and I mention in that speech – unfortunately I haven't got a reference – that in

1976 goodwill in relation to the acquirer's pre-acquisition net worth was 1%. By 1987 it was 44%. So if you've got a couple of big acquisitions and write off goodwill against reserves you could blow your net worth away. And that's really why there was this pressure. And another thing: I notice that Ray Hinton said in his dissent to FRS10 that 95% of companies that had goodwill used the write-off to reserves. So you had major problems, with the accounts looking completely bizarre with this goodwill write-off policy and this was a huge issue. I remember Michael Renshall, who was chairman of ASC, felt that this was the biggest issue that the committee faced. And they put out ED47 (Goodwill), and later ED52 which dealt with intangibles, and they proposed writing off goodwill, and intangibles, over a period not exceeding 20 years and, as Allan said, in no circumstances more than 40. ED47 got more responses than any other Exposure Draft since Current Cost Accounting. It was absolutely hammered. 93% of corporates objected; 73% of all respondents. ED52 was similar: 80% of corporates objected, and 62% of all respondents objected. That was the ASC's last attempt to resolve the issue and we were then left to pick up the pieces. And I think probably one of the most sensible things we did was: we left it. And we got on with other issues which we've already dealt with in the book; and, in a way, made our name first by dealing with those abuses while, quietly in the background, we were looking at the options for goodwill. And by the time we issued anything on goodwill, we had calmed things down, and also we had a certain reputation at this stage. If we had gone straight into the issue I think we would have been crucified.

**AVC** I think our first move was the Discussion Paper at the end of 1993. We'd already achieved FRS3 by then, and we were pretty well down the road to getting out FRS4 and FRS5. So, as David says, yes, we had definitely made our mark.

**GM Well that leads nicely into the question of whether the ASB had problems getting its solution accepted.**

**GW** Wasn't it the first standard on which we held public hearings?

**Dog Tweedie** interjected loudly at this stage, with a deafening complaint that this had been the only occasion when he had been able to air his views publicly, and noting that other standards were the worse for not benefitting from his wisdom in these matters.

Eventually, having made his point, he subsided.

**GW** That's what I call a public hearing.

**AVC** It was definitely the first. I'm not sure there was ever another. I can't recall another one.

**GW** I can't remember any others. I remember we held it at Kingsway Hall. And I remember Ray Hinton being put in his place by Will Baxter. Will was 90 then. He gave evidence to us on this standard. And he saw goodwill as a sort of quasi-asset – the perspective I was giving you just now – whereas Ray was the great advocate of the dangling debit. But, of course, he was also Will's former pupil, so taking Will on was a serious business for him. But he wanted to question Will on this and asked a long and convoluted question – possibly because he was a bit worried about tackling his former teacher. And Will attempted to answer this question. Ray had got a bit more confidence by then so he said, "I'm sorry, Professor Baxter, but I can't quite understand your answer. Could you amplify it please?" And Will replied – as quick as a flash – "Well, G K Chesterton once said, if you get a question you don't understand, give an answer you don't understand, so I expect you're right". David intervened and said, "Thank you for your contribution, Professor Baxter. Are there any other questions?", as Ray recovered his composure.

**AVC** I was at Will's table during lunch, and he'd used the example in his paper of jointness, and he talked about a Dresden Shepherd and Shepherdess, which are worth more together as a pair. And I said to him, "There's surely a market for odd pieces of Dresden Shepherds and Shepherdesses; so that spoils your argument, doesn't it?" He said, "You think so, do you?" He came on immediately after lunch, and he didn't use that example. He said, "I'm a film director, and I have the option of hiring either Mr Laurel or Mr Hardy". And that, of course, was perfect, because there is no market for Laurel on his own and Hardy on his own. He'd thought that one up between lunch and the start of the session immediately after lunch.

**GW** They have since been succeeded by Morecambe and Wise, of course. And Wise continued to earn his living after Morecambe died. You know, they are very difficult, those problems of jointness. But you can see what he was getting at. The aggregate, certainly, is what you would go for if you were selling them. Would you sell them individually, or would you sell them as a pair? Of course, you would sell them as a pair because the pair would be worth much more than the sum of the two individuals. And that difference is the jointness, the 'goodwill' if you like.

**DPT** I remember we put out the Discussion Paper in '93, and we actually listed all the possible ways we could deal with goodwill. We had six.

The first was capitalisation with amortisation over a finite period (the US and IASC position).

The next one was capitalisation with just impairment testing.

The third one was combining those two – method 2 only being used where goodwill had an indefinite life or a useful life believed to be more than 20 years.

The fourth one was immediate write-off against reserves.

The fifth one was the dangling debit (the goodwill write-off reserve).

And the sixth one was transfer to a goodwill reserve – a negative reserve – and impair that. In this case, whenever goodwill was impaired, the loss was charged through the P&L account.

Well, the reaction was: 34% wanted the goodwill write-off reserve; and about 25% each wanted either capitalisation and amortisation or capitalisation and impairment. And I remember the staff member who was running the project saying, "Well, it's clear that the biggest support is for the dangling debit". And I said, "No, it's not. If you look at the first two, there's

50% who want capitalization and either amortisation or impairment". And that's when we put them together. And, having worked up this proposal to capitalise goodwill and allow either amortisation or impairment alone under strict conditions, we had it field-tested by seven major companies who were big acquirers – and they supported the idea. Overall, we got 59% support for this idea in responses to a Working Paper "Goodwill and Intangible Assets" published later (June 1995), including 58% from preparers. So we really knew we were on track now. We had turned industry around. I remember they were so hostile to amortisation, on the basis, as Allan said earlier: 'I've got this investment. It's not losing value. Why then am I writing it off in the P&L account?' They just did not understand the write-off.

When I was with KPMG we pioneered the impairment test with Grand Metropolitan, who had just bought Smirnoff. And they were very hostile to the brand being treated as a form of goodwill – partly because they had no reserves left, to write it off against and also as they had offers to buy the brand at amounts higher than they had paid. We then said, well, how are we going to measure this thing for depreciation? What's the life of Smirnoff? And we asked how they had worked out the price for the vodka brand. They'd done it on a discounted cash flow basis. So we used their plans and calculations and then kept updating them in later years with the actual cash flows, to see if, in fact, the value of Smirnoff was less than the purchase price. And that's where the impairment test came from. Jeannot Blanchet and I wrote it up in Accountancy (Tweedie and Blanchet, 1989). We'd seen an impairment test in action, and we knew it could work. So there were all these issues flying round and we put the acceptable solutions together. And that's how we ended up with FRED12 and FRS10 and later FRS11 (Figure 7.1).

*Figure 7.1* A goodwill Christmas card sent by Accountancy Age at a time when accounting for goodwill was being vigorously debated in the UK with kind permission of editor Aaran Fronda.

### *Goodwill and intangibles*

**GM Did the ASB consider different treatments for goodwill and for intangibles?**

**DPT** Basically, we felt that some intangibles were so close to goodwill that it was going to be arbitrary if somebody identified an intangible as a separate asset, and then had a completely different treatment for goodwill. So we really felt that we had to make sure that they didn't play the games that they had done earlier by creating a brand or something and therefore reducing the goodwill figure. We required them to treat them both the same. In the 1993 Discussion Paper, we had proposed that since certain intangibles such as brands and publishing titles couldn't be disposed of separately from a business – which was the Companies Act requirement for identifying an intangible asset – and given that there was no generally accepted method of valuing these intangibles, and the dividing line with goodwill was unclear, such intangibles should be subsumed into goodwill.

All Hell broke loose. That proposal didn't work at all. There was strong opposition to it. Companies argued that intangibles could be critical to their business (possibly remembering Rowntree's experience of being taken over by Nestlé in 1988 while arguing vociferously that their extremely valuable brands, which were not on the company's balance sheet, were not being recognised by investors when considering the bid price) and therefore it was important to account for them separately. We accepted that and in the 1995 Working Paper proposed that intangibles could be recognised separately from goodwill if they met the legal and conceptual requirements for identifiability and could be measured reliably on initial recognition. But the condition was they would be treated in the same way as goodwill to prevent a company's results being reflected in a more favourable light simply by classifying expenditure as goodwill or as an intangible. The same rules were to be used for both.

**AVC** Interestingly, if they split them out, it does make it easier, I think, because then you can see whether they are behaving differently. For instance, it fits in very well with the idea of income-generating units that we used for our impairment tests. I'm not against the idea of having a host of intangibles, provided that the treatment is the same as goodwill.

**DPT** It was interesting. We said that intangibles could be reliably valued if there was a ready market for them. But the trouble is, most of these very valuable intangibles, such as brands, were unique. And then we eventually allowed companies to record these intangibles provided that there was a generally accepted method of valuing them–which tended to be on a discounted cash flow basis, multiples of turnover or royalties or something like that. So we did restrict it. They had to jump through several hoops before they were allowed to show a separate intangible. But as we've said before, the treatment was going to be exactly the same as for goodwill.

**AVC** The project director, Shân Kennedy, spent a lot of time working with companies to develop criteria that would identify intangibles that qualified for individual recognition under our proposals and whose continuing value could be reviewed for impairment under practicable impairment tests.

**GW** If you take the view I was putting earlier, that goodwill is an asset, but a really difficult one to detect, recognise and measure, then it's a spectrum between tangible fixed assets and goodwill. Tangible fixed assets you can see and it's much easier to identify them physically. Often it's easier to identify a price as well. And then, as you move along the spectrum, intangibles that you can sell separately are much like tangibles, except you can't touch them. You know, their legal rights are the same and they've got a traded value the same. And then you move along the spectrum until you get to a really nebulous thing like goodwill and you get things close to goodwill – such as customer networks and things like that, which sometimes can be identifiable and sometimes not. And it's not a question of principle, it's a question of application. And what struck me when re-reading FRS10 and FRS11 is the detailed guidance in them. You could in some ways say they are rules rather than principles, but they are not; they are good examples of principles-based standards. And that particular issue of goodwill impairment illustrates the really fundamental problems that standard-setters have. They do have principles, but just telling people to go away and do good and apply the principles would lead to all sorts of inconsistency, manipulation, and lack of comparability. That's why the standards are what they are.

### *Wider implications of provisions standard*

**GM FRS7 was obviously a critical step in the regulation of acquisition accounting. Did it have wider implications for other aspects of financial reporting?**

**AVC** Yes, indeed it did. As we've said earlier, it is built on the definitions of assets and liabilities. And those implications had to be carried through to all aspects of reporting. The way this was done was through a Standard, FRS12, which was called Provisions, Contingent Liabilities, and Contingent Assets. Now we are looking here at the effect of FRS7, so I'm speaking only of what FRS12 had to say about provisions.

I think it had three particular features that were really important. The first was that it defined a constructive obligation. The idea that you could have an obligation other than by operation of law had long existed, but there had been no clear definition of what that would be. And we defined it as an obligation that derives from an entity's actions either by an established pattern of past practice, published policies, or a sufficiently specific current statement that the entity has communicated to other parties that it will accept certain responsibilities; and, as a result, the entity has created a valid expectation on the part of the other parties that it will discharge those responsibilities. That proved to be an extremely useful definition, particularly in relation to the practice of restructuring. I think we mentioned earlier, restructuring was often done, especially when senior management changed, with what was loosely called 'big bath' provisions. You put into them everything you could conceivably think of that might be related to the restructuring that you intended to undertake and consequently buried potential future costs thereby presenting a rosy picture in later years.

We attacked that at two levels. First of all by defining restructuring pretty tightly as being a programme that is planned and controlled by management and materially changes either the scope of the business undertaken by an entity or the manner in which that business is conducted. So that meant that what we were about to say about restructuring only applied to major reorganisations. We then went on to spell out exactly what could be included in such reorganisations. Essentially that definition insisted on a detailed formal plan, not just a broad announcement to the market that they were going to restructure. The people affected had to be informed – not necessarily every individual, but at least the trade unions – with details of where it was and when it was likely to happen. So that put a stop to a lot of these so-called big bath provisions.

Secondly, the Standard backed up its rules on constructive obligations by giving 12 examples of situations which either were or were not constructive obligations. For example, if you had to decommission an oil platform or a nuclear plant, that was an event where you had already incurred an obligation because you had done something which would have to be removed, under the law, at some future date. And you had to take that into account. On the other hand, if a change in tax legislation meant that you had to retrain your staff, that was an event of the future. You didn't owe an obligation to anybody. An obligation requires a third party to whom you owe responsibilities.

And then the third item was that this Standard gave guidance on measurement. The term 'fair values' must be measured at best estimate. That 'best estimate' wording had existed for many years. We defined it more narrowly as expected value, which means you take into account the relative probability of the various possible outcomes. And you may have to do that even for single items – a single best guess of, say, a lawsuit judgement, is not necessarily what you should be providing for, because there could be a range of possible outcomes, and you have somehow to reflect that. That was an idea that might have been new to quite a number of people in that situation. And we also gave guidance on discounting. We said that it should be at a pre-tax rate, and that the tax effects should be reflected under the tax standard.

## *The international position*

### *Defining fair value*

**GM As I understand it, ASB was the first standard-setter to put Fair Value into operation. Then FASB and IASB adopted it, but with some differences. Could you tell us about these developments?**

**GW** Yes – of course, 'fair value' has been around for quite a long time as a concept. But nobody had defined it operationally in a standard until

FRS7, and FRS7 went into some detail about how you might handle it for different types of assets, and so on. For instance, this issue of fixed assets that you'd value at depreciated replacement cost, where you had a unique asset that didn't have a ready market value. So all that stuff was addressed, and later on, of course, FASB standards adopted fair value in a number of roles, not just acquisition accounting, notably the financial instruments project. And the G4+1 also, I think, got into measurement and discussed fair value. So it got through to FASB standards, and the FASB standards, of course, got through to the International standard. And the International standard on fair values still has a lot in common with FRS7, although there are important differences. Notably, the IASB standard (IFRS 13) adopts the FASB assumption that fair value is a selling price, and other measures are allowed only as proxies for this. FRS 7, on the other hand, was grounded in the ASB Statement of Principles, which regarded value to the business as the measurement objective. This approach allowed replacement costs rather than selling price, in appropriate circumstances, and it allowed for costs of acquisition or disposal to be included in the fair value calculation.

I think the differences – I would say that – make FRS7 superior because FRS7 locks into the idea that it is the actual value to the firm. It does allow values to be entity-specific. That's not the same thing as incorporating management expectations of future events. It's saying that looking at the consequences of what we've got now, we reflect what the position is the entity is in. For example, if we have a market that's not very big and the entity has a lot of a certain asset – say a commodity stock – so that it would depress the price if it unloaded it, we allow a lower value, or require a lower value, because that's what the entity would be capable of realising. We don't just take the spot price for a small volume. And there are a lot of different applications where the ASB approach does differ; but it's all based on this idea of entity-specific valuation. And the FASB and IASB instead concentrated on this rather abstract concept of open market value, which, of course, we have in FRS7. We do use the definition that it's an arm's length transaction between well-informed buyers and sellers, but the FASB and IASB took this to imply that there is *a fair value,* a unique value, whereas if you read FRS7 carefully it's based on the idea that there is a unique *objective* to work out what this thing is worth in its context. But its context matters, and you might switch methods of valuation, for example between replacement cost and net selling price, depending on the circumstances. That's based on our Statement of Principles, of course, which does start with value to the business, whereas the FASB framework, which of course influenced the FASB standard, and later the IASB standard, uses this rather abstract idea of fair value; and it leads to different results in some cases.

Nevertheless, a lot of FRS7 is in those later standards, and for the better. And I think if they had taken the whole of FRS7 it would have been better still.

*The treatment of goodwill*

**GM How did the ASB's proposals on goodwill compare with the existing international standards?**

**DPT** Well, it was interesting, because when we started discussing this at the IASC, where I was one of the two UK and Irish representatives at the time, the UK was almost laughed at for its goodwill treatment. The IASC had abolished the option to use write-offs against reserves. We were one of the few countries that still used the policy, so we were really at the back of the heap. And, as Steve Zeff put it, we went from there to being the world leaders on goodwill accounting; and IASC came along and followed us (Camfferman and Zeff, 2007). And it was really quite interesting watching it happen, because I remember Michael Sharpe, before he became chairman of the IASC and before I joined that committee, getting hold of me when I was presenting to IASC as chairman of ASB, trying to persuade me to give up all these ideas about an impairment approach and to accept a 20 year write-off period – which I refused. And then, shortly afterwards, I was speaking in Sydney to the Hundred Group of major companies in Australia. I deliberately – to save Michael – had not mentioned goodwill. And he then turned around and said, "David, you've got to give up these ridiculous ideas you have about goodwill". And one of the guys in the audience said, "What's this idea of goodwill?" So I explained what we were trying to do. And you heard from the audience, "Bloody good idea!" We ended up with a bit of a debate, and the chairman asked for a vote. Michael was the only one voting for a 20-year write-off. All the rest of the audience supported the UK proposal. And I think that probably turned Michael's view on the issue: he then started to support our position.

We did have differences even though they accepted great chunks of FRS10, and it's still there. FRSs10 and 11 were among the most internationally influential of ASB's projects. IASC suggested initially that normally they'd expect a five-year life of goodwill, and perhaps they could go up to 20. That view revealed a different view of goodwill to ours. We looked at it as the period over which the value of the underlying business exceeded the value of the identifiable assets. They tended to look at goodwill as a separate asset; therefore it should be written off like a tangible asset over a fixed period though they did eventually accept a version of our impairment test. Eventually, the IASC allowed a rebuttable presumption that the useful life of intangibles and goodwill does not exceed 20 years but, unlike the ASB, required the useful life to be finite. Because we identified intangibles and goodwill similarly we allocated the impairment losses to both goodwill and intangibles, whereas the IASC wrote all losses off against goodwill first, and then pro rata to tangible assets and intangibles.

There was a major argument between the ASB and the SEC in the IASC meetings. The SEC was very keen to keep a 40-year maximum amortisation period. Mike Sutton, the Chief Accountant, appeared about three times, I think. And he got quite frustrated by the fact that the IASC was coming around to the ASB point of view. It got quite heated at one stage.

And I remember him saying that the US had found the answer about 20 years ago to deal with things like brands and goodwill: and that was to amortise them over 40 years. As Bruce's Foreword notes, I said that "in the UK we've got brands such as Gordon's Gin and Johnnie Walker that are actually older than the United States. And in my humble opinion, they had done more for the sum of human happiness than the United States, and that personally I would amortise America before I'd ever write off Johnnie Walker Black Label". I remember someone later asking me about my relationship with Mike Sutton and I said "well, Mike doesn't send me any Christmas cards". Obviously, that got back to him: sometime in the following summer a Christmas card appeared from him saying "I'm terribly sorry, I found this in my desk".

Anyway, there was a big argument, and I think the SEC was quite shocked that we got our view accepted by IASC. There were some fundamental differences between us and FASB. They didn't use discounted cash flows in their impairment tests; they just used cash flows – regardless of the time value of money – which I found bizarre. But the other thing that happened: at the IASB we had a huge argument over whether in fact goodwill should be shown as not just the bit you bought of the business, but also the bit that was owned by somebody else – minority interests. And the majority of the IASB wanted to bring the hypothetical internally generated goodwill of the unacquired part of the business into the accounts as well. And this, of course, completely blew away our concept of the bridge to the original investment in a company that Allan mentioned earlier – the North Americans just did not accept that notion. Fortunately, I had enough blocking votes to stop the standard being published if the majority view became part of the standard, so the Board reluctantly had to give an option: you either could show acquired goodwill or, in addition, add the goodwill of the non-acquired part of the business. The basis of conclusions revealed the argument, mentioning that the preference of the majority was to show all of the goodwill but, while the IASB believed that alternative accounting methods reduce the comparability of financial statements, to ensure the standard was promulgated, an option was allowed. Neither view was supported by a sufficient number of board members to enable a standard to be issued but in view of other accounting improvements in the standard and the benefits of convergence between the IFRS and US GAAP, a choice was accepted despite the disadvantages of optional treatments.

### *The impairment test*

**GM What was unique about the ASB's impairment test?**

**DPT** When it came to calculating impairments the ASB was much tougher and introduced the "embarrassment disclosures". We believed that we should use a company's budget to estimate cash flows for, say, five years and then thereafter only increase these estimates by the growth rate in the economy or industry. And we required companies to disclose what they did if they didn't stick to our proposals, i.e. if they had a longer budgetary period than five years, or they used different growth rates. IAS36 didn't do that. Similarly, we required the previous estimates to be looked at. If the estimates were wrong, we would require the actual cash flows to be substituted. And then, if that led to an impairment, companies had to take it. And these were quite tough requirements. It meant you could only fool people so long because we made them disclose where they had used a policy more advantageous to them so there was a question mark over their honesty. That wasn't in the International Standard either. So I think our standard was tougher, but there was no doubt about it that, to a large extent, IAS36 and the IASC's goodwill standard were copying the ASB's requirements.

**GW** I think that the ex post impairment test, substituting five-year cash flows: the actual for the forecast, was very important because you've got to be honest about this. There's a huge incentive to lie when you are marking your own homework; and the impairment test gives you a huge capacity to predict future cash flows. If you can choose what cash flows you like then you can get the impairment that you like, probably zero I imagine. So that was the biggest one from my perspective, but there were also the other details and disclosures: all meticulously thorough, designed to make the test reliable and transparent from the user's perspective, and discussed with the constituencies as well to ensure practicality. For example, all the constraints on growth rates of cash flows that could be assumed beyond the initial five-year forecasting horizon. They were in the later IFRS standard as well, but not as tight as ours. I think the uniqueness of the ASB test was the care that was devoted, and the amount of negotiation with preparers to make sure that it was practical. All these constraints were there to stop people being, if you like, over-optimistic, which, after all, is a natural frame of mind you're in if you're about to make an acquisition or have just made one.

Interestingly, the world has never caught up with that particular issue – particularly the ex post impairment test. The Americans, of course, had to abandon any idea of it because of concessions to American industry. And then the IASB followed the American line when the IASB came to do its business combinations standard. So we've ended up internationally with a weaker impairment test and no amortisation.

[*Interviewer's note: as this book project was coming to an end, FASB and IASB reported on their recent reviews of the treatment of goodwill. Allan Cook prepared a summary of the IASB decisions in an endnote*[1] *to this chapter. Chapter 10 comments on the deliberations of FASB and IASB and the UK Endorsement Board.*]

**GM Why, unlike FASB, did the ASB choose both amortisation and impairment tests?**

**GW** I think that the combination of the impairment test with amortisation was a very good one, because it gave people an alternative if they thought the impairment test was too complicated for them. It allowed them the option of choosing a realistic time period, and doing what they do with tangible fixed assets. I always thought that amortisation had got rather a bad press in all this, mainly because people's idea of what was realistic became rather stretched. You've heard David mention the 40 years from the SEC and a suggestion of five years from the IASC. And obviously, this was a problem, but we do amortise fixed assets quite happily, always have done, and we understand what that means. It doesn't mean that the cost less accumulated depreciation is actually what the thing's worth. It means, well, we did pay this amount for it in the past, and we've charged a certain amount to profit, and this is what remains to be charged to profit. This is our accountability for fixed assets. And that's really what that standard was all about. It was about accountability for expenditure in acquisitions on goodwill.

Steve Zeff wrote an excellent paper on what happened at FASB and the background to it (Zeff, 2002; see also Beresford, 2001). And, basically, they compromised with American industry. American industry would accept capitalisation, but not amortisation. They wanted the looser impairment test – of course, on the grounds that impairment reflected business reality and the true length of life and the value of what they had acquired, that sort of thing. And no doubt also they were quite pleased with the flexibility it gave them – to score their own exam paper, basically. And obviously when the IASB came to discuss that issue, the Americans were already ahead of the IASB in developing a standard, and it incorporated the 'impairment only' approach and weaker constraints on impairment tests than those of FRS10 and 11. I don't think their standard was quite out, but it was in draft. And the IASB (with strong American representation) followed FASB rather than ASB – wanting at that time to converge with American standards so that the SEC might be persuaded to give greater recognition to IASB standards.

That, I think, was a sad thing: what the ASB was doing in the nineties has still not been done by the rest of the world, though it makes a lot of sense to add amortisation ***with*** the impairment tests. That combination is not just a compromise, it's a very sensible adaptation to the realities and the difficulties of identifying and measuring goodwill.

**AVC** One of the things that contrasts with the way that the FASB approached impairment in FAS142, which was published about four or five years later, was that we went for as low as possible a level for income generating units, whereas the FASB said that you should go for a high level, one level below the definition of a reporting segment. Well, that could be pretty high. So I think our test – while it required probably much more work – was more realistic as a test of impairment. One other thing is: when the FASB allocated the purchased goodwill to the income-generating units, I don't think they also allocated the internally generated goodwill. We said that if part of an acquisition was merged with part of the acquirer's own business, an estimate of the internally generated goodwill in that business had to be apportioned as well so that a failing acquired business could not escape impairment by sheltering under a possibly larger part of the acquirer's business, which did not have to account for its internally generated goodwill. Consequently, an impairment would be more likely to occur under our test than under theirs.

**DPT** Nevertheless, we should point out that, although impairment of the combined businesses was identified as you say, no internally generated goodwill was recognised in the balance sheet and the impairment charge put through the profit and loss account was limited to the pro rata portion of the combined businesses that stemmed from the acquired business.

The other aspect I thought we did well was that we said that, if the presumption that the useful life is 20 years or less is rebutted and a life that was either indefinite or over 20 years was selected, an impairment test had to be used annually. And there were two conditions before the presumption could be rebutted. One was that the durability of the acquired business, or intangible could be demonstrated. And the second was that the goodwill or intangible was capable of continued measurement, because, obviously, if we couldn't measure it, we didn't want them to use this test. And the durability would depend on the nature of the business, the stability of the industry, typical life spans, etc. And the measurement test: we said that if you merged the acquisition with another business, you had to be able to track that goodwill. If you couldn't track it then you couldn't use the impairment test. Similarly, if the management information system wasn't good enough to identify and allocate cash flows you couldn't use the rebuttable presumption either and would have to amortise over a period of 20 years or less. So we did put constraints on it. You weren't just given a free run at it. On the other hand, we did say that if you sailed over the tests quite easily, you probably wouldn't have to work through everything the next year: you'd just be able to look at it and say, well, it's almost the same, so we're clearly not impaired. Though we did always insist on an impairment test the year after an acquisition, to make sure that you weren't just amortising something that was already impaired – even if you were using a useful life of less than 20 years. Additionally, those using a period of 20 years or less would be required to use an impairment test if events or changes in circumstances indicated that the carrying values might not be recoverable.

Getting completely original goodwill and impairment standards accepted both in the UK and internationally after all the angst suffered by the ASC was probably one of the ASB's greatest achievements.

### *Wider implications of provisions standard*

**GM The more general provisions standard was unique in being jointly developed with the IASC. David, how did you find the experience of holding together two separate Boards in this joint project?**

**DPT** FRS12 was really an absolute guidepost for the future. It actually probably led to the IASB, funnily enough. The reason we had the G4+1 was that I had mentioned to Denny Beresford, the Chairman of FASB that we were both working on provisions – wouldn't it be a good idea to get together and talk about it? And he said, well why don't we invite other standard-setters to join us? And he then sent out an invitation which was quite apocalyptic – to join a 'Post World Congress'! And it was actually that a World Congress of Accountants was being held in America, and since the national standard-setters might be there, why don't we all get together? And the Canadians, Americans, Brits, and the Aussies – plus the Dutch – came along. The Dutch fell away eventually, but that began the G4. We discussed provisions then we went on to discuss other things. And the Standard really emerged from a G4+1 document largely drafted by Andrew Lennard and Sandra Thompson. And we went on from there. There were no substantial differences between IAS37 and FRS12. Andrew was the staff person working on both, and I always remember he sent me a note about when, as Chairman of the IASC Provisions Working Party, I first introduced him to IASC. It says:

> *AL* I am pleased and privileged to be presenting to you today.
> *DPT* Really, Andrew, you must be mad.
> *Laughter*
> [*AL* At this time, time slowed down. I thought David has destroyed my credibility. It's imperative to get it back.]
> So Andrew said:
> *AL* That may be true, David, but at least I'm polite.
> *Much laughter*

But it worked very well that way, and clearly, we made sure that the two standards (FRS12 and IAS37) ran together. It was fought all the way, for the same reasons we had to fight on business combinations, including the fact that in IAS37 we banned future losses for all provisioning. One point I found quite amusing during it was that on one issue in the IASC deliberations, I could get only eight votes out of sixteen. So I said, right, as chairman of the working party I'm going to use my casting vote, and we're going to ban these things, and on we go. So on we went and Michael Sharpe, who was chairman of IASC at the time, leaned across and whispered: "You don't actually have a casting vote, but never mind – keep going". So we did!

The UK standard was slightly more detailed in that it dealt with discount rates, but apart from that it was almost word for word the same. And what I thought was very significant was that there was the acceptance of the IASC Framework, and our Statement of Principles: a liability was defined precisely, as an obligation, and that was a massive change. And you could see accounting was starting to move onto an entirely different basis after that. So I think this was a very critical standard, not just for us but internationally as well.

## Note

1 **AVC note:** At the time of writing (November 2022), the latest position is that in June of this year the FASB decided to abandon a project begun four years

previously to improve the goodwill impairment test procedures in preference to reintroducing goodwill amortisation. Responses received during the project had been divided, though there was virtual unanimity that the FASB and IASB should have the same accounting for goodwill.

At the September 2022 meeting of the IASB, the Board gave tentative approval to a package of disclosure requirements including a statement of the strategic rationale for undertaking the business combination and quantitative information about expected synergies. For strategically important business combinations, information would be required on management's objectives for the combination and the metrics and targets it would use to identify whether those objectives were being met; then in subsequent periods, for as long as management monitored the combination against its objectives, whether those objectives were being met using those metrics. Strategically important business combinations were defined as those where the acquiree's operating profit, revenue or gross assets including goodwill exceeded 10% of those of the acquirer in its last annual report, or which took the entity into a new geographical area or major line of business. Limited exemptions would be allowed for disclosures that might lead to the provision of commercially sensitive information. These, however, would not cover the requirement to disclose the strategic rationale for the business combination nor the actual performance in subsequent periods using the metrics that management was using to monitor whether the objectives for the combination were being met. A high threshold would be required for claiming the exemptions, which would have to be justified on a case-by-case basis.

At its November meeting the IASB decided that, in the light of widespread disagreement over the nature of goodwill among all classes of stakeholders, with strongly held opinions on both sides, it would not be an efficient use of its resources to continue to explore whether to reintroduce amortisation of goodwill at that time. Board members stressed that their decision was taken in the context of the debate on the subject over recent years and did not necessarily reflect how they would decide the issue if starting again. Furthermore, by remaining with the status quo, they made it easier, rather than more difficult, for a later Board to re-examine the issue in the possibly changed circumstances of a different time. Their decision was based on the thorough research by the IASB staff but also reflected their desire to maintain convergence with the FASB where possible. They added that their conclusion vindicated their decision at an earlier stage of the project to prioritise improving disclosures before attempting to resolve the intractable issue of the subsequent accounting for goodwill.

It is expected that a decision to move its tentative decisions on disclosures to the standard-setting phase of the project will be taken by the IASB in December 2022.

While we, including our interviewer, who raises many objections in Chapter 10, have found the above conclusion an underwhelming outcome to three to four years of research and debate by both the FASB and IASB, and more recently the UK Endorsement Board, we suppose it at least has the merit of making progress where progress is possible. By focusing on relatively straightforward metrics for comparing the performance of an acquired business with the strategic rationale for its acquisition, the IASB is opening a new door to improving investors' understanding and management's accountability. In the context of this book it is also worth noting the similarity between FRS10's insistence on ex post updating of estimates of future performance, mentioned by GW in the last paragraph of the discussion above, and the IASB's current proposal to report actuals against estimates of the metrics justifying a major acquisition.

## References

### *Books and articles*

Beresford, D.R. (2001). Congress looks at accounting for business combinations, *Accounting Horizons*, 15(1), 73–86.

Camfferman, K. and Zeff, S. (2007). *Financial Reporting and Capital Markets,* Oxford: Oxford University Press, p.381.

IASB. (2022). https://www.ifrs.org/news-and-events/updates/iasb/2022/iasb-update-july-2022/.

Meeks, G. (1977). *Disappointing Marriage: A Study of the Gains from Merger,* Cambridge: Cambridge University Press.

Tweedie, D.P. and Blanchet, J. (1989). Brands, goodwill and the balance sheet, *Accountancy,* January, pp. 20–22.

Zeff, S. (2002). 'Political' lobbying on proposed standards: a challenge to the IASB, *Accounting Horizons*, 16(1), 43–54.

### *Standard-setters' publications*

ED47 (1990). *Accounting for goodwill,* ASC.

ED48 (1990). *Accounting for mergers and acquisitions,* ASC.

ED52 (1990). *Accounting for intangible fixed assets,* ASC.

ED53 (1990). *Fair value in the context of acquisition accounting,* ASC.

FAS142 (2001). *Goodwill and other intangibles,* FASB.

FRED12 (1996). *Goodwill and intangible assets*, ASB.

FRS3 (1992). *Reporting financial performance*, ASB.

FRS4 (1993). *Capital instruments*, ASB.

FRS5 (1994). *Reporting the substance of transactions*, ASB.

FRS6 (1994). *Acquisitions and mergers*, ASB.

FRS7 (1994). *Fair values in acquisition accounting*, ASB.

FRS10 (1997). *Goodwill and intangible assets*, ASB.

FRS11 (1998). *Impairment of fixed assets and goodwill*, ASB.

FRS12 (1998). *Provisions, contingent liabilities and contingent assets*, ASB.

FRS17 (2005). *Retirement benefits*, ASB.

IAS22 (1983, revised 1998). *Business combinations*, IASC.

IAS36 (1998). *Impairment of assets*, IASC.

IAS37 (1998). *Provisions, contingent liabilities and contingent assets*, IASC.

IFRS13 (2011). *Fair value measurement,* IASB.

SSAP22 (1984). *Accounting for goodwill*, ASC.

SSAP23 (1985). *Accounting for acquisitions and mergers*, ASC.

SSAP24 (1988). *Accounting for pension costs*, ASC.

# Appendix

*Table A7.1* Mergers and Acquisitions: Issues and Solutions

| *Issue* | *Previously permitted practice* | *Device* | *FRS* | *Requirement* |
|---|---|---|---|---|
| **Merger accounting vs Acquisition accounting** | | | | |
| Choice of merger or acquisition accounting | Free choice if merger conditions met | | 6 | Not an option |
| Uneven parties | Not prohibited | | 6 | i Neither party portrayed as acquirer or acquiree.<br>ii All share in determining new management structure, etc<br>iii Neither party dominates through relative size |
| Prior shareholding | Up to 20% | Bed & Breakfast deals | 6 | Previous two years taken into account |
| **Means of achieving merger accounting** | | | | |
| 1 Consideration for equity shares acquired.<br>2 Consideration for voting non-equity shares acquired | At least 90% of FV of consideration is equity shares.<br>At least 90% of FV of consideration is equity or voting non-equity shares. | | 6 | Any consideration in form of non-equity or substantially reduced voting rights must be immaterial proportion. |
| | | Vendor placings<br>Vendor rights | 6 | Related arrangements taken into account |

| *Issue* | *Previously permitted practice* | *Device* | *FRS* | *Requirement* |
|---|---|---|---|---|
| **The flexibility of acquisition accounting** | | | | |
| Boost future profits: | Fair value using acquirer's perspective (with detailed disclosures per acquisition) | i Provide for intended reorganisations<br>ii Provide for future losses | 7 | Liability requires existing obligation |
| | Fair value using acquirer's perspective (with detailed disclosures per acquisition) | Inventory write-downs | 7<br>6 | MV for market traded;<br>Lower of RC and NRV for others<br>Disclosure of exceptional profits determined using fair value on acquisition |
| | Pre-acquisition decisions by acquiree | Persuade acquiree to provide for future costs. | 7<br>6 | i Acquiree must be 'demonstrably committed' regardless of the takeover bid outcome.<br>ii Question acquisition date.<br>iii Disclose previous 12 months. |
| Protect reserves from excessive depletion: | Fair value assets | Overvalue non depreciable assets | 7 | FV not to exceed recoverable amount |
| | | Recognise new assets, intangibles | 7 | FV is replacement cost, ie normally MV |
| Treatment of goodwill (the balancing item) | Immediate w/o of goodwill | Permitted option | 10 | Not permitted |
| | Capitalise goodwill | Excessive amortisation period | 10 & 11 | i Annual review of useful life<br>ii Detailed impairment test compulsory if life indefinite or exceeding 20 years |

# 8 Pension obligations

FRS17 was issued in November 2000, at the end of David Tweedie's chairmanship of the ASB. It was a fitting conclusion to the formative decade of the ASB and contained most of the ingredients which had been characteristic of the ASB's work during this period: it addressed an important issue in financial reporting which had been subject to creative accounting practices; its measurement and recognition proposals were grounded in the ASB's Statement of Principles; it made use of FRS3's format for presenting gains and losses outside operating profit; it developed in step with, and ultimately ahead of, international standards and those of the US; it involved another profession (in this case, the actuaries rather than the lawyers or bankers); and it was controversial, requiring a great amount of tact to bring different interest groups to acceptance of a common solution.

## The problem

The problem of reporting the cost to employing companies of defined benefit pension schemes was at the heart of FRS17. Retirement benefits other than pensions, such as health care, were included in the scope of FRS17 but were treated according to the principles applied to pensions, which was the emerging international consensus. Pensions were classified into two categories, defined benefit schemes and defined contribution schemes. The latter involve regular payments into the pension fund by the employer, and possibly the employee, and the pension is an annuity based on the value of the fund and the market interest rate at retirement date. The employee therefore bears the investment risk (the uncertainty of investment returns and the interest rate on which the annuity would be calculated). FRS17 and international standards dealt with defined contribution schemes, in the accounts of the employer company, by charging the contribution becoming due in the period to operating profit, with the balance sheet recording merely the cumulative difference between amounts paid and amounts incurred. Defined benefit schemes, on the other hand, involved the employer making a promise of the amount of the pension that would ultimately be paid, thus bearing the investment risk and the other

DOI: 10.4324/9781003346920-8

actuarial risks (such as the length of life of the employees) of the scheme. Typically, the pension would be based on the employee's terminal salary, and possibly enhanced by indexation to compensate for price changes. The result of running a defined benefit scheme was often to create a substantial liability, and sometimes a substantial asset, in company accounts. The problem of reporting these liabilities or assets, and the associated revenues, expenses, gains, and losses, was the central issue in FRS17 and the associated debate, so defined benefit pension schemes are the focus of the rest of this chapter.

## Alternative accounting models

There are three basic models for the recognition of defined benefit schemes in company accounts:

1 *Flow through*. This recognises the contributions payable by the employing company during the period as an expense chargeable to profit. The balance sheet reports any balance at the end of the period due to unpaid contributions (a liability) or prepayment (an asset). This approach is easily and reliably measurable, but it does not reflect the cost and burden of the pension promise. In particular, it allows employing companies to take 'pension holidays' for periods in which they do not make contributions to the scheme, no pension cost being charged against profit during the holiday. This method also hides the size of any deficit or surplus in the pension fund, which would be potentially an important factor in determining the terms of a take-over bid. The flow through method was common practice in the UK in the period before there was an accounting standard on the subject (SSAP24, issued by the Accounting Standards Committee in 1988).[1]

2 *Actuarial cost*. This provides a more sophisticated estimate of the periodic cost of the defined benefit promise. Its objective is to estimate the cost of pension obligations incurred during the accounting period. Unlike the flow through method, it focuses on the creation of the obligation rather than the payments made to meet it. In a world of certainty, this method would charge the profit and loss account with the amount necessary to cover the additional future pension obligations incurred in each period. In a realistically uncertain world, the relevant assumptions about such matters as investment returns, interest rates, and the employees' expectations of life will change over time, giving rise to 'actuarial gains and losses': changes in the net value of the pension fund due to changes in the assumptions. The actuarial approach does not recognise such gains or losses immediately but spreads them over the future service lives of the members so that an actuarial loss will increase the pension cost in the year in which it occurs but most of the loss will be recovered as part of future pension costs. As with the flow through

approach, the balance sheet records only the cumulative difference between pension costs charged in the profit and loss account and the amounts actually paid to the fund. This method smooths out the volatility that can result from recognising the periodic fluctuations in the net value of the pension fund (current value of investments less current value of obligations to pensioners). Traditionally, it was favoured by actuaries and requires actuarial modelling techniques (projecting and then discounting future cash flows of the pension fund) to estimate the pension cost. It was the approach favoured by the UK's standard SSAP24. By spreading forward the actuarial gains and losses that have already been incurred, this method fails to report, in a timely manner, the full economic exposure of the employing entity. Moreover, irrespective of the smoothing method, it can be argued that the actuarial valuation method is misleading because it ignores the current market prices of pension fund investments and substitutes subjective assumptions about future returns on investments.

3 *The Fair Value, or Balance Sheet, approach*. This attempts to report, in a timely manner, the full economic burden of the pension fund on the sponsoring company. It therefore estimates the current market values (often referred to as 'fair values', although they are broader in scope than the selling price concept of 'fair value', subsequently adopted by the IASB) of the obligations and assets of the pension fund and reports the net amount in the balance sheet of the sponsoring employer, in the absence of any restriction on the employer's obligation to the fund (such as requirements for employees to contribute to the elimination of a deficit). The consequence of reporting current values is that the changes in the value of the pension obligation, including actuarial gains and losses, must be included in the accounts. There were (and are) concerns that reporting these items in the profit statement can dominate and even distort the apparent profitability of the operations of the business because the finance of the pension fund is separate from the core activities and includes a significant element of random 'noise' reflecting the fluctuations of markets which are outside the control of the business. The first accounting standards to adopt the 'fair value' approach (the FASB standard and the international standard) acknowledged this volatility problem and dealt with it by arbitrary smoothing formulae for the recognition of actuarial gains and losses. The ASB, when it issued its 'fair value' pensions standard (FRS17, 2000) had the advantage of having previously issued FRS3, which provided for the separate reporting, outside operating profit, of gains and losses such as revaluations of operating assets. This enabled the ASB to avoid arbitrary smoothing mechanisms, which would have been inconsistent with its Statement of Principles, and to report actuarial gains and losses in full, outside operating profit, as other gains and losses.

## The background to FRS 17

Defined benefit pension schemes provided by the employing company became very popular amongst large UK companies during the twentieth century. The number of companies having such schemes rose rapidly during the period following the Second World War, and they were common practice until the late 1980s, when a variety of factors reducing their attractions, particularly to employers, started to appear (Munnell, 2005). In their heyday, generous pension schemes were seen as a way of attracting and retaining a skilled labour force, and they were encouraged by generous tax concessions.

Pension obligations were not seen as onerous, because they were generally believed to be covered by the investment funds accumulated from contributions: these were typically equity investments which were expected to grow in value sufficiently to cover such threats as inflation or rising wage rates. Thus, the cost of pensions was not seen as a potential threat to employing companies, and in some cases, it was a potential asset. Griffiths, in his 1986 book 'Creative Accounting', entitles his fourth chapter 'How to Pilfer the Pension Fund', providing examples of how pension funds could be used to benefit the sponsoring company. The most popular was the 'pension holiday', described earlier, whereby the company could boost its profits by making no contribution to the pension fund for a period, thus avoiding a pension charge against profits if it was reporting under the flow through method. Pension funds were also potentially valuable to take-over bidders; for example, a well-endowed pension fund would be able to fund post-takeover restructuring by offering early retirement pensions. Pension fund surpluses could also, in some circumstances, be used by the employer as tax-free reserves (contributions to the fund being tax deductible and investment income received by the fund, tax free).

However, these advantages to the sponsoring company depended upon the pension fund showing a surplus of recognised assets over obligations, and this possibility was challenged from several directions. First, the 1986 Finance Act restricted the ability of employers to over-contribute in order to avoid tax, thus, ironically, in the short term, encouraging some companies to take 'pension holidays' in order to reduce excessive surpluses. Second, bear markets from the late 1980s challenged the cult of the equity, which had sustained the optimistic view that over the long-term pension liabilities were effectively hedged by their equity investments. This blow was reinforced by the government's withdrawal of pension funds' tax relief on dividend income (1997). This changing environment led to a debate within the actuarial profession which questioned the traditional actuarial model, based on projecting assumed growth rates of investment returns, and advocated instead a 'financial economics' approach, which made greater use of current market prices, as in model 3 above (Exley et al., 1997). Third, the reported obligations of defined benefit schemes were increased by the publication of revised life tables, which were used by actuaries to project the lives of pensioners. These reflected a general increase in the life expectancy of the population, and therefore in the period over which pensions would be payable. Fourth, public concern about the financial security of the schemes, following the Daily Mirror Group scandal, in which Robert Maxwell misappropriated substantial funds from the company pension scheme, led to much tighter regulation of pension fund investment, funding policy, and stewardship (Pension Act, 1995).

From the employees' perspective, too, the apparent attractions of a pension based on final pay after a lifetime of service with the same employer began to diminish. The need for a more mobile labour force made the personal pension more convenient than one tied to a particular employer, with whom the employee would remain for only part of a working life.

As a result of these developments, by the time that the ASB addressed the issue in FRS17, defined benefit pension schemes were seen more often as a burden on sponsoring companies, rather than an asset. In many cases, this burden, as reported under FRS17, represented a significant proportion of the reported net assets of the sponsoring company, and in some cases, it eliminated net assets entirely (Harris et al., 2003).

## The development of FRS 17

The limitations of the flow through model caused the ASC to address the issue of pension costs in the context of the creative accounting of the 1980s and its efforts culminated in one of its later standards, SSAP24, 1988. This was the first UK accounting standard on the subject, and it required a switch from the generally accepted practice, flow through, to Model 2, the actuarial approach. By distinguishing between funding (the need to make payments in accordance with the actuary's recommendations) and accounting (the need to present a true and fair view of pension obligations in financial statements) SSAP24 closed the creative accounting loophole of the pension holiday. However, because actuarial practice allowed considerable flexibility in the choice of method and assumptions, significant factors such as the discount rate applied to future pensions could vary widely across companies. Moreover, costs recognised as a result of changes in the actuarial assumptions were spread forward over the expected service lives of existing members of the pension scheme, so that only a small proportion of the cost was recognised immediately, and the balance sheet did not record the current best estimate of the company's exposure to the pension scheme. The latter problem was brought into sharp focus by the ASB's standard on fair values in acquisition accounting (FRS7, 1994) which required the pension funds of acquired companies to be measured at fair value, a Model 3 'balance sheet' method. Thus, SSAP24 was a progressive step but contained the seeds of further progress.

The ASB recognised the need for improvement in SSAP24, but it was a relatively new standard which did improve practice and there were more pressing issues, so the ASB's only early pronouncement on the subject was UITF6 (1992) which confirmed that SSAP24 should apply to all post-retirement benefits, including health care costs. Its first pronouncement on the core issue of defined benefit costs was a Discussion Paper (1995) which considered two alternative models for accounting for pension costs: one based on improving SSAP24's actuarial approach to make its application more consistent and transparent and the second based on the more radical fair value approach of Model 3. The ASB's preference at that time was the more conservative actuarial approach, but this was superseded by international events.

The IASC published an Exposure Draft, E54, in 1996 and a revised Standard, IAS19 (revised), in 1998. These followed broadly the fair value model, as adopted in the US standard SFAS87 (1985), including smoothing using the 'corridor' method to eliminate some of the volatility arising from actuarial gains and losses by deferring recognition of those which fell within an arbitrary percentage (the 'corridor') of the value of the pension fund. The ASB responded with another Discussion Paper (1998), which indicated that the changes in international standards and in opinions within the actuarial profession (the emergence of the financial economics approach, mentioned above) had persuaded the ASB that a change to the fair value model was now appropriate. This was followed by an Exposure Draft, FRED20 (1999), which addressed the practical details of the new model, and FRS17 (2000), which implemented it as a replacement for SSAP24. In recognition of the radical change required by the new standard, full implementation was not required for three years, although early adoption was encouraged.

The core of FRS17 was the balance sheet method: the current value of the pension fund liabilities was deducted from that of the assets and the resulting surplus or deficit was recorded in the balance sheet, which, under previous standards such as SSAP24, had shown only the accrued difference between pension costs charged (on a basis that did not reflect economic reality) and amounts paid to the fund. The change in the surplus or deficit over the accounting period was now recorded in full in the performance statement, but in different parts of that statement, as permitted by FRS3. Only the service cost of providing pensions earned in the period was charged to operating profit. The expected return on investment was offset against the interest charge on the pension liabilities and reported in the 'financing' section of the profit and loss account (approved by an amendment to FRS3, June 1999). The difference between the actual and expected returns on investment was reported, together with other actuarial adjustments, in the Statement of Total Recognised Gains and Losses, i.e. outside profit and loss, but within total performance. Both the bifurcation of investment income and the protection of operating costs against elements other than service costs recognised the concern of those who feared that the balance sheet approach would introduce volatility (due to the fluctuations of stock markets) which would mask the underlying profitability of the core operations of the business. They enabled the ASB to introduce the fair value approach whilst avoiding the arbitrary and convoluted smoothing methods of the IASC standard and its American predecessor.

Measuring the basic components of the FRS17 methodology, the assets and liabilities of the scheme, was complex and involved some difficult decisions and compromises. The net surplus, the deficit or surplus in the pension fund, is the difference between two large numbers, both subject to error and volatility, so that an observation at a single point in time or a comparison between two points in time, is unreliable: this was the motivation for the smoothing devices that remained an option in the international standard and for FRS17's use of FRS3 to dis-aggregate the elements of pension fund performance. The pension fund assets are the most reliably measurable. They tend to be listed on markets and therefore have reasonably objective prices, although markets are sometimes volatile, and there has, in recent decades, been an increasing tendency to invest in unlisted assets, such as private equity. The liabilities of the scheme pose much more difficult problems. There is no complete market for pension fund liabilities: the reinsurance market offers limited scope for laying off some liabilities or portions of them but moral hazard issues make it difficult to establish a market for entire schemes, e.g. an employer who is relieved of the cost of early retirement has an incentive to offer more early retirement than would otherwise be expected, and relief from the cost of a terminal salary pension promise might create an incentive to offer exceptional pay rises in the final year of employment. Moreover, each pension fund has unique characteristics, and its consequences occur in a distant and uncertain future. Hence, even a 'fair value' approach, such as that of FRS17, must resort to actuarial methods to estimate the current value of the pension obligation by projecting the future payments incurred by present obligations and discounting them back to the present (to allow for the fact that a deferred obligation is a lesser burden than a current one). This inevitably requires that assumptions be made.

Two contentious assumptions made in FRS17 with regard to the measurement of the pension obligation were that the rate of interest used to discount future pension payments would be the yield on a high-grade corporate bond, and that employers with terminal salary schemes should base commitments on the expected terminal salary. Both of these decisions would, relative to the alternatives, increase the reported obligations. Under SSAP24, actuaries had tended to use as a discount rate the higher rate of return on equities, thus reducing the reported liability. On the other hand, that standard had, like FRS17, required estimates of terminal salary to be used for calculating the employer's commitment in a terminal salary scheme, but the ASB did discuss the proposition that this was inconsistent with the Board's Statement of Principles, which required that there must be an irrevocable commitment before a liability (in this case, the additional pension earned by future pay rises) could be recognised. These issues were thoroughly debated by the ASB and research evidence was considered, but the arguments and evidence were not conclusive on either issue. The ASB's final decision, in both cases, was to follow the international consensus of IAS19 (revised): a high-grade corporate bond rate for discounting pension liabilities, and the projected unit credit method (which recognises projected increases in pension liabilities due to future salary increases) for the recognition of liabilities. This pragmatic solution has survived, as the international consensus, for over two decades.

Another issue which required thorough discussion was that of surpluses in pension funds, and the ability of sponsoring companies to benefit from them: clearly a matter of public sensitivity, following the Maxwell scandal. It was decided to allow recognition of a pension fund surplus as an asset of the sponsoring company only if the company was able to benefit from it, e.g. by taking a contribution holiday or by lowering future contributions. The closer regulation of pension schemes at that time meant that the existence of a recorded surplus was not sufficient to guarantee a benefit to the company.

However, pension fund surpluses were becoming much less common. By the time FRS17 was issued (2000), the concern was with deficits and whether companies could continue to sponsor defined benefit schemes.

## The legacy of FRS17

FRS17 was probably the ASB standard which had the greatest impact on the general public. This was because it related to the incomes, current or prospective, of a significant proportion of the population. Defined benefit schemes were already declining in number, under pressure from declining investment returns, less favourable tax treatment, more demanding regulation, and increasing life expectancy. The effects of these factors could be smoothed out, at least for a time, by using actuarial methods, but the fair value approach affected them with brutal and occasionally arbitrary suddenness. Some actuaries and pension fund managers accused FRS17 of destroying defined benefit schemes, as the reported deficits continued to grow, further fuelled by the World Financial Crisis (2007 onwards) which led to a sharp decline in interest rates (reducing the discount applied to pension fund liabilities) and also lowering investment returns. It was these factors which led to the further decline of defined benefit schemes, not FRS17's reporting of their consequences. Indeed, it might be argued that, by providing a prompt warning of the true cost, FRS17 prevented companies from entering into further commitments that they would not have been able to meet, thus avoiding detriment to both their pensioners and their shareholders.

Within the world of accounting standards, FRS17 survived as an option in the IASB's 2004 revision of IAS19, which, although maintaining the option of the 'corridor' smoothing method, also allowed the alternative FRS17 approach of immediate recognition of actuarial gains and losses in the statement of total recognised gains and losses. A subsequent revision of IAS19 (2011) led to the withdrawal of the 'corridor' approach, so that the FRS17 model is now the basis of the international accounting standard. It is arguably the approach that is most consistent with the conceptual framework, and it has raised awareness, amongst users of accounts, of the dangers lurking in an apparently simple defined benefit pension promise.

## Geoffrey Whittington

### *Discussion*

#### *Origins*

**GM Why did the ASC originally develop a standard on accounting for retirement benefits? And why did SSAP24 choose a partial reform, the actuarial approach, rather than full recognition (the FRS17 approach)?**

**AVC** The debate in accounting for pension costs went back a long way. It began in 1976, I think. I became involved, along with actuarial colleagues, when my employer, Unilever, was commissioned by the ASC to write one of two papers on the whole subject of pension costs. After that, I was drawn into the Working Party, which I eventually ended up leading. And that, as you'll see later, probably accounted for my initially very strong support for spreading variations in the regular cost rather than recognising them instantly. But in 1976 spreading was the treatment required by the only standard on pensions, which was APB8 in the US. It was quite different from the one that was subsequently developed during the period that we're looking at.

SSAP24 grew out of the great increase in pension schemes that had taken place after World War 2. But, as Geoff has described in his introduction to this chapter, by the time that the standards that we are talking about were being discussed, some of their attractiveness was beginning to wear off. By the mid-eighties, those new schemes were beginning to mature and building up sizeable assets by comparison with the employer companies' own net worth. So even small changes in the experience or assumptions of the pension scheme could have a dramatic effect on the company. And it was quite natural that accountants should take refuge in the expertise of the actuaries, which went back further than the expertise of accountants, starting from the mathematical advances of the seventeenth century, to guide them on what the pension cost should be.[2]

But you have to remember that the approach of the actuaries was targeted on funding. The actuary was trying to devise a method that would be a reasonable, and not too volatile, way of setting aside funds to reach the desired objective of maintaining the security of the promised benefits far into the future. Unless the scheme was significantly overfunded, the financial strength of the sponsoring company was an important consideration. For this reason, the actuary might sometimes accept a relatively weak basis of funding rather than force the company to put additional contributions into the fund under a strict timetable that could imperil the company's financial position. So the actuary had a much more flexible approach to developing an actuarial valuation than an accountant would in measuring cost. Also, although they were experts, and constantly developing their methods, the actuarial profession as a whole had not at that stage got to grips with the developments in financial economics of the early 1970s (any more than had the accountants). So it really wouldn't have been a practicable proposition for the ASC to move far away from reliance on actuarial techniques. The important issue that the ASC addressed was to separate funding from cost. And they did make a serious attempt to do that. Their success put a stop to the major problem of that period, described in Geoff's introduction, which was that companies were taking contribution holidays, and then finding a few years later that their fund had collapsed in value.

I'm afraid that's a rather long response to your question.

**GM Not at all – it's very concise and informative. Next question. FRS17 was one of the last standards of the Tweedie era. What was ASB's initial position on SSAP24, and when did retirement benefits first appear on the agenda?**

**AVC** Well, David, you probably remember that you and I discussed the programme of the ASB very early on, even before the Board started, and pensions were one of the things we knew we had to address at some point. We didn't rush into it, because SSAP24 was very recent. We finally put it onto the agenda sometime during 1993. It's mentioned in the FRC Report for that year.

**GW** Why did you think it needed addressing at all, Allan, because SSAP24 had fixed the pension contribution holiday, which was, if you like, the abuse problem. Were deficits apparent at that time? You know, FRS17 deficits weren't reported in SSAP24. What was it that made you think it was something that needed dealing with?

**AVC** Several people were saying there was too much flexibility; and also the disclosures were not enough to adjust for that flexibility – to re-compute, if you like. Now, an actuarial valuation – certainly in those days – was a very complex thing and took many, many man-hours of work, even with computers, so it wasn't a realistic proposition for users of the employer's financial statements to completely re-work the valuation. And different valuation bases produce quite different results. What they could do with enough disclosures was get some sort of sense of the degree of optimism or pessimism – perhaps optimism or conservatism, we should say – in the approach that the actuary had taken. So there was the flexibility, aggravated by the inadequacy of disclosures, which inevitably could not enable a re-computation of the actuarial valuation.

The ASB's initial position – I think it was a 6:3 majority – was in favour of the actuarial approach. The three were rather important members: they included David and Geoff, Geoff pushing against it, and David supporting him. I have to say that I think the minority case, with hindsight, was very well argued and converted me in the end. But I put up a strong and rather too long a battle to preserve the actuarial basis. It's interesting when we come to it why it was that we changed our opinions.

The main difference in accounting terms between the approach of SSAP24 and the position adopted by the minority, which eventually became FRS17, was that the old ASC and those that supported that approach adopted an accounting objective of maintaining the pension cost as a constant percentage of pensionable pay. So you got a level premium over the service period of the current employees. That seemed very reasonable at the time. The Statement of Principles had not been developed. Probably, if you asked an accountant what was a sensible principle, he would have thought about the profit and loss account before thinking about the balance sheet. And a constant percentage of pensionable pay seemed an ideal solution for the accountants to aim for. And then go to the actuaries and say, "Now, how do you do it?"' This eventually was challenged and the period in which we were developing our standard was exactly the period when other criticisms were coming in.

There was the very influential paper (Exley et al., 1997) mentioned in the Introduction to this chapter. It was published in April 1997, but Exley had been making other contributions in the Institute of Actuaries before then, and I expect that in all of those he was pushing for the insights of financial economics to be applied to pensions.

*Development*

**GM Given that preparers and the actuarial profession and a majority of the ASB were initially for the actuarial model, why did the more radical FRS17 fair value model prevail?**

**DPT** What I always hated about SSAP24 was that a company could show a prepayment, an asset, simply because it had paid more than the actuarially determined amount, while in fact, it might have a monster deficit that was completely invisible. And maybe, OK, you could deal with that with disclosure, but that really wasn't the ASB's way of dealing with things. We wanted to present the economics. What in my view killed SSAP24 was Gordon Brown's raid on the pension funds when he removed the tax credits that the funds could reclaim on the dividends from UK companies. Well, that took £5 billion out of the pension funds every year. And there was not a flicker in the amounts that were being charged in the accounts of the pension scheme sponsors. I thought, the actuaries are bound to change their assumptions. And they didn't. They stayed exactly the same. And I thought, this is completely phoney; the whole thing is being managed. Public sector pensions were invisible, and still are, of course:[3] it was reported by the Times in 2021 that the real annual cost to the taxpayer of providing public sector pensions amounted to £95 billion and is not shown anywhere. We all just don't see them. And because you don't see them you don't manage them. And that's really what upset us about company pension schemes. At the same time we were being warned by the Americans, who had just produced their standard dealing with healthcare. And it shocked and just about destroyed their car companies. General Motors, apparently, had a healthcare liability of $32 billion, which was 78% of its net worth. Ford's liability was $12 billion, which was 40% of its net worth. All they had actually been doing until then was recording the pay as you go costs. And healthcare costs were rising far faster than general inflation, which seems to have been ignored by the companies.

So that was the position. And I think also we were already coming around to consider accounting differently. We believed in assets and liabilities on balance sheets – that was FRS5. We believed in showing the components of income – FRS3. Tell it as it is with FRS4, with debt and equity, and so on. Fair values. Disclosures on derivatives are already coming through by this time. And it was interesting that with the first Discussion Paper (1995) that we put out, all but one actuary supported the use of actuarial valuations. In the responses to the second one (1998), only one actuary did not support the use of market values. So there was a complete swing in that area. We also persuaded our overseas colleagues. The G4+1 in April 2000 came out with a statement saying, we think the way the ASB is going about this is probably the right way to go in the future. So the whole momentum was moving in our direction at this stage. So I think that's basically why it all swung around and at that stage, we were starting to have a straight run to the finish. Well, not entirely straight!

**GM So, Allan, can you explain to us how opinion shifted within the ASB? David has told us what was going on in the outside world.**

**AVC** Well, they did shift. I think they were chiefly influenced by what was going on in the outside world.

**DPT** Nonsense, Allan, it was the argument of Geoff and myself that did it!

**AVC** Yes, it was that too, because the project director, Anne McGeachin, was beginning to put up papers that really firmly pressed for the balance sheet approach. I think most Board members readily accepted one part of the proposed solution: the idea of recognising the market value of assets in the balance sheet, and taking the strain in the STRGL. However, they were divided over whether to recycle those changes into the profit and loss account over the remaining service lives of pension scheme members. The second big issue was: the discount rate to use for the liabilities. And that they were pretty hesitant about. We searched for a long time to try to find what would be a suitable theoretical portfolio of matching assets the return on which would serve to discount the liabilities. And we were trying to find evidence that equities could provide such a return. That idea was finally scotched when no one could prove a correlation. And so we did then start saying, well, maybe we should just go along with the international version. One was dealing here with real imponderables. I'd like to ask Geoff and David: how sound, they believe, was the conceptual basis for the use of the corporate discount rate on AA bonds?

**GW** Well, it was essentially a compromise.

**DPT** I think the basic thing was that we agreed that ideally, we should use a discount rate for liabilities based on the return on assets that broadly matched the liabilities. The question was what should those assets be?

Some of our constituents wanted a rate that wouldn't cause substantial fluctuations in the measurement of the liabilities. But that wasn't the real world. I was one of the few people at that time on the Board who did not have a company pension. I had to finance my own, and I was very aware that if I wanted a 10,000 pound pension, and annuity rates were 10%, I needed a capital sum of a 100,000 pounds. If rates fell to 5%, I needed a 200,000 capital sum.

There was an obvious problem with using the rate of return on so-called 'matching assets' in the scheme if a correlation with changes in the liabilities could not be proved, i.e. if the assets did not truly match the liabilities. The actuaries at the time used a prudent but expected rate of return on the scheme's actual assets – usually equities. I remember we taunted them, saying, well, what happens if the company fills the pension fund with junk bonds? Because of the return required on such bonds, the discount rate would have been so high that companies would have had almost no pension liabilities whatsoever. But, as Allan just mentioned, there was research by the Institute and the Faculty that demonstrated from past data that the correlation between equities and salaries wasn't even close. And the best match for the final salary liability was probably inflation-linked bonds, but there were very few of those about.

We were looking for a discount rate that reflected the time value of money and the risk of the future payments. What would it be? I remember being invited to the Institute of Actuaries where they presented four papers, all with conflicting views on what this interest rate should be. And the President asked me if I would like to comment; and I did comment, "What on Earth am I supposed to do with that? It would be rather nice if the actuaries could come up with one answer, instead of four" – whereupon somebody said, "When you come up with a definition of profit, we'll come up with a definition of a liability". Touché! We just couldn't get agreement and defaulted to the international measure. The Americans were using it. The IASC was coming forward with it. It's difficult to argue against international compromise when you haven't got a better answer. So we ended up with the high quality corporate bond rate, the AA bond rate, of equivalent currency and term as the scheme liabilities which reflected the time value of money and a small premium for risk. Just to show there were no hard feelings, at the end of 1999 the Institute of Actuaries elected me as an Honorary Fellow – possibly so they could have the opportunity to expel me later for bringing the profession into disrepute!

**GW** That was the best we could do within a reasonable time horizon. We could have spent years arguing over niceties of risk, and who should bear what risk, and how you estimate it – because hidden under there is of course the famous problem of own debt: that, implicitly, if you choose the corporate bond rate you are putting in the value of the liability the possibility that you won't have to pay it, you'll get away with not paying it. That's quite controversial actually. So you could argue with all these things. But the corporate bond rate at least got everybody marching in line, and comparability is very important. It stopped people manipulating the discount rate to suit their position. If you wanted to hide a big deficit you could just have said, "oh, we've just taken a different view of interest rates". And that was also a problem for SSAP24, of course. The corporate bond rate was a necessary compromise; and it was not an unreasonable one given the range of options: it lay midway between the equity return, favoured by some, and the risk-free return, favoured by others!

The equity return was the old resort; but, as explained earlier, by the start of the nineties the cult of the equity had rather fallen flat on its face, as stock market returns declined. Also, there was surprisingly little evidence to support the traditional view that equities hedged pension obligations.

In a presentation on FRS17 that I gave in Edinburgh in 2006 I said there was an assumption of mean reversion in a lot of the actuarial approach – you know, "it will all come right in the end". That's why we take the long-term view. But what will come right? If equities are low at the moment and the actuarial approach says they should be higher, why aren't people buying equities if they are such a bargain? Equally, with the expectation of life, we don't know what it is. I suggested rather complacently that everyone isn't suddenly going to have a shorter life, which would be very good news for the pension funds if not for the pensioners. And I said, rather facetiously, well, maybe there will be a plague of bird flu or something – but of course, we are now in the midst of a pandemic of something which is very similar to bird flu. This is a graphic illustration of the risks associated with actuarial projections! With regard to the discount rate, it is very difficult to find a concrete answer, but certainly choosing an objective measure, like the corporate bond rate, does at least reflect important aspects of economic reality – fundamentally the time value of money – and it isn't manipulable, and it is comparable across firms. That was a lot better than doing nothing.

**GM What was the attitude of the actuarial profession? The valuation of pension funds was traditionally their role, so was there tension when accountants adopted the fair value approach?**

**DPT** It was quite interesting – I mentioned before that only one actuary did not support the smoothing approach of SSAP24 in our first (1995) Discussion Paper. But when we issued FRED20, they suddenly woke up to what the implications of going in a different direction might be. I had a meeting – well, it was supposed to be a lunch, the invitation coming from a former partner of mine – only to find I was faced with a bunch of actuaries and journalists. The *Financial Times* (2000) described it as an ambush and it was! But it was quite interesting: the points that came up there were exactly what we kept hearing from the actuaries.

They were concerned that what we were proposing would change the way that companies would behave. Well, absolutely right – they were sleepwalking into disaster – we wanted to show them the consequences of their actions (or rather inaction!).

Their comments were as follows:

"This was nowhere near the international standard". Well, that was rubbish. The big difference was the smoothing mechanism that was in place internationally, but apart from that we were pretty close to the international standard.

"The right standard, but the wrong time". This proved the old aphorism – i.e. the usual conservative comment, "Don't do it at all" while the liberals would say "Do it, but don't do it yet". So we didn't believe in that. We said, there's a debate about how we measure things, but we are going ahead with this standard.

"This is just a snapshot. It's fogging the process that really needs to be looked at with a longer exposure". Well, our view was, we should expose what's there and then explain it, the volatility, and all.

"Shareholders can't get their hands on these surpluses". Well, we didn't actually allow companies to show all the surpluses. They were only allowed to show the amount that could be utilised by the company to the extent that it is able to recover a surplus either through reduced contributions in the future or through refunds from the scheme.

"The market movements make it hard for companies to plan ahead what their results should be". The whole point was to stop them planning what their results should be. We didn't want them to manipulate their pension funds and contributions and things like that.

The last one they tried was, "The small shareholders wouldn't understand it".

Well, the small shareholders, as Tom Lee and I had proved (Lee and Tweedie, 1977), didn't understand very much about accounting anyway. But the actuaries zeroed in on the effect on profit, and one thing FRS17 did was to try and protect profit. People had to overcome the shock of seeing the idea that we were going to show the deficits and surpluses in the balance sheet (Figure 8.1).

**GM What were the international developments at the time? How did they affect the ASB and how did the ASB participate in them?**

**DPT** That was interesting because the IASC had made a quantum leap forward when it prepared to abolish the actuarial method. It was really looking towards the US, and also to how it could reduce the number of reconciliations with US GAAP. The IASC was also concerned with the problem of dealing with the effect of stock market volatility on the pension fund but the IASC and the ASB were really working in different directions. And it was quite interesting how they listened to our position but they were really wedded to the American one. And they produced a similar corridor to the FASB when they revised IAS19 in 1998. What people do forget is that the FASB had another smoothing mechanism, not simply the corridor. They allowed market values to be averaged over a five-year period, whereas we were saying here's the value now. We made a big fuss – I was on the IASC at the time. The Australians and the Brits voted against the revision of IAS19. I remember

*Figure 8.1* Cartoon published by the *Financial Times* on 4 November 1999 during the controversy over accounting for pension funds, with kind permission of artist Nick Baker and the *Financial Times*.

Warren McGregor complaining that "there was a lamentable condoning of income smoothing".

I had great fun rubbishing the corridor approach. My standard line was:

> suppose a pension fund was in equilibrium, having liabilities of $40 million matched by assets of a similar amount. If the value of the assets were to fall to $30 million and the liabilities remained the same, the fund would have a deficit of $10 million.

Under the most commonly used option of IAS 19, derived from the US standard, the deficit is reduced:

First, to remove market 'noise' by a reduction of 10% of whichever is the higher of assets or liabilities – in this case liabilities, leading to reduction in the deficit of $4 million;

Second, by spreading the remaining deficit of $6 million ($10 million minus the $4 million) over the expected working lives of the employees – say ten years for this example.

The result is that the deficit shown in the financial statements becomes $600,000.

As Robert Bruce's Foreword notes, I used to play to the gallery (unusual for me) by saying, "Explain that to your granny. You may as well take the $10 million, divide it by the cube root of the number of miles to the moon, and multiply it by your shoe size. The number doesn't mean a thing!"

Part of the problem was that the IASC didn't have an FRS3. It really didn't have a good performance reporting standard. So the delegates voted to maintain the corridor. It was indicative of future possibilities that we managed to get them to state in their Basis for Conclusions that the UK approach was perhaps better and might be considered in the future. The interesting thing a few years later was that British companies, having got used to FRS17 were really pressing the IASB to ensure that they were allowed to continue to use it. So in the revisions to IAS19 in 2005, Geoff and I, as members of IASB, persuaded the others to enable British companies to continue with the FRS17 approach. But the standard also allowed two other approaches: the corridor, or a policy enabling all changes in the pension fund to be shown in the P&L account which, of course, could lead to great volatility in profit. To my great delight in June 2011, my last month as IASB Chairman, I persuaded the Board to remove the latter two approaches, and we adopted the ASB approach so the long-term gain and loss now went into what IASB called Other Comprehensive Income – the STRGL equivalent. So ASB won in the end. It took a long time – it took ten years after we had produced FRS17, but we did get there.

One of the other things that IASB didn't allow was the recycling of gains and losses from Other Comprehensive Income to profit or loss in later years – always a big issue.[4] And we did that by saying we hadn't got any logical policy regarding the timing and amounts for recycling, and it was difficult to identify a suitable basis just on one standard. So we ducked explanation of that one altogether. But the main thing IASB did in 2011 was to knock out the charge of the whole thing to profit and loss; remove the corridor approach; make any change in the funds' deficit or surplus be shown in comprehensive income.

So, in the end, the Goodies won.

**GM Leading on from that answer: the ASB was the only standard-setter to require immediate recognition of actuarial gains and losses. Why was this?**

**GW** The obvious answer is that we had a vehicle for softening the blow by taking it in the FRS3 Statement of Gains. But I think behind that you've got to say we were a new standard-setting body without the burden that FASB have got with all their past massive 'legislation', if I can call it that; and their continuing membership, and their continuing staffing. Most of their staffs were quite long-term people. They were thought into the idea of smoothing and were happy to apply it through an actuarial approach. It was also very difficult for them, having American industry breathing down their neck and wanting to keep in control of the profit and loss figures. By contrast, the position we were in also helped us not only to gradually push through FRS3 but also to apply its consequences to issues like pension accounting. And, of course, we had our shiny new Statement of Principles, which was similar to the FASB's, but we actually tried applying it; and it was very clear what a liability was. And we saw the liability of the pension fund as being much more than some weird accrual, an actuary's estimate of what in the long term might be appropriate for paying the pension. And that fundamentally is why we were able to achieve what we did.

**AVC** What we did was to give people hard numbers clearly drawn from current conditions to enable them better to understand the dynamics of changes in a company's pension cost and improve their assessments of the implications for future periods. One of the strong points made by some actuaries – I am thinking of the Exley paper we have mentioned – was that the balance sheet approach gave numbers that tallied with other circumstances where they were needed. So, for example, when people were considering whether they were being offered a good transfer value or a poor one, it was the balance sheet approach they would use. They argued that firm figures tied down to market values could actually be used with advantage and improve the decision-making in many different circumstances. We've already acknowledged the fact that, under the regime of SSAP24, companies used to use point in time values for things like transfer values, because these were current transactions. And we had made the same point in FRS7: in a takeover you should be valuing a pension fund on a fair value basis. It all tied up very much better that way.

**DPT** The key to gaining acceptance of FRS17 was to differentiate between what was to go into the Profit and Loss Account and what would be shown in the Statement of Total Recognised Gains and Losses. FRS3 required that profit and loss account income and expenses would involve non-holding activities, internal events – trading activities of the entity that really added value. In the case of pensions, FRS17 therefore proposed that the normal costs of employment would go to the profit and loss account. Into the Statement of Total Recognised Gains and Losses would go non-operating activities with less predictive value such as holding activities, external events – price movements and things like that – for pensions this would involve actuarial gains and losses. FRED22, a proposal to develop FRS3 further – mentioned earlier in Chapter 3 – was also lying in the background. So it was all moving in the same direction at the time of the pensions standard.

**GM Why did the ASB choose the projected unit credit method to measure pension obligations when it includes the effect of future pay rises to which the employer is not currently committed? Is this not a violation of the Statement of Principles and inconsistent with the provisions standard (FRS12)?**

**AVC** FRS17 answers that very clearly. It says that there is a difference between a present commitment to pay a pension based on present salary and a present commitment to pay a pension based on final salary, which the Board believes should be reflected in the measurement of the liabilities. The promise has already been made; and the right to the promised benefit has already been earned. You don't have to wait for the fact that the cost of that promise in respect of a particular individual has yet to be calculated. The pension fund rules say that we will give you a pension based on the pay that you are receiving in the last few years of service, whatever it is - sometimes just the last year, the last 12 months before you retire. And the ASB had no difficulty in accepting that as a liability.

**GW** But you have difficulty with that, Allan, because, looking at it in terms of our definitions of liabilities, it isn't a commitment on the company yet because the company has to do something before it creates a liability. In other words, it has to give you a pay rise. But there's no commitment by them to give a pay rise. There's an expectation that they might, but is the expectation strong enough to create a liability?

**AVC** The liability is there, the measurement may not be, perhaps. Once the liability is there, you do your best to measure it.

**GW** Are you saying it's an option, the liability, is that what it is? It's an option of the company, not on the company: it's the company's option to decide to give a pay rise and therefore raise the accrued pension as well. The company can choose not to exercise the option, and therefore there is not an irrevocable commitment that would create a liability.

**AVC** The promise is made to every individual member of the pension scheme but it is valued by reference to the group. It would not be realistic for the company to shut its eyes to the near certainty that some of those members will earn more in the future either from rising up a pay scale, cost of living adjustments or promotion.

**GW** Realistically, they could sack everybody. A well-known company is reported as doing that at the moment. They have created a new vehicle to employ the employees, and they are transferring them to the new vehicle which doesn't have the same pension scheme. It's a different kind of pension scheme altogether – a defined contribution rather than defined benefit scheme. And this sort of thing is happening all over the place at the moment. Companies are using their power – under the pressure of a big liability, they will do fairly ruthless things, disappoint expectations. People used to think they'd got a job for life if they went to big companies. That was the philosophy of companies like the ones you worked for, Unilever and Shell. And the idea of a defined benefit scheme was to encourage employees to go into that sort of environment and to stay loyal to the company for life. Nowadays the story is a bit different: the labour market is different. People don't think about jobs for life, and companies certainly don't.

**AVC** I think your analysis of the position as an option held by the employer is certainly helpful but, to exercise it, the employer needs to take further steps to extricate itself from a commitment it already has: for example, to negotiate with trade unions and pension fund trustees. That seems to make it a matter of measurement rather than recognition of a liability. I grant you, however, that the ease with which companies have managed to close their defined benefit schemes and persuade employees to transfer to defined contribution ones may suggest that the option is worth more these days than when FRS17 was first issued.

**GW** My view is that the option to give a pay rise lies with the company. Hence it does not have an irrevocable commitment; it need not exercise the option.

**DPT** I was sympathetic with Geoff's view – and used a similar argument against the international consensus on deferred tax – why provide tax on unremitted foreign earnings when no liability would arise unless they were remitted? This will emerge in Chapter 9. However, I wonder if there is a simpler explanation for using the projected unit credit method. IAS19 revised in 1998 required only this method as it was the most widely used (and it still does). Did we simply follow international practice? Allan, can you remember?

**AVC** On your first point, I think that the comparison with unremitted foreign earnings is not an exact parallel. For any company, the normal assumption is that retained earnings are to be reinvested in the company to improve its financial position or expand its business. The same is true of multinationals. No commitment is normally given to remit the retained earnings of foreign subsidiaries; indeed local governments generally encourage retention and reinvestment in the local economy. For pensions, the opposite is true. A commitment to third parties has been given that can only be avoided by negotiations to change the terms of employment, or at least the understanding of those terms created by the long established practice of the employer.

But, to answer your question on whether we simply followed international practice in requiring use of the projected unit credit method, I think the answer is a guarded "Yes". We followed the practice but accepted the arguments on which that choice was based. From a pragmatic point of view, we would also have been concerned at the apparent understatement of the pension liability if it was measured on a basis that assumed the winding up of the pension scheme at the reporting date, with no provision for any future cost of living or other increments.

**GW** I'm just putting the counter-view, Allan. You've correctly stated the majority view. It's just that I was in a minority in that I didn't think there was a commitment there that would justify a liability under our framework. I still support the minority view.

**GM The bifurcation of investment returns into expected and actual seems to be very subjective and open to abuse. Would it not have been in the spirit of a fair value approach to report actual investment returns in the P&L account?**

**GW** Under FRS17 we wanted obviously to report the investment returns and we wanted to include the total return, interest, dividends, and changes in value; FRS17 tries to show you the total position. But this raises the question that, particularly if you're invested in equities, annual investment value can fluctuate a lot, and part of the return is the change in value of the investment rather than dividends or interest. So total return is going to be very strongly fluctuating. Yet you do have a very long-term view as a pension fund manager that you are investing to get a total yield over the lifetime of the investment. So why not split up the actual return into the expected return, which tells you what the managers of the fund, or the company, think they are going to earn over the lifetime in order to pay pensions, and then the residual, which is a more 'below the line' sort of thing, an unpredictable fluctuation, which goes with the actuarial gains and losses, and isn't charged in the profit and loss account. And you could argue that that's a useful piece of information.

I can imagine critics of smoothing things, like Jim Leisenring, denouncing this as giving the company the opportunity to just say what it wants in the profit and loss. But I think that's a misinterpretation of FRS3, although perhaps not of the way some people might misuse it. The message of FRS3 was: you should look at the full performance statement, and gains and losses are still gains and losses, even if they are not expected to recur. So you should take note of all those things: they just have a different interpretation and a different weight. Volatility does sometimes mean revert, but you can't assume it's going to. So the actual investment return of the year is a profit or loss, but it's a different nature of profit or loss from what you expected as the steady return over the lifetime.

That was the reason for doing it. The trouble is that you've got then to have some method of deciding what's the expected return – one that's comparable across companies and one that they won't manipulate to their own advantage. And we tried to deal with that by disclosure, by saying they have to report a run of years and the variation between the actual and expected over those years. And if you find that every year the expected return is way above the actual return, then, of course, you become rather sceptical of the bifurcation, and you look at the total. So that's the way we thought we'd handle it. And I think it's the only way you can handle that. I don't think that the bifurcation is a useless piece of information, but it can be in the wrong hands.

**DPT** I should say, Geoff, that right up to the end on IASB we had the zealots who wanted the whole lot in the profit and loss account. Warren was one of them. And he managed to persuade some of the staff, and I remember an acrimonious meeting where I told them that I would vote against the standard if they did that because it would blow the whole thing out of the water. Nobody would accept that volatility in the P and L. We were quite fortunate in the UK because we had the mini crash in the stock market in 1997; and I used to use the example: if your profits in '97 and '98 were 20 in both years, and the stock market crash led to your fund falling by, say, 33 in '97 and fully recovering in '98, what do you want to show? Do you want to show minus 13 (20–33) in 1997 and plus 53 (20+33) in 1998, or would you rather show 20 profit in both years, and show the swing of 33 of the pension fund in the STRGL? It struck me as fairly obvious. I remember a very foggy day in Bristol when I was stuck at the airport and Allan and I had a long discussion for about an hour or more on the phone, because at the time there was a lot of pressure on us to adopt the corridor approach. And it was, how could we reject the corridor– but still get the standard accepted while preventing hugely optimistic expected returns going through the profit and loss account? And, as Geoff said, it was the disclosures which convinced us – the embarrassment disclosures again – we were quite good at those because we used them with business combinations as well. And we required a five-year table showing the difference between the actual gains and losses and the company's estimated returns used in the profit and loss account for both pension assets and liabilities. We then made the reasoning for this disclosure requirement clear. The relevant paragraph stated:

"A consistent trend of experience losses/gains in the statement of total recognised gains and losses may indicate that the assumptions have been over-optimistic/over-pessimistic and may cast doubt upon the reliability of the amounts reported in the profit and loss account. Where such a trend has emerged it is important that careful consideration is given to the choice of assumptions in the future". i.e., stop cheating!

That paragraph was in there deliberately. It was there not only to warn companies but to alert the Review Panel.

It's interesting – that disclosure was not supported by respondents to the Exposure Draft. But we kept it, and we kept it because we believed it helped to place in context the actuarial gains and losses reported in the year, and hence played an important role in the Financial Reporting Standard. We refused to back off on that one even though it was opposed.

Other information which helped convince us it was necessary was supplied by the Americans who informed us of the heroic assumptions of the S&P 500 between 2000 and 2004 when the estimated return by these companies was $498 billion; the actual return was $197 billion. So there was a phoney $301 billion flowing through their profit and loss accounts (The Analyst's Accounting Observer, 2005). That's why we had our disclosures. If I remember correctly, we couldn't persuade them to include similar disclosures in the International Standards.

**AVC** I was going to say I think this last discussion brings out quite well the difference of understanding of what we call the STRGL and they call Other Comprehensive Income. We invented the STRGL – invented in one sense, as we explain in our discussion on FRS3 – we had this clear vision of what the STRGL was doing. It was a part of financial performance. And I think other countries didn't really see it in that light. They saw it rather as just some sort of subdivision of the analysis of movements in shareholders' funds. They didn't present it as clearly as we did as a primary performance statement. That made them very reluctant to put things into the STRGL, and it made them insist that, if they did that, they had to recycle them into profit and loss at some stage. It was our understanding of the STRGL that eventually convinced me that it offered the most effective way of providing the clear information that was so much needed. The STRGL enabled us to do that in a very open way. We weren't hiding gains or losses from anybody by slipping them into some sort of glorified movement in reserves.

**DPT** Internationally, Other Comprehensive Income was looked upon as a 'dumpster' where you put unwanted losses and (rarely) gains. They never saw it the way we did which probably explains why the IASB's performance reporting project got completely bogged down.

*Legacy*

**GM Finally, looking back at FRS17: What was FRS17 intended to do, and did it achieve it?**

**GW** FRS17 gave a message which was very unwelcome, but of great practical importance. It came at a time of switch-over from the average pension fund being an asset to the company – because of the boom on the stock exchange and favourable valuations of pension obligations, the value of investments was typically more than the estimated pension obligation – to being a significant liability, particularly for former public sector firms that had been privatised: firms like BT, which still has, as I understand it, one of the biggest pension liabilities of any firm in the UK. It was a time of switch-over, so the Defined Benefit pension schemes were declining already for reasons we've just been discussing. And so it delivered the message that in this uncertain world, with all these alarming uncertainties that lay ahead concerning such matters as investment returns, interest rates, inflation, and life expectancy, it was very expensive to give a promise to somebody that, when they retire, they would have a pension based on their terminal salary, and which was typically indexed. To make indexed defined benefit pension promises is just incredibly expensive and FRS17 drew attention to that. So it gave an early warning of a coming crisis is the way I would put it. And that was a benefit – giving time for taking evasive action both by employers and employees. The subsequent restructuring or re-funding of many final salary schemes is evidence of the impact of FRS17.

Its original intention was not to convey any particular message, but rather to do good company accounting and say how the company's obligation to the pension scheme had changed. One of the interesting things about this relates to the interests of members of the pension schemes. Of course, FRS17 was not concerned with pension fund accounting. It's the pension fund typically that owes the pension to the pensioner, not the company. The company stands behind the fund and gives a guarantee, and FRS17 looks at the question of what burden the company's covenant creates for the company that we should be reporting in the company's accounts. We are not looking specifically from the pensioner's perspective, but the 'early warning' information that FRS17 provides is of obvious interest to pensioners and to those who manage pension funds on their behalf. The pension schemes, incidentally, do show, in their own accounts, the net assets of the pension fund at an estimate of current market value on a similar basis to FRS17. But they don't show any pension liabilities, leaving the total funding position to the reader's imagination. It's the strangest set of accounts I've ever come across, designed purely to show the trustees' stewardship of the fund assets, not whether those assets are sufficient to pay the pension obligations.

**DPT** I'd just like to mention a couple of points. Firstly, did it contribute to the decline of final salary pension schemes? I remember after we put out FRS17 the Daily Mail showed photographs of Gordon Brown and me and headed it, "The men who destroyed your pension". So some certainly blamed FRS17. I also remember looking at the BA accounts. And the ones for 2001/2002 mention that they were moving from a defined benefit, final salary basis to a defined contribution scheme, taking account of the changing environment, including new accounting rules, (they mentioned FRS17). And in 2005/2006 Martin Broughton, the chairman, in his Chairman's Statement (he'd just newly taken over as Chairman, and he was an accountant) said "the stark reality is that your Company has the biggest deficit of any company in the FTSE100 relative to its size and it is growing, despite equities at a five year high. Not surprisingly, commentators have described British Airways as a 'pension fund with wings' …It is an issue that must be tackled if we are to grow our business, invest in new aircraft and restore the dividend." At that stage the newly created obligation was £1.8 billion. And the company's net worth was £2 billion. So you could see the effect of the new standard.

Just as a final point, I remember going to the Hundred Group to tell them what we were about to do regarding pension accounting – I think probably before we issued the Exposure Draft. And there was uproar. The FRC Chairman even lobbied to stop the standard as it developed but refused to intervene as the ASB was independent. I was summoned by a minister responsible for pensions who had clearly been lobbied by major companies. He put pressure on me to cut the effect on companies' balance sheets of the deficits being shown by the proposed standard. I told him we could cut the deficits in half. He visibly brightened until I said it involves adding a requirement – take the right answer and divide it by two – would he like to write to me with his request which, of course, we would have to make public? We never heard any more.

At the Hundred Group meeting, I have just mentioned, the finance directors voted on our proposals but they split 50:50. And what I found was very interesting probably about four or five years after we issued FRS17, one of the most vociferous opponents came up to me and said, "You know, once FRS17 came in we started discussing pensions in the boardroom. We never ever mentioned pensions till then". And that's exactly what FRS17 was designed to do. It forced companies to determine how to fund their pension deficits and how to disclose their plans to the market.

We started to get comments in annual reports on the lines of: "the pension deficit is £40 million. The company intends to pay an extra £5 million per annum into the fund over the next few years; the assets in the fund are expected to grow at a rate of 4% per annum; and the pension scheme will be changed in the following way… it is expected that the fund will be in equilibrium by 20XX". They were starting to manage their pension liabilities.

**AVC** That's what happened in America, of course, on healthcare. Nobody had thought about healthcare. If you asked them questions, they'd say, "Well, we can't estimate that, so we do it on a pay as you go basis". What an answer!

## Notes

1 This did not mean that the amount recognised for pension cost was entirely discretionary. Larger companies would engage an actuary who, after conducting an actuarial valuation, usually every three years, as described in Model 2, would agree with management a recommended pattern of future payments called a 'funding plan' designed to ensure that adequate funds were built up to pay the promised benefits to all members of the scheme at their eventual retirement dates. Particularly for a well-funded scheme, the actuary had sufficient discretion in selection of the actuarial method and assumptions, as well as the pattern of funding, to be able to offer significant alternative funding plans.
2 Pensions Management Institute, Briefing Note 86.
3 Although ONS provides estimates from time to time, e.g. ONS (2021).
4 Recycling involves showing in profit or loss a gain or loss recorded in other comprehensive income in an earlier period. A corresponding debit or credit would be shown in other comprehensive income when the recycling took place.

## References

### *Books and articles*

Exley, J., Mehta, S. and Smith, A. (1997). The financial theory of defined benefit schemes, *British Actuarial Journal*, 3(4), 835–938.

*Financial Times*. (2000). 'Tweedie's Gladiator Show'. *Financial Times*. 24 February 2000.

Griffiths, I. (1986). *Creative Accounting*, London, Unwin.

Harris T., Michaelides, L. and Weyns, G. (2003). *UK Pensions: Is It Just a Storm in a Teacup?* London: Morgan Stanley.

Lee, T. and Tweedie D. (1977). *The Private Shareholder and the Corporate Report*, London, ICAEW.

Munnell, A. (2005). Employer-Sponsored Plans: The Shift from Defined Benefit to Defined Contribution', Chapter 18, pp. 359–380 of Clark, G., Munnell, A., and Orszag, G. *The Oxford Handbook of Pensions and Retirement Income*, Oxford: OUP.

ONS (2021). *Pensions in the National Accounts, a Fuller Picture of the UK's Funded and Unfunded Pension Obligations*, London: ONS, 8 February 2021.

The Analyst's Accounting Observer. (2005). Pondering Pensions: How They Affected the S&P 500 in 2004, May 27 and (revised) June 27 2005.

### *Standard setters' publications*

APB8 (1966). *Accounting for the Cost of Pension Plans*. Opinion No. 8, APB.

Discussion Paper (1995). *Pension Costs in the Employer's Financial Statements*, ASB.

Discussion Paper (1998). *Aspects of Accounting for Pension Costs*, ASB.

E54 (1996). *Employee Benefits*, IASC.
FRED20 (1999). *Retirement Benefits*, ASB.
FRS3 (1992). *Reporting Financial Performance*, ASB.
FRS4 (1993). *Capital Instruments*, ASB.
FRS5 (1994). *Reporting the Substance of Transactions*, ASB.
FRS7 (1994). *Fair Values in Acquisition Accounting*, ASB.
FRS12 (1998). *Provisions, Contingent Liabilities and Contingent Assets*, ASB.
FRS17 (2000). *Retirement Benefits*, ASB.
IAS19 (1996 and 1998). *Employee Benefits*, IASC.
IAS19 (2005 and 2011). *Employee Benefits* (revised), IASB.
SFAS87 (1985). *Employers' Accounting for Pensions*, FASB.
SSAP24 (1988). *Accounting for Pension Costs*, ASC.
UITF Abstract 6 (1992). *Accounting for Post-Retirement Benefits Other Than Pensions*, ASB.

# 9 Other issues

This chapter seeks to "fill in the gaps" through brief mention of other standards and proposals that help to illustrate driving themes in the work programme of the ASB over its first decade.

## The statement of principles

The primary influence on that work was the Board's Statement of Principles. Although issued only in December 1999, individual chapters had been published for discussion from as far back as April 1991.[1] Moreover, the Board was able to draw upon earlier conceptual developments by overseas standard setters (notably the FASB and the IASC) and its predecessors in the UK (notably David Solomons' *Guidelines for Reporting Standards, 1989,* which was commissioned by the ICAEW). Although these sources were not in unanimous agreement on every issue, they did represent a broad emerging international consensus which the ASB's own principles reflected. The primary purpose of articulating such principles was to provide a coherent frame of reference to be used by the Board in the development and review of accounting standards. The Statement was not an accounting standard but, by setting out the conceptual underpinnings of the Board's view of the key issues in financial reporting, it was the basis for most of the Board's standards. An appendix at the end of this chapter shows that the greater part of the Board's work programme derived from the Statement of Principles in the sense that key arguments in its FRSs were, as intended, drawn from that Statement or the published drafts that preceded it.

The Statement dealt with the eight major issues (set out in general terms) below:

The objective of financial reporting (to provide information that is useful in assessing stewardship and for making economic decisions);

The reporting entity (determining which entities are controlled by a parent);

The qualitative characteristics of Financial Information (materiality, relevance, reliability, prudence, understandability);

DOI: 10.4324/9781003346920-9

The elements of Financial Statements (assets and liabilities and changes in them, i.e. gains and losses);

Recognition in Financial Statements (required if sufficient evidence exists that a new asset or liability has been created or there has been an addition to an existing asset or liability and it can be measured at a monetary amount with sufficient reliability);

Measurement in financial statements (historical cost or lower recoverable amount; or up to date current value)

Presentation of financial information (the statement of financial performance; the statement of financial position/balance sheet; and the cash flow statement);

Accounting for interests in other entities (the effects of control, joint control, significant influence, and lesser or no influence).[2]

## Accounting policies

Perhaps the standard flowing most obviously from the Statement of Principles was FRS18 Accounting Policies (December 2000). It took the opportunity of the publication of the Statement of Principles one year earlier to replace one of the earliest of its predecessor's standards, SSAP2 Disclosure of accounting policies, which by then was nearly 30 years old. SSAP2 had set out four "fundamental accounting concepts", one of which, "accruals", was stated in terms that appeared to conflict with the ASB's Statement of Principles. After clarifying that revenues and costs were recognised as they were earned or incurred rather than when they were received or paid, it went on to say, "they are matched with one another so far as their relationship can be established or justifiably assumed and dealt with in the profit and loss account to which they relate...". Those words founded recognition on potentially subjective judgements of matching, whereas the Statement of Principles relied on the more objective grounds of its definitions of assets and liabilities, which by that point had proved their effectiveness in numerous FRSs.

A further important update introduced by FRS18 was in the definition and role of prudence in selecting accounting policies. The FRS noted the potential conflict between prudence and neutrality and made the point that prudence only comes into play under conditions of uncertainty. It concluded that the competing demands of the two principles "are reconciled by finding a balance that ensures that the deliberate and systematic understatements of assets and gains and overstatements of liabilities do not occur". By contrast, SSAP2 had defined prudence in terms that constrained profit recognition more narrowly, insisting that revenue and gains should not be anticipated but recognised by inclusion in the profit and loss account only when realised in the form of cash or other assets whose ultimate cash realisation could be assessed with reasonable certainty. The ASB noted that, over the 30 years since SSAP2 had been issued, the development of markets had reduced the significance of realisation, or prospective realisation, as the sole determinant of whether a gain should be recognised. There was also greater awareness of the distorting effect on reporting financial performance of devices that allowed the smoothing of profits. An inbuilt bias in the concept of prudence had encouraged the undervaluation of assets and overvaluation of liabilities, thus creating hidden reserves that could be drawn on in later periods to achieve the profit trend desired by management.

## Cash flow statements

As explained in Chapter 2, the Board issued FRS1 Cash Flow Statements little more than a year after its own formation, after reviewing comments received on an exposure draft published by its predecessor, the ASC. The principal innovation in the standard was to introduce into UK financial reporting the international shift to reporting changes in cash and cash equivalents rather than changes in funds available to the entity required by the former statement of source and application of funds.

After companies had had two years experience of implementing FRS1, the Board called for comments on the operation of the standard. The result of this consultation was a revised standard, issued in October 1996, which updated the original in three significant respects:

- The focus of the cash flow statement became cash rather than cash plus cash equivalents. Respondents to the consultation had echoed the long-standing divisions of opinion over what should be included in "cash equivalents". Instead of attempting to redefine cash equivalents, the Board simply refocused the statement on cash.
- Acknowledging that cash balances alone less overdrafts were normally not significant components of corporate treasury management, the Board created a new subdivision of the cash flow statement entitled "management of liquid resources".
- Responding to requests made to the consultation preceding the original FRS1 and to the exposure draft of its replacement, the Board required a reconciliation to be provided of the movement of cash to changes in Net Debt/Net Funds. This could be presented either adjoining the Cash Flow Statement, but distinguished from it, or in a separate note.

The requirement for a statement of "movements in net debt/net funds" standardised a reporting metric that had long played a prominent role in presentations and discussion of UK financial reports. The introduction of a section on the Management of Liquid Resources distinguished accumulation or reduction of Treasury investments from longer-term financial transactions, as well as providing insight into how the entity managed its Treasury. Finally, despite the innovatory nature of these amendments, the greater information provided enabled the standard to continue to comply with that of the IASC and remain broadly compatible with other international requirements.

## Associates and joint ventures

Equity accounting[3] for associated companies ('associates') formed the subject of the UK's first accounting standard SSAP1, issued in 1971. It responded to the desire of certain companies to reflect in their accounts a fuller presentation of the performance of some of their trade investments than was given by reporting only dividends received. The criterion adopted for equity accounting was that the investor should be in a position to exercise significant influence over the operating and financial policies of its investee.

Unfortunately, the range of investments falling within the SSAP1 definition was too broad, reaching from joint control at one end to a fiercely protected arm's length relationship at the other. Furthermore, application of the standard often stretched the limits of what could be considered significant influence. The consequence was severe embarrassment of some investors who had insufficient knowledge of their investee's financial policies and controls to detect misreporting of profits that had a significant effect on their own results.

The ASB attacked the problem in two ways: first, by developing an analysis, presentation, and improved disclosures for joint ventures; and second, by tightening the definition of associates and increasing their disclosures. FRS9 Associates and Joint Ventures defined a joint venture as an entity in which the reporting entity held an interest on a long-term basis and which was jointly controlled by the reporting entity and one or more other venturers under a contractual arrangement. An 'entity' had to carry on a trade or business of its own that was not just part of the trades or businesses of entities that had interests in it. Joint ventures were to be presented under the 'gross equity method', which, in addition to information required for associates, noted the reporting entity's share of its joint ventures' turnover, both in total and by segment, and, in the balance sheet, its share of the assets and liabilities making up its net investment in joint ventures. Profit and loss amounts above profit before tax were separately presented from those for the group. Joint arrangements that were not entities were accounted for as part of the reporting entity's own assets, liabilities, and cash flows.[4]

FRS9 tightened its definition of associates by requiring a reporting entity to demonstrate actual rather than potential exercise of significant influence over its investee's operating and financial policies. For both joint ventures and associates, the standard introduced a range of improved disclosures, especially where either class in aggregate, or in individual entities, exceeded threshold ratios to certain group reported amounts.

These reforms enabled the ASB to construct a much improved standard that both clarified public understanding of the various interests an investor might have in operations carried out with or through other entities and ensured consistent application of its detailed requirements. They were widely welcomed by all sides of the UK financial community.

## Deferred tax

By contrast with almost all the other standards issued by the ASB during the decade, FRS19 Deferred Tax was reactive rather than innovative. For over 20 years UK companies had reported under a standard, SSAP15, that required only partial provision for their deferred tax liability. The justification had been that capital allowances (tax depreciation) granted for the purchase of plant and machinery (100% in the year of purchase) and inventory (inflation adjustments) were so generous that there was in practice no prospect of the notional tax liability becoming payable (in accounting terms, "of the tax timing difference reversing"). By the mid-90s when FRS19 was being developed, the generosity of these allowances had diminished. Furthermore, experience had shown that judgements on whether and when the timing differences would reverse varied widely for similar situations. The consequence was that partial provision, as well as the then practice of writing off goodwill on acquisition to reserves, was damaging the reputation of UK accounting standards in the eyes of other standard setters and weakening the perceived quality of financial statements produced under those standards. International pressure to change the UK standard increased with the revision of the international standard IAS12 in 1996, itself closely modelled on a revised US standard FAS109 Accounting for Income Taxes issued in 1992.

Anxious not to become an outlier in the movement to international convergence, and mindful of the fact that partial provision seemed inconsistent with its own Statement of Principles, which required liabilities to be recognised on the basis of past, not future events, the ASB issued a Discussion Paper in 1995 advocating a change to full provision for all timing differences. Although the majority of respondents disagreed with this proposal, the Board persevered and, after informal consultations, published an exposure draft in 1999 proposing a form of full provision that was reluctantly accepted by the majority. FRS19 followed in December 2000.

The reason why FRS19 did not completely align with the international consensus was a fundamental difference of understanding of the nature of the deferred tax item. IAS12, following its US model, regarded deferred tax as a "valuation adjustment" which reduced the assets and liabilities with which it was associated to a net of tax basis. The idea was that recovery of the value embodied in an asset inevitably resulted in payment of tax on the recovery of that value, whether from the profits earned through use or from its eventual sale. The difference between the carrying value of an asset and its tax base was called a "temporary difference". Although all timing differences were temporary differences, the converse was not true. There were also permanent differences between profits reported in financial statements and those recognised for tax purposes. These arose because certain types of income and expenditure were not taxable or tax-deductible at all, or because certain tax allowances or charges had no corresponding amount in the financial statements.

FRS19 regarded deferred tax as a liability, recognised in common with all other liabilities as an obligation resulting from a past event and measured at its most probable outcome. Valuation adjustments, on the other hand, had no such constraint and, accordingly, provided for deferred tax in virtually all circumstances on the grounds that the eventual tax implications of transactions giving rise to assets and liabilities at their carrying amounts must be included in the financial statements. A common example of a transaction giving rise to a permanent difference under FRS19 was a property attracting UK Industrial Buildings Allowance, which could be rolled over to a new property when it was sold. Unless and until the option to apply for roll-over relief was allowed to lapse, there was not even a prospective liability. Not providing for deferred tax in these and other situations was much simpler to explain when it was seen as a liability than it was under IAS12's valuation adjustment approach.

The Board's decision to develop its own version of full provision, despite the fact that international convergence had been a prime motivation for the standard, illustrates a significant aspect of its policy in seeking that goal. Its representatives negotiated strongly with other standard setters, challenging arguments that seemed weak or excessively cumbersome (see Camfferman and Zeff, 2007, p.361). When voted down on an issue that it believed important, it did not acquiesce in convergence for its own sake but included in its Development of the FRS section a rigorous examination of the issue from all sides. FRS19, authored by staff member Joan Brown, is the prime example of that policy, running to 146 paragraphs of closely argued text, almost as much as in FAS109, in order to preserve the arguments for another day.

## ASB statements

In addition to the accounting standards mentioned above, the ASB had also looked at the reporting process, having issued Statements designed to have persuasive rather than mandatory force on the subjects of Interim Reports (September 1997) and Preliminary Announcements (July 1998). In February 2000, it even issued a Discussion Paper on 'Year-end financial reports: improving communication'. With the privatisation of previously nationalised utilities, the Board was aware that for many shareholders the opportunity to purchase shares in these utilities was probably their first foray into equity investment. While it was widely acknowledged that changes made by the Board in financial reporting requirements had improved the quality of information provided to institutional investors and analysts, there had also been concerns that as financial statements became longer and more complex they were becoming less accessible to private shareholders. There was evidence that many such shareholders did not read or understand the primary financial statements (Lee and Tweedie, 1977). The Board, therefore, coinciding with the independent Company Law Review being coordinated by the Department of Trade and Industry, proposed that companies with very large numbers of shareholders might offer them either summary financial statements or even a simpler narrative review that reported on a standardised set of financial highlights in plain language without including tabular profit and loss accounts or balance sheets.

The Board was not only concerned to make the reporting process simpler for readers of accounts but also to help preparers of financial reports. It had earlier (November 1997) introduced 'The Financial Reporting Standard for Smaller Entities' (FRSSE), a single, simpler accounting standard that smaller entities could choose to adopt as an alternative to the full set of FRSs and UITF Abstracts. At the end of the period covered by this book, the Board issued (February 2001) a further Discussion Paper seeking views on the salient features of the FRSSE and whether improvements could be made.

## The international dimension

Increasingly during the 1990s, the ASB's work was becoming dominated by collaboration with other national standard setters in tackling controversial issues. The four Discussion Papers outstanding at the end of December 2000 dealing with specific accounting issues were all fiercely debated matters of international concern.

The first Discussion Paper, 'Derivatives and other financial instruments' had been issued by the ASB in July 1996. It addressed two main groups of issues. First, it dealt with disclosure to provide information about the impact of financial instruments on the entity's risk profile, how the risks arising from financial instruments might affect the entity's performance and financial condition, and how these risks were being managed. The ASB had held discussions with the Hundred Group of Finance Directors, the Institute of Investment Management and Research, and the London Stock Exchange, all of whom agreed that guidance on disclosure and accounting for derivatives and other financial instruments was needed. The Board noted, when issuing the Discussion Paper, that it believed there was an urgent need for the improvement of financial instrument disclosures. However, the second group of issues in the Discussion Paper was far more controversial. The Board expressed as its preliminary view that all financial instruments should be measured at current value with all gains and losses recognised as they occur.[5] The Board acknowledged that the radical nature of this proposal meant that it would be several years before the second part of the Discussion Paper could be issued as a standard on measurement and hedge accounting.

In due course, the Board issued the relatively uncontroversial FRS13 'Derivatives and other financial instruments: disclosures' in September 1998. Dealing with the opposition (mainly from the banking sector) to measurement and hedge accounting proposals, however, would last for many years and would even bedevil the IASB's attempts to have its predecessor's standard on the subject (IAS39) widely accepted. The ASB quickly realised that the way most likely to gain acceptance of a standard on the subject was to work in collaboration with other major standard setters and, with others, formed the Joint Working Group of Standard Setters (JWG)[6] which was tasked with producing a draft standard. A consultation paper incorporating the JWG's draft standard proposing a full fair value model for financial instruments was published in December 2000 but ultimately was only used to inform the IASB in its revision of its predecessor's IAS39. The full fair value model has not to date been made mandatory by an IFRS.

Three other Discussion Papers were published by the ASB by December 2000, all of which, unlike that dealing with derivatives, were developed by the G4+1 group of accounting standard setters.[7] While, initially, the G4+1 focused on attempting to harmonise accounting standards among its members, it began to operate as a 'think tank' to agree broad principles from which each sponsoring standard setter was encouraged to develop its own policy. Several of the group's published papers had a profound impact on international accounting. For example, IAS37 and the ASB's FRS12 owed much to the G4+1 paper 'Provisions: Their Recognition, Measurement, and Disclosure in Financial Statements', 1995 (authored by the ASB's Andrew Lennard and Sandra Thompson) while 'Accounting for Share-Based Payment' (2000) discussed further below, was reissued by the IASB when it began work on the project that culminated in IFRS2, Share-based Payment.

All of the three outstanding ASB Discussion Papers, none of which was debated at length by the Board, were based on G4+1 position papers. The first, 'Business Combinations', was issued in December 1998 and concluded that the use of a single method of accounting for business combinations was preferable to two (or more) methods and that the purchase method was the appropriate method to use. It proposed that the pooling (merger) method should not be used for any business combinations. As discussed in Chapter 7, the ASB had issued FRS6 in September 1994 which set out strict criteria to be met before merger accounting rather than acquisition accounting should be used. While other members of the G4+1 were supportive of eliminating the former accounting method, in issuing the Paper the ASB commented that it was not aware of a general demand for a revision to FRS6; "however", it added, "concerns about the application of FRS6 have been expressed overseas". The Board, consequently, asked its constituents whether changes should be made to the criteria given in the UK standard but, with an eye to the future, sought views on whether the prohibition of merger accounting would be supported if that were to be the predominant international practice.

Following the restructuring of the IASC, the subject was placed on the IASB agenda and, consistent with the views of the G4+1 paper, IFRS3 (2004) required that all business combinations were to be accounted for using the purchase method. From 2005, this applied to UK listed companies as a result of the requirements to follow IASB standards.

Unlike the business combinations proposals, the other two G4+1 inspired Discussion Papers were in the main supported by the ASB. The Board agreed with the thrust of 'Leases: implementation of a new approach' issued in December 1999 (authored principally by Hans Nailor and Andrew Lennard of the ASB with a significant contribution from Clark Anstis of the Australian Accounting Research Foundation who had been seconded to the ASB) that the arbitrary distinction between operating and finance leases that was required by existing standards (SSAP21 in the UK) was unsatisfactory and that the usefulness of financial statements would be enhanced by an approach that applied the same method to all leases. Under SSAP21, operating lease accounting treated the deal as a rental with the annual rental/lease charge in the profit and loss account being the only accounting effect of the lease contract, whereas finance lease accounting treated it like a purchase associated with a loan. In issuing the Discussion Paper, the ASB noted 'the common and growing practice of analysts of recasting financial statements on a basis that is similar to that proposed'.

While the 'purchase and loan' approach proposed was supported by users of financial statements, it was fiercely opposed both by lessors and lessees. Operating leases were a highly effective off-balance sheet device that enabled companies to hide both the assets employed in the business and the related liabilities incurred. In aggregate, these figures were huge[8] and enabled companies, especially those such as airlines with considerable equipment leases, to display far more favourable gearing ratios and return on assets than would have been the case if all leases were treated as finance leases.

As the ASB Chairman commented when the Discussion Paper was published: 'The existing model is very much an 'all or nothing' approach. It is ridiculous that, for example, a lessee should recognise all (or nearly all) of an asset if the minimum lease payments amount to 91% of its value and none if the minimum lease payments amount to 89%.[9] The practice of structuring leases to avoid showing leased assets and the resulting liabilities on balance sheet is a natural consequence of a standard that draws a bright line between similar transactions. The proposals should lead to a new standard that extracts leases from the straitjacket of inadequate accounting and reflects them by showing the true scale of the assets and liabilities involved.'

A new standard was not, however, a forgone conclusion. The leasing industry, whose existence was largely tied to delivering off balance sheet financing, lobbied hard against the new proposals. A measure of the extent of opposition, mainly from leasing associations, can be gauged by the fact that from the earlier G4+1 Special Report on the subject, authored by Warren McGregor (1996), which explored the conceptual foundations for revised leasing standards to the publication of the IASB's standard on the subject (IFRS16) 20 years would elapse – and the date for implementation of the IFRS was for accounting periods commencing on or after 1 January 2019!

The last of the three G4+1 inspired Discussion Papers issued by the ASB before the end of 2000 was the highly controversial paper 'Share-based payment' (July 2000), the principal author of which was Kimberley Crook with a significant contribution being made by Kathryn Cearns – both project directors with the ASB.

Share schemes were a common feature of director and executive remuneration. In the UK, the Government had recently announced a tax-advantaged share scheme to encourage more companies to offer shares to all employees. Companies whose shares or share options were regarded as a valuable 'currency' commonly used share-based payment to obtain employee and professional services. Yet in the UK there was no comprehensive guidance on accounting for such payments. It was not uncommon for share options to be granted to employees at an exercise price that was equal to or higher than the market price of the shares at the date the options were granted so the options would have no 'intrinsic value' at grant date and no charge would be made in the profit and loss account in respect of employee services purchased by the issue of share options.

The paper proposed that transactions involving the purchase of goods or services from other parties, such as employees or suppliers, with payment made in shares or share options issued by the entity to those other parties, should be recognised in the financial statements, with a corresponding charge to the profit and loss account when those goods and services are provided. The transaction should be measured at the fair value of the shares or share options at the date upon which the other party, having performed all of the services or provided all of the goods necessary, becomes unconditionally entitled to the options or shares (the vesting date). In most cases, an option pricing model should be applied to establish the fair value of the option. Where performance by the other party occurred between the grant date and the vesting date an estimate of the transaction amount was to be accrued over the performance period.

The G4+1 members' standards boards expressed differing degrees of interest in implementing the proposals in the Paper. The FASB, which had only recently weathered a major political storm while developing a standard (SFAS123) on the subject and had been forced by Congressional pressure to allow, in addition to its preferred proposal of expensing the fair value of all stock options, an option simply to give disclosure in the notes of the effect of the fair value-based expense, immediately stated: "the FASB has no plans to reconsider its existing guidance".[10] The ASB's approach, however, was more aggressive than other G4+1 members and, after noting that the Board had been actively involved at all stages of the Paper's development, stated that it intended to develop an accounting standard on share-based payment, taking account of the comments received on the Paper.

The scene was set for a bitter fight between standard setters and large sections of the corporate community whose concerns not only involved exposure of previously hidden levels of executive remuneration but also the threat of significant additional charges in the profit and loss account.

In September 2001, the newly instituted IASB added share-based payments to its initial agenda and invited comments on the G4+1 Discussion Paper. In February 2004, despite intense lobbying against the project, IFRS2

'Share-based Payment', was issued requiring companies to recognise the fair value of employee stock options (albeit calculated at the date of the grant of the option rather than the vesting date proposed by the G4+1) as an expense in arriving at earnings. All G4 standard setters followed suit – the FASB revised SFAS123 in December 2004 removing the disclosure only option.

## The G4+1 and the IASC/IASB

The success of the G4 +1 in bringing together the major Anglo-Saxon standard setters and their interest in harmonising their standards was undoubtedly a threat to the IASC. Some of the national standard setters began to speculate about possible alternatives to the IASC should the G4 or an expanded version of G4 or FASB start to issue joint standards in the countries involved. The IASC's Chairman and Secretary-General at the time, respectively Michael Sharpe of Australia, and Sir Bryan Carsberg, with the backing of the SEC and the tacit support of the EU, worked to bring the two groups together and appointed a Strategy Working Party to look at various options for the future of international accounting standards and to set out a blueprint for a future high quality international standard-setting board. The result was the creation of the IASB which began work in 2001. The G4+1 disbanded the same year.

Even before the IASB was instituted, debate in the UK concerning the future role of the ASB had begun. The creation of the IASC's Strategy Working Party signalled the prospect that the standard-setting agenda would in the years to come be dominated by a global standard setter. Should the ASB's objective now be to narrow the differences between its standards and those of the International standard setter? Should the latter's standards become the core standards for listed companies, with, possibly, national requirements being added by the ASB as necessary? Should UK standards continue with a reconciliation to international standards added? The international focus of the ASB was leading to a completely different standard-setting era from that considered by the Dearing Committee.

These problematic issues were resolved more quickly than anyone expected when in March 2000 the European Council at its Lisbon meeting set the deadline of 2005 to implement the Commission's Financial Services Action Plan and urged that steps be taken to enhance the comparability of financial statements prepared by publicly traded companies. The Regulation (EC) No 1606/2002 of the European Parliament and of the Council on the application of international accounting standards (IAS) (known as the IAS Regulation), was duly enacted on 19 July 2002. It required the financial statements of both domestic and foreign companies issuing equities or debt on a regulated EU market to comply from 1 January 2005 with international accounting standards issued by the IASB. Financial statements prepared under certain other accounting standards were deemed to be equivalent to the IASB standards. A process of review and endorsement of IASB standards for use in the EU was set up but, to date, has made few departures from the IASB original.

With the IASB now firmly supported from both sides of the Atlantic, the role of the ASB inevitably reduced from that of standard setter to standards consultant, though it remained the formal authority for regulating the accounts of companies not subject to the IAS Regulation. Henceforth it might expect to influence the IASB, particularly with respect to issues on which it had itself worked, but it would no longer decide on the outcome. This bitter sweet ending to a unique decade of reform and innovation marked the close of its activity as the UK's powerful accounting standards setter but also the success of its efforts to help bring to birth an authoritative international standard setter with the same high ideals as its own.

## Allan Cook and David Tweedie

### *Discussion*

**GM Did you feel you had to compromise too much in achieving the widespread approval you describe for your standard on Associates and Joint Ventures?**

**DPT** I'm really sorry we didn't get rid of associated company accounting. I've never liked it. Interestingly enough, SSAP1 only came into being because the Accounting Standards Steering Committee had to produce something quickly. And they got hold of the technical work of the English Institute, who were doing something on associates and made that their first standard. It was a surprising choice because, even as the ICAEW admitted, only nine companies out of the top 300 actually used associated company accounting. All the rest of them in their financial statements just showed dividends received and investments in the associate. So it was a bizarre choice, but we were stuck with it. I could understand its use when we hadn't got anything on off balance sheet subsidiaries: it at least gave you a clue what was lying out there. But then it became enshrined in company law, which said that 20% holdings were presumed to be a participating interest, and that you were presumed to exercise a significant influence unless you could show the contrary.

FRS9 toughened this. I think we probably couldn't abolish associates because of company law. And it was the case that after FRS9 you had to prove that you had influence by participation in the expansion or the contraction of the business, or in determining the balance between dividends and reinvestment – you were really involved in the management. So I think the ASB's standard did try, but frankly I think we would have been better off just showing dividends received and the investment in the company. I really don't like associate accounting at all.

**AVC** The ASSC's decision to develop the standard at this time seems likely to have been influenced by the issue in the US in March 1971 of APB18 The Equity Method of Accounting for Investments in Common Stock.

**GW** I don't really understand your animosity to it. I see the complication, but, logically an associate is just another device for raising finance from outside, and running the company in a separate way from a subsidiary (which implies complete control) but nevertheless within the group. But there is a spectrum, like those which we came across later in various forms of creative accounting. The associated company captures the situation where you're not just a passive investor drawing dividends; you have got a lot of clout. If you sold out, it would really move the management and so on. So you do have power whether you care to exercise it or not. And yet it's not a controlled subsidiary. For a controlled subsidiary, you consolidate the thing, you show the lot. For an investment you just show the dividend. And there's something in between. Logically, there is something in between. If you want to put it there and make life complicated or not is another matter, but I don't quite understand the animosity to it.

**DPT** My problem, Geoff, is that you can't necessarily get your hands on those profits you are showing, whereas you can in the subsidiary. And you can in a joint venture the way we did it in FRS9. But for associates, you cannot get those profits unless they pay you dividends. That's why I don't like it.

**GW** So it's a realisation idea actually

**DPT** Not quite. It's the fact that it's giving a misleading impression of what your profitability is. I think a company's profitability is artificially enhanced by including profits of associated companies, which the investing company can't use.

**GW** Yes, we've got an interesting example of that now with Rosneft and BP. BP have recently said they are going to sell their holding in Rosneft. They have exactly a 19.75% equity interest in Rosneft and had two directors on the Rosneft Board (who have just resigned), which amounted to a 'significant influence', allowing equity accounting as an associated company, under current IASB standards. And they have been drawing a big dividend. They have been showing their proportionate share of Rosneft's earnings as part of BP's earnings, under equity accounting. This is a big slice of BP's total earnings.

So you are saying that it is actually nonsense and they should have been reporting only dividends received. Well I suppose with hindsight that's true, given what's happened. But if they had carried on in their normal way, they had a major influence there in Russia, which was more than just a passive investor interest. They had two seats on the board as well as a significant shareholding.

**AVC** I think one of the problems with the original equity accounting for associated companies standard was that there was no separate distinction of joint ventures. I think that FRS9 did a service by showing the different levels of connection with the investee. One of the things that I also think is quite important is the fact that in a controlled company, and also in a joint venture, the investor does have quite a lot of knowledge about what is going on inside the company. With associated companies, some of them were fiercely defensive of their own rights, and didn't disclose. Some major disasters occurred within those companies. And it was the investor that was then blamed, because, as David said, a big slice of their profits turned out not to be there. That's not just that they had refused to pay the dividend – it's that they had an internal scandal of which the investor was unaware.

### *Deferred tax*

**GM Thank you. With respect to FRS19 now, if the end result of providing for 'temporary' and 'timing' differences was so close, why did the ASB not go along with the international consensus?**

**GW** I don't think the 'temporary' and 'timing' differences were close anyway if you are referring to the difference between FRS19 (based on a timing difference approach) and the revised international standard (IAS12, which adopted the approach of the US standard, SFAS109), which used 'temporary differences'. You are talking about quantitative closeness at a particular moment in time. But conceptually they are miles apart. One approach (temporary difference) attributes the deferred tax liability (or asset) to the individual asset (or liability) in the balance sheet, claiming that the item's tax position (its future deductibility for tax purposes relative to its carrying amount) should be fully reflected in the deferred tax provision, leading to 'full provision', even when the item is unlikely to affect the entity's future tax bills. The other approach (timing difference, favoured by the ASB) regards the deferred tax position as arising from the difference between accounting profit and taxable profit in the profit and loss account. The two approaches lead to similar results in many cases, but some 'temporary' differences do not arise from 'timing' differences, and these do not give rise to future tax effects, so that providing for deferred tax seems to have no meaning in such cases. The ASB wished to avoid tax provisions for such items and developed the 'incremental liability' approach to justify this whilst adopting a standard (FRS19) which was otherwise largely harmonised with international practice.

I personally would prefer the flow through method to either of the IAS12 or the FRS19 approaches. This could be described as the 'no provision' method! It does not recognize deferred tax in the accounts. It reports the actual tax assessment for the current year as the tax charge in the accounts. Deferred items, such as the future increase in taxes likely to be incurred as a result of accelerated tax deductions in the current year, should be disclosed in supplementary notes. The deferred tax position of an entity depends on many uncertain factors, such as the future position of the entity (whether or when it makes future taxable profits) and the future tax system (future changes in rates and in the tax base), and these do not provide sufficient certainty to justify a deferred tax asset or liability consistent with the ASB's Statement of Principles.

I think the whole debate on deferred tax was confused because people didn't think clearly, right from the start, what it is that we are providing for. Instead, our earlier UK standards were pragmatic reactions to events. The reason for the then existing standard in the UK, SSAP15, was that we had got to a situation where we gave such generous capital allowances, with rollovers and things, that there were lots of entities that were unlikely ever to pay the extra tax that was being deferred under the previous full provision approach. So it was being deferred forever. So the UK had adopted the partial provision method in SSAP15, which was more consistent with a timing difference approach, although the standard did not articulate that very clearly. In developing FRS19, we were trying to harmonise with an emerging international consensus which was based on the temporary difference approach, so that SSAP15 was no longer viable. We had to compromise by adopting a standard which preserved our self-respect by not providing for unrealistic 'temporary differences' (justifying this by the 'incremental liability' approach), whilst trying to be as consistent as possible with the international consensus.

**AVC** I would just say that I think that the Americans were reacting to the idea that there were only two things in life, and one of them is taxes. So they wanted to see the whole of the accounts through the lens of ultimate taxes. And that is, as Geoff says, a completely different attitude, and one that we didn't accept.

**DPT** Just on that, I agree with Geoff on flow through. I think we both probably agree to a modified flow through, which would be not just the tax paid but also that related to gains shown in revenue and which would be paid in the next accounting period. If, for example, you brought in some accrued dividends that you received you would provide the tax due on that too. So it's like a minor change. But it's not the system that we ended up with. I used to say, I remember, at the time that what we should probably do in accounting is take the deferred tax provision, the goodwill figure, and the provision for pensions and net them together, then we'd only have one damn silly figure in the balance sheet instead of three! But it was an issue where we had a major argument with the Americans at the IASC. I was put on the IASC when they had already issued the exposure draft and I came in as they were finalising the standard. Jim Leisenring and I had a huge row which lasted over an hour – well, a full and frank debate I suppose you'd diplomatically call it or as Accountancy Age (25/4/96) put it "blood and feathers were flying…insiders said they had seen nothing like it for years". We both enjoyed being very rude about the other's view and it was exactly on the point that Allan has just made about the Americans – saying they were looking at it through the tax prism. I thought it was absolutely ridiculous. I thought their view was contrary to the Statement of Principles. Where was the obligation? You ought to have no realistic alternative but to pay – we were very precise on that with provisioning. Yet, for example, with revaluations there's no tax involved in that at all. And similarly with unremitted earnings from overseas subsidiaries. If you don't remit them, then there's no tax, ever. And it's these sorts of things where I just felt it was breaking with the Principles – that's why we had the big row at IASC. I'm sorry we ended up with the standard we did.

**GW** It would have been best to deal with deferred tax by disclosure actually: flow through plus disclosure. The trouble with deferred tax provisions is that future tax rates and regimes aren't set yet and future taxable profits are not yet earned. It doesn't meet the definition of a liability; the measurability and certainty are not there.

### *Financial instruments*

**GM So shall we move on? The ASB never completed a standard on financial instrument measurement and hedging. Why not? How did the Joint Working Group (JWG) advance the project?**

**AVC** Well the ASB knew from the start, when it issued a discussion paper on the subject in 1996, that the work would take some time. It didn't propose to move swiftly to a regime where all financial instruments were recognized and measured at fair value. In fact, what happened was that the whole structure of setting accounting standards changed between 1996 and 2000 when the document came out. And the JWG was required to finish its document by the end of 2000, which it did. But that may also have led to some of the opposition – the very fierce opposition that it faced. I think that the genesis of the JWG was that every time there were proposals on financial instruments, the standard answer was, "It's too difficult, we can't do it, there are no clear values". And the JWG was set up in order to answer those points – to assert that it was a workable possibility; and to show in some detail how it could work.

The main proposals of the Group were:

- all financial instruments should be measured at fair value;
- all derivatives had to be on balance sheet.
- There could be no hedge accounting of future transactions, for example, where an English company intending to buy a German machine buys the necessary currency and defers any subsequent gain or loss to be incorporated into the cost of the machine at the point when the purchase is made, and
- all gains and losses on financial instruments had to go to the income statement.

The above recognition and measurement requirements were supplemented by disclosure requirements, especially:

- a description of each of the financial risks that was significant to an enterprise in the reporting period and the enterprise's objectives and policies for managing those risks;
- information about the balance sheet risk positions and financial performance effects for each of these significant risks; and
- information about the methods and key assumptions used to estimate the fair value of financial instruments.

One of the useful things that it did was to set out a hierarchy of how to determine fair value. You first of all had to take the market value if there was a market value for the same instrument. The next level was – if there was a market value for something similar, you used that, with adjustments for the difference between that item and yours. Then the third – and many opponents wanted that to be second – was that you used a valuation model that was consistent with accepted economic pricing methodologies and using estimates and assumptions that market participants would use. So it was quite tightly defined there. And I think some of that has continued into IAS39, but I leave David and Geoff to opine on IAS39.

It also looked at special circumstances – for instance, securitisations, which we had already dealt with in FRS5; stock lending, which came to the curious conclusion that the stock didn't remain yours; and unusually large holdings, where it said you cannot discount the price because of a large holding. It made the point that if you had an instrument where there were associated intangibles, those were not part of the measurement of the instrument. For instance, demand deposits of banks or credit card receivables had quite a lot of intangibles because the seller would expect to be paid for the benefit of future business that would come from operating those bank deposits or other receivables.

Of the 284 responses, 75% were opposed; and two-thirds of those that were opposed came from, not surprisingly, preparers, particularly, of course, the banks. One of the remarkable things was that, whereas normally when an issue comes up in successive consultations, there is some shift of opinion, on these proposals there was no such shift. It was the same arguments, no new views were offered. The strongest opposition came from the banks. The investment banks were happy with it, and the retail banks were not. I can understand why the retail banks would have been so anti because their whole asset management and control of their business was being turned upside down. The essential business of a retail bank is to match, and sometimes intentionally mismatch, the maturities of the deposits that they have got against the instruments that they invest in. And they managed that by looking specifically at the extent of mismatching. If we had put in the volatility of market values and asked them to manage on that, they would lose control because that had nothing to do with the relatively stable average maturity of the deposits. It's true it would reflect it, but it would reflect it with a lot of other factors thrown in which they didn't actually need. And so management of their deposits would pretty well collapse and have to be reconstructed on a completely different basis.

Now I think the draft never addressed that point properly. I think it concentrated on saying that all these things were possible. You know, when they were intentionally mismatching, they could control that to a certain extent by the positions they took in the market. But that didn't mean that the whole deposit book had to be valued on that basis. So I did have some sympathy, and I think the fact that we didn't address it in the JWG led to more hostility than we need have had. I think the JWG was quite clear in its principles and didn't want to enter into that sort of detailed discussion.

**DPT** I remember telling the Chairman of the JWG, Alex Milburn, when I had been appointed Chairman-elect of the IASB, that if he thought he was going to hand that document over to me and I was going to make that the first publication of the IASB, he was completely mistaken. It was going to go on the shelf. He had to publish before we started because it was like the goodwill debate: at ASB we deliberately did not tackle goodwill first. If we had to try to tackle financial instruments first, IASB would never have got off the ground. It was exactly the same sort of situation.

Going back to our own discussion paper, which wasn't dissimilar from that of the JWG, derivatives can completely transform a situation – the performance/risk profile, etc. of a company – and it wasn't apparent within the accounting framework we had then. We had a complete mixture of values. We used current value for trading investments and we had current asset investments at the lower of cost and value, fixed asset investments were written down if there was a permanent diminution. It was a mess. And the mixed attribute system – it just meant that if we kept that, and used current values for derivatives, we had to get into hedge accounting. That is horribly complicated. What do you do with the gains and losses in these hedging derivatives? Where do you put them if they don't put them in the income statement because the instrument they were hedging wasn't measured at fair value? It was a mess – chaotic and hugely controversial. It was quite clear that historical cost wasn't suitable for most financial instruments. First, entities could cherry pick. If their financial instruments were valued at historical cost they could choose what profit they wanted by selling at a moment of their choosing. Secondly, almost all derivatives had no cost – it was a contract – so the initial cost was nil. The derivatives were completely invisible. A mixed attribute system just didn't work: it had to be current value. And that's what we came out within the discussion paper. We believed that financial instruments should be at fair value – all financial instruments. And we should not have hedge accounting – exactly the same as the JWG. To show what happens if you don't do that, you just have to look at IAS39. I used to say that if you understood it you hadn't read it properly. It was a nightmare. And we were absolutely castigated for that and it wasn't an IASB standard – we had inherited it from IASC. The French banks loathed it. The British banks weren't much better. In fact, I remember my "farewell from the ASB" dinner that the British Banking Association threw for me. Instead of a speech by the Chairman of the Bankers politely saying, what a great job we'd done, etc., he launched an attack on financial instruments at current values. So my gracious speech in return ended up being thrown away and we ended up in a complete brawl at the top table. But it was indicative of what was going to happen. The French banks even lobbied their President. And Chirac in 2003 wrote to the Chairman of the European Commission saying that these current value standards would have dire consequences for financial stability. In 2008, in the middle of the financial crisis, you got Sarkozy calling a meeting of the G8, and the G8 agreed that the accounting rules had got to change, so that people could shift out of current values down to historical cost. I used to be asked around this time, 'How do you feel about the French?' I had a standard response. "Well, if I go to France I am treated like a king – and you know how the French treat their kings!" It was a constant fight. So you can realise why I did not start off IASB with that particular issue. It was just not on.

**GW** Yes. On the other hand that shows also why something did need to be done. I mean we did eventually have the financial crisis. And there was a vast increase over that period in the amount and variety of derivatives actually created. The banks put themselves at risk terribly, so they weren't exactly angels. I can understand them being disturbed by the prospect of changing their well-established practices and so on. But the world was changing, and the practices that were needed were probably changing. And bringing about change in that environment of course is extremely difficult. But I don't think the IASB was on the wrong track there, or the JWG before them. They were genuinely, honestly, trying to think about how to deal with these things. And certainly the work the ASB did, I was very impressed by – notably the work that Sandra Thompson did in the early days; all those discussions we had about hedge accounting. Finance directors got engaged and auditors got engaged. There was a real problem there and we were really trying to solve it. Of course, potential solutions looked a bit frightening to people, and they don't like change. And the fact that there wasn't a simple solution, an obvious solution, made it all the more difficult. We didn't have an easy solution to give them.

### *Leasing*

**GM Shall we turn to leasing?**

**The proposals of the leasing discussion paper seem to follow directly from the Statement of Principles. Why was this project so controversial when similar projects based on the Statement (such as provisions) had been generally accepted?**

**GW** There is a very straightforward answer to this, in some ways – that with leasing there was a very powerful lobby there, a very well-established group of people making money out of this, and on both sides of the market (Dissanaike et al., 2022). Preparers of accounts and other people who were lessees not only got a decent form of finance here, they got a very decent method of accounting for it if they wanted to improve their gearing ratios, and so on. And it was to some extent discretionary as well. If they wanted to show what a powerful company they were and what great assets they had, they went for finance leasing. And so it gave them nice options. And on the other side, there was the leasing industry, which, of course, was big money. Some of them were specialised in that area: obviously their business was potentially being undercut by this standard because if we changed things so that operating leases were treated the same as finance leases, the accounting advantages weren't there. People might go for other forms of finance, and they'd lose their business entirely. So there was well-established practice there – not necessarily good practice – but nice options that some people liked. And, of course, there wasn't a major scandal to drive it immediately. There was bad accounting perhaps, but not a major scandal.

David is very fond of this story about Ron Dearing saying that David would go across a motorway for a fight. But, of course, the role of Ron Dearing in relation to David, and later Sidney Lipworth (they were wise old heads) – they were there to restrain David from going across the motorway for a fight he was going to lose. And I think battles with the leasing industry at the early stages were a fight he was going to lose. And I'm sure Ron had a quiet word – or Sid, or whoever it was at the time – and said, you know, just leave it a bit till you've had a few victories, and they are a bit more scared of you, and your reputation is better established.

**DPT** It was quite funny. One of the lines that I always used to use was that one of my ambitions before I died was to fly in an aeroplane that was actually on an airline's balance sheet. And I remember being in Australia, and the CFO of Qantas was quoted as saying he was checking my travel schedule to make sure they could put one of the few aeroplanes they actually owned on my flight so that I wouldn't ever again be able to use that line.

I gave a talk in 2008 and stated that at that time the US had 18 standards dealing with some form of leasing, 11 FASB Technical Bulletins on the same subject, and 32 Emerging Issue Taskforce Issues on leasing, and almost nothing on balance sheet. It just wasn't there. And I remember when we were trying to get Principles-based standards, and the Big Six, I think it was then, asked if I could go to their senior partners' meeting (this was when IASB had just started) and give them an example of one. So Trish O'Malley and I went and we gave them a four-page standard on leasing. And they were horrified. It said show the liability incurred by signing the lease contract and from which you can't escape, and the rights to the asset you have obtained thereby. That basically was the standard. And we had a bit on renewal options and that sort of thing. Look at the size of the standard that came out. But the thing I thought was really interesting was a paper quoted by the FT written by Vivien Beattie et al. (2000). They said that on average the unrecorded liability on leases represented 39% of long-term debt; while the unrecorded asset was 6% of total assets. Their conclusion was: "the magnitude of the change astonished us, with gearing rising from 20% to 72%, an increase of 260%." So you can understand why any leasing standard was fought: it was a huge off balance sheet device. This was why we felt we had to do something about it.

### *Share-based payments*

**GM Why did the share-based payment proposals arouse such heated debate?**

**DPT** Evidence from Credit Suisse First Boston in the year 2000, looking at the S&P500 showed that the latter were worried about the dilution effect of issuing share options. Of the companies CSFB surveyed, 69% had repurchased shares to try to avoid this dilution effect. And of the 69%, each spent an average of $479 million buying back these shares presumably to avoid the dilution effect of the options (Credit Suisse First Boston, 2001). Other research around the same time (National Center for Employee Ownership) showed that of the options that were issued 75% of them went to the top five executives of the companies, 15% to the next 50 executives, and all the other employees shared 10%. Now you can't quite conflate these two points about the amount that's been repurchased with the destinations of these options. But, looking at it, if you take 75%, which is the share of the senior executives of that $479mn, then divide by 5, you get a figure of about $72 million each, and that's a lot of value that's being given to these people. So you can understand why we had these scandals like Enron, where management were desperately trying to keep the share prices up – and obviously the value of their options up (National Center for Employee Ownership, 2002). The other point brought out by the analysts was that shareholders were ceding an ownership stake in the company. In other words, management was taking over the company by stealth. They mention that $71 billion fair value of options in the information technology sector amounted to a transfer of wealth roughly equivalent to the year-end capitalisation of PepsiCo (*Analysts Accounting Observer*, 2001). If that company had changed ownership, it would have been big news, whereas this was being done by stealth – people did not realise what was happening underneath. The fact was that the value of issued options wasn't being charged in the accounts. The American standard allowed either expensing the value or disclosing it. Among the S&P 500 only two companies charged the value of options given as an expense. Analysts, using the methodology of the US standard and referring to the S&P 500, estimated that, as a result of not expensing the value of the options granted, in 1999 earnings were overstated by 6%; it was 9% in year 2000 and 31% in 2001 (earnings were lower in 2001). The amount of the 2001 overstatement was nearly $47 billion. The main group that took the options, unsurprisingly, was the information technology sector. In 2000 the analysts reckoned the earnings of these companies were 30% overstated (25% in 2001) (*Analysts Accounting Observer*, 2002) because options weren't charged. And the analysts commented, "small wonder that these firms were at the forefront of the opposition to the FASB's proposals to book the expense". It went on to say, "The wars that have been fought between the FASB and the corporate sector are usually framed as disputes about the right accounting. Nothing could be further from the truth: these are battles over keeping at bay any effective governance by investors. Recognising stock comp. expense in the income statement would cause investors to more quickly question abusive compensation structures that affect their interests". And here's a classic example of stewardship, what financial reporting is used for. FASB always argued that it was really only about information for decision-making; but here's an obvious stewardship example.

The basic argument used against expensing was the fact that there was no cost to the company –therefore there shouldn't be a charge. We refuted that.

The employees provided services in return for options. If you paid them cash, or had given them shares and let them sell the shares, you'd have recorded that. An option is simply a variant of an issue of shares. And if every time you issued shares there was no cost, then how would we account for business combinations, if shares are worth nothing! The other argument, of course, is that if they are worth nothing, why don't you give them to everybody, and we'll all get rich!

A second argument is that earnings per share are hit twice. Of course it is: you increase the number of shares and basically you are getting a service. Well, the service should be charged. And if you've issued shares for cash, and the cash wasn't used to generate earnings to the same level as existing earnings levels, earnings per share would fall. And a similar effect occurs if the resources an entity received were not being used entirely to generate earnings to the same level as before, again it would affect performance. So issuing options is obviously going to affect both the denominator and the numerator of earnings per share.

And finally the argument was that there'd be adverse economic consequences. Well, there would be for the senior executives! People would see exactly what they were getting! (See Figure 9.1.)

*Figure 9.1* Cartoon published by the *Financial Times* on 3 July 2000 during the controversy over share option remuneration for executives, by kind permission of the artist Nick Baker and the *Financial Times*.

Warren Buffett was frequently quoted as saying:

> If share options are not remuneration, what are they?
> If remuneration is not an expense, what is it?
> And if expenses don't go to the profit and loss account, where do they go?

**AVC** Did SEC take sides on this? I would have thought that it would have been in their interest to have that standard.

**GW** I remember the SEC wasn't entirely enthusiastic in its support, and that was probably because the SEC itself is politically appointed, and there were strong lobbies of Congress by the financial executives and similar pressure groups against expensing stock options. I remember even Congressman Oxley, of Sarbanes-Oxley fame, addressing the IASB and warning us against intervening in the issue.

**DPT** Arthur Levitt was the SEC Chairman. He is reported as having said later that was the biggest mistake he made. He repented afterwards: he shouldn't have told FASB not to press the expensing of stock options too hard.

### *Internationalisation*

**GM As I've listened to your discussions in earlier chapters of the ASB's work in the 1990s, I've been struck by the evolution over the decade from a largely domestic, UK perspective to an international one. With the earlier standards, the challenge was to persuade the main UK interest groups – auditors, finance directors, analysts, ... In the later discussions, alignment with different national and international standard-setters became a major concern. This is not surprising given that the 1990s were a period of rapid corporate and financial globalisation. But did you regret the loss of your coherent constituency – most of the major players within a mile or two of your office; and did the loss of autonomy lead to less satisfying standards?**

**AVC** I agree very much with the trend that you've detected there. When the Dearing Committee was first discussing what would be the role of the ASB, an early draft suggested that the international aspect was important because if we had good standards this would provide opportunities for British accountants to gain clients abroad. I urged the influential member of the Committee whom I was assisting to make the point that the international aspect was a great deal more than that. The next draft looked very different. The UK had always taken a lead internationally. If you think about it, IASC was founded by Sir Henry Benson, Lord Benson as he later became. In 1966 he went to the leaders of the US and the Canadian institutes and persuaded them to participate in an informal group, the Accountants International

Study Group (AISG), that would examine differences between accounting practices in their three countries and publish their findings. Six years later, after 20 publications by the AISG, he persuaded the executive committees of the accounting institutes in those three countries that there needed to be a more broadly based international body that would set 'basic' international accounting standards. And he was the one who set up the IASC, originally with members representing nine countries, though a further two were soon added and more later. It is interesting to note the similarity between the AISG's role in preparing the ground for the IASC and that of the G4+1 some 30 years later in doing the same for the IASB.

From the early '70s ASC, senior accountants, and multinational businesses in the UK began to press for harmonisation of accounting worldwide. The OECD held a special meeting of standard-setting bodies on that subject in 1985. And I remember Don Kirk, who was the chairman of the FASB, came to that meeting and said, "I don't know what harmonization means". What he wanted was convergence, and that indeed was a sensible line to take, but it was beyond the ability at that time to talk about convergence, because that would have meant convergence with US standards; and nobody was prepared to give way on that at that point. But the SEC was also taking an interest in bringing together standards, and it made an offer that, if IASC was prepared to improve its standards, the SEC would allow International Accounting Standards instead of US Standards to be used as the basis for the reconciliation required from a foreign company's original financial statements. Now the SEC's requirement was not only a reconciliation of key items in your financial statements to US Standards; it also required you to draw up your original financial statements on the basis of a coherent set of standards. If International Standards were used for those financial statements, the SEC would accept them without the need for a reconciliation. But they dangled this carrot for years and years, giving way not an inch. And only when the ASB had developed its own standards, and IASC had embarked on a thoroughgoing reform of its standards moving far away from Benson's idea of 'basic' standards, that the SEC began to take an interest in creating IASB. David will know much more about that than I, so I won't attempt to describe it.

So ASB was, I think, very instrumental in bringing about the birth of IASB, and played an important role. The IASB was also fortunate in securing the services of four outstanding ASB staff members, namely, Joan Brown, Kimberley Crook, Anne McGeachin, and Sandra Thompson, who took over the important projects of service concession arrangements (for the Interpretations Committee), share options, pensions, and financial instruments respectively. David has to answer your question whether it was easier in IASB or ASB. It's true that ASB had fertile ground. It was set up at exactly the right moment when things couldn't get much worse. And there was a general recognition – with quite a push from the more high-minded finance directors, to change things. I think it was because British accounting before ASB came along had sunk to such low esteem internationally that it would have been very difficult for us to have had a strong influence on International Standards, as they subsequently turned out to be. The ASB, by getting its own house in order first, but continuing to keep good links with others, managed with them to launch the IASB. The ASB was chivvying the IASC to improve its act and then participated in getting IASB launched.

## GM David, Geoff – Anything to add?

**DPT** We didn't set out to get rid of the ASB. We set out to bring standards together worldwide. That's why we picked the big issues with the G4+1 and did them together. That raised the obvious question of why should standards be different, why should accounting in America, Australia, Europe, etc. get different answers for exactly the same transaction? And the coordinating body, IASC on its own hadn't the resources to bring us together, which led to the IASB. What I regretted was, there was perhaps too strong a North American influence on IASB – brilliant technical accountants but understandably wedded to the North American style of standard-setting. Consequently, the standards moved to a sort of American format. We managed early on – you will remember, Geoff – to kill the notion that every standard should have a great list of questions and answers. We flatly refused, on the basis that every one of those was going to be a rule. But it was just the detail they poured into it. The ASB standards are much shorter; they are clear; they don't go into the depths that the IFRS went into. I feel bad about that. We just hadn't the votes to stop that sort of thing happening. It was a shame, but what I thought was really bad occurred in 2012. ASB was abolished, and taken over by the Accounting Council or something – run by the FRC itself. It wasn't independent anymore. It didn't feed into IASB the way that other countries did. So the British influence on international standards diminished rapidly. And that was a real shame. The ASB had been a major force on the IASC. I felt that the informed, independent British voice was silenced. I argued against it at the time, with the Chairman of the FRC – fairly vigorously, I don't think she liked the comments I made. But it's turned out that the UK has now no influence.

**GW** Obviously I saw all this happening. And I remember vividly that we had an ASB Away Day in June 2000 – the year of the Lisbon agreement. We had this Away Day somewhere up the Thames Valley. And David told us then that, following up on the Lisbon Agreement by the Council of Ministers in March that year, the European Commission was about to publish its proposal that all publicly traded Community companies prepare their consolidated financial statements in accordance with one single set of accounting standards, namely International Accounting Standards (IAS), at the latest by 2005. That, of course, included the UK, which was committed to following EU regulations. I thought this meant the ASB was finished. I remember Ken Wild and I were both the ones who were distraught about this. I don't know why us two.

It was obvious once Europe had said that for listed companies we were going to have to do international standards, and they gave a date which they ultimately kept to, then, once that was done, setting standards for big companies was in the hands of another body, and the ASB's influence would diminish enormously. The standards that would follow for small companies would be cut-down versions of the big ones: there wasn't going to be a huge, striking conceptual difference. We lost the battle for survival at that stage. In a way, if you look at the sweep of history, it's an inevitable development – deeply unpleasant but nevertheless inevitable. The globalisation of markets and internationalisation of companies means that they do want to speak a common international language, and that can't be done by a standard-setting body based solely on the UK. We thought, and I still think, that for UK purposes we did an excellent job producing standards that met our situation. As David has said, the only problem with the thing was that we had to hand over to the new dominant commercial nation in the world – the US – and we were going to have to put up with a lot of standards that accept their conditions. I remember those incredibly detailed interpretations of IAS39, with such things as "regular way transactions", and all these things the Americans do. There was mind-bending detail and their parochial nature reflected the way Americans think and do business.

I didn't care for the level of detail involved in dealing specifically with such things as regular way transactions. But that was the way history took us, and the environment took us, being part of an international community took us. It's easy to look at individuals and times and say "if only I'd done this and that", but I'm afraid it's the inevitable course of history. I agree about the UK recently: they haven't done the best they could with the ASB. But I was the IASB's representative on the ASB in the early years, when there was supposed to be a special 'liaison' relationship with some national standard-setters, including the ASB. And I was supposed to be the ASB's medium for this. And I had an awkward time working with Mary Keegan (David's successor as ASB Chair) because Mary, who I sympathised with, wanted to set standards for the UK. And she saw that she couldn't do it direct (the UK, having handed authority to the IASB, subject to adoption of individual IFRSs by the EU) so she wanted to influence the IASB. She hoped that I might act as her agent to go to the IASB and tell them what to do. Well, that was actually not on. First of all, I didn't want to be anybody's agent: IASB Board members were supposed to be independent, not delegates. But secondly, even if I had wanted to be (and I did support most of the ASB's views), I couldn't have gone to the IASB and told them what to do – I was one of a Board of fourteen members who all needed persuasion. And there was a big American bloc, which David referred to. It was inevitable: they were paying for it. They were the people who saw the real benefit of world markets because they were selling into them all. They were the most deeply involved in world markets and were putting the greatest resources into accounting standard-setting.

But it wasn't a comfortable job being the representative of the IASB to the ASB, because I liked the ASB, I liked what they were doing. I understood Mary's position. But it wasn't my job to represent her; it was my job to exchange information and tell her what the IASB's thinking was. And I'd go back and tell the IASB what the ASB's thinking was, and most of them were not at all interested, I can assure you. That was the way it turned out. And the ASB had eventually to collapse. I didn't like the subsequent reforms of the FRC any more than David did. I don't approve of the way the FRC has changed or of this proposed new regulator which will replace it. But that's a separate issue because that's about the whole of corporate governance, it's not just about accounting. Accounting is really in the hands of the IASB, not the FRC now. The FRC is a disempowered body from an accounting standards point of view. From the auditing and corporate governance points of view, it still has an important role, actually. But that's another story.

**GM Thank you.**

## Unfinished business

**GM So shall we go around each of you asking which business unfinished at the end of your ASB spell do you most wish you had brought to completion?**

**DPT** First, not getting rid of associates, which we've discussed already.

Second, I would really have liked to finish the revision of FRS3 which was one of our best standards. But the exposure draft we issued at the end of our first ten years would have improved it. It basically combined the statement of recognized gains and losses and the profit and loss account into a single statement with three categories: operating, financing and treasury, and other gains and losses. The other gains and losses were those on assets and liabilities held for the long term in order to carry out the activities of the business, rather than being there to gain from their changes in value. These gains would be revaluations, gains, and losses on disposal of assets, actuarial gains and losses from FRS17, gains and losses on the disposal of continuing businesses, that sort of thing. The Board was very clear about having a holding/non-holding distinction. Some sorts of holding gains such as trading gains would go through operating, but most of the holding gains would go into the other gains and losses. The Board agreed it wasn't helpful to mix operating results with gains and losses arising from long-term items held for operating and financing purposes because such gains and losses, essentially reflected the length of time that the item happens to be held and the price changes that have taken place while you've held it. Under historical cost, such gains and losses were recognised only in the year of disposal and represented accumulated gains from previous years. So the Board therefore decided 'other gains and losses' should pick up all these things to avoid, if you like, contaminating the operating section. It banned recycling, which we've discussed before. The argument there was that gains and losses shown in the performance statement under the principles in the Statement of Principles should only appear once, and once recognized, that was it – they shouldn't be transferred from one part of the statement to the other in a later period. And transactions with owners should not appear in that statement: there should be a reconciliation of ownership interests as a separate statement. Respondents were very supportive. But could we get IASB to buy into it? We just couldn't do it. But I still think that's the way accounting should go.

**GM Allan, do you have your 'regrets'?**

**AVC** I'm not sure that I was as keen as David on having it all in one statement. But the principles that he's just set out, I am fully behind.

I think the one that I particularly wanted to see was share-based payments. And that in the end came about. I'm very pleased with that. It had long annoyed me that the figment of 'no cost' was allowed to persist for so long. I think I would leave it at that.

### GM Geoff?

**GW** I agree with David and Allan about FRS3. You know I'm very keen on FRS3, and I would have liked to see it develop in the light of experience and so on. So that's very straightforward. I agree with Allan too on share-based payments. It was such an obvious – intellectually – quick kill. You can see very easily what you ought to do about it, there's no struggle there. Of course, it's not politically a quick kill at all. That's why we couldn't do it as easily as that. We might have done it a bit better than the IASB if we had done it though. I was always a bit sad about the IASB's effort. They made it very complicated and they were inconsistent in using grant date rather than vesting date for measuring employee options.

The other thing that I think we lost but we couldn't have turned into a standard in time was the groundwork we did on financial instruments, particularly the work Sandra Thompson did. I was very impressed by the progress we were making there and I think if the ASB had been put in charge of the IASB project, they might have produced a much better standard on financial instruments. But that would have taken quite a long time – it's a big project.

So my two would be FRS3 and share-based payments.

### Notes

1 The Discussion Draft of the Statement of Principles chapter on Presentation, published in tandem with the first proposals on restructuring the profit and loss account, was discussed in Chapter 3 of this book.

2 The ASB's Statement of Principles deserves a study in itself, both because in a number of aspects it went beyond the Concepts Statements of the FASB and the IASC's Framework, which derived from them, and because a number of its principles were showing their effectiveness in practice even as it was being developed. Unfortunately, such a study is beyond the scope of this book. Future researchers, however, may find useful insights in a comparison of the points of difference between the ASB's Statement and the FASB/IASC equivalents, including:

- stewardship named by the ASB as one of the objectives of financial statements;
- a Reporting Entity chapter in the ASB's Statement that distinguishes direct from indirect control of an entity and examines the various forms of control; supplemented by a chapter on Accounting for interests in other entities;
- a fuller treatment of measurement than in the IASC Framework, including a decision tree for determining which basis to use for which purpose and guidance on the use of discounting.

3 A method of accounting that brings an investment into its investor's financial statements initially at its cost, identifying any goodwill arising. The balance sheet carrying amount of the investment is adjusted in each period by the investor's share of the results of its investee less any amortisation or write off for Goodwill, the investor's share of any relevant gains or losses and any other changes in the [investor's] investee's net assets, including distributions to its owners, for example by dividend. The investor's share of its investee's results is recognised in the investor's profit and loss account.

4 This treatment differed from the international equivalent, IAS31, which required proportional consolidation for such arrangements. The ASB found that proportional consolidation could overstate the reporting entity's interest in the arrangement, in particular by representing a share of its cash flows as its own.

5 The Board did not propose that all gains and losses on financial instruments should be reported in the profit and loss account. For example, gains and losses, both realised and unrealised, on fixed rate borrowings were to be reported in the Statement of Total Recognised Gains and Losses.

6 The standard setters involved were from Australia, Canada, France, Germany, Japan, New Zealand, the UK and the US, and representatives of the Nordic Federation of Public Accountants and the IASC.

7 Formed initially in 1992, the founding G4 members were: the Australian Accounting Standards Board; the Canadian Accounting Standards Board; the UK Accounting Standards Board; the United States Financial Accounting Standards Board + (as an observer) the International Accounting Standards Committee. The New Zealand Financial Reporting Standards Board joined the Group in 1996. For a report on the G4+1's activities during its nine years of existence, see Street (2005).

8 For example, by 2021 the Leasing and Finance Association's Monthly Leasing and Finance Index was reported to be 'based on a cross section of the $900 billion equipment finance sector'.

9 SSAP21 stated that a lease was presumed to be a finance lease if, at the outset, the present value of the minimum lease payments -discounted at the interest rate implicit in the lease – amounted to substantially all of the fair value of the leased asset. The standard indicated that "substantially all" was normally 90% or more.

10 FASB's disclosure option was chosen by virtually all publicly traded companies, only two choosing to expense the cost of the options.

## References

### *Books and articles*

*Analysts Accounting Observer.* (2001). July 31, 2001.

*Analysts Accounting Observer.* (2002). July 27, 2002.

Beattie, V., Edwards, K. and Goodacre, A., (2000). (Stirling University) quoted by Michael Peel, *Financial Times*, 22 February, 2000.

Camfferman, K. and Zeff, S. (2007). *Financial Reporting and Global Capital Markets*, Oxford: OUP, p.361.

Credit Suisse First Boston. (2001). *Stock Compensation: A Primer*, 27 November 2001.

Dissanaike, G., Jayasekera, R. and Meeks, G. (2022). Why do unsuccessful companies survive? US airlines, aircraft leasing, and GE, 2000–2008, *Business History Review*.

Lee, T. and Tweedie, D. (1977). *The Private Shareholder and the Corporate Report*, London: ICAEW.

McGregor, W. (1996). Accounting for Leases: A New Approach, AASB, AcSB, IASC, FRSB, ASB, FASB.

National Center for Employee Ownership. (2002). Distribution of US stock options: Outstanding options as of 2000, quoted in the *International Herald Tribune*, July 19, 2002.

Solomons, D. (1989). *Guidelines for Reporting Standards*, London: ICAEW.

Street, D. (2005). *Inside G4+1: The Working Group's Role in the Evolution of the International Accounting Standard Setting Process*, London: ICAEW.

### *Standard setters' publications*

APB18 (1971). *The Equity Method of Accounting for Investments in Common Stock*, APB.

FAS109 (1992). *Accounting for Income Taxes, FASB.*

FRS1 (1991, Revised 1996). *Cash Flow Statements*, ASB.

FRS3 (1992). *Reporting Financial Performance*, ASB.

FRS5 (1994). *Reporting the Substance of Transactions*, ASB.

FRS6 (1994). *Acquisitions and Mergers*, ASB.

FRS9 (1997). *Associates and Joint Ventures*, ASB.

FRS12 (1998). *Provisions, Contingent Liabilities and Contingent Assets*, ASB.

FRS13 (1998). *Derivatives and Other Financial Instruments: Disclosures*, ASB.

FRS17 (2000). *Retirement Benefits*, ASB.

FRS18 (2000). *Accounting Policies*, ASB.

FRS19 (2000). *Deferred Tax*, ASB.

FRSSE (1997). *The Financial Reporting Standard for Smaller Entities*, ASB.

IAS12 (revised 1996). *Income Taxes*, IASC.

IAS37 (1998). *Provisions, Contingent Liabilities and Contingent Assets*, IASC.

IAS39 (1998). *Financial Instruments: Recognition and Measurement*, IASC.

IFRS2 (2004). *Share-based Payment*, IASB.

IFRS3 (2004). *Business Combinations*, IASB.

IFRS16 (2016). *Leases*, IASB.

SFAS109 (1992). *Accounting for Income Taxes*, FASB.

SFAS123 (1995). *Share-based Payment*, FASB.

SSAP1 (1971, revised 1974 & 1982) *Accounting for Associated Companies*, ICAEW.

SSAP2 (1971). *Disclosure of Accounting Policies*, ICAEW.

SSAP15 (1978, revised 1985). *Accounting for Deferred Tax*, ASC.

SSAP21 (1984). *Accounting for Leases and Hire Purchase Contracts*, ASC.

*Statement of Principles* (1999), ASB.

# Appendix: ASB's major projects

## Projects stemming from ASB's overall plan as relating to its Statement of Principles

| *Statement of principles* | *Date* | *FRS or other documents* | *Rationale* |
|---|---|---|---|
| ***Elements*** | | | |
| Performance | 1993 | FRS3 | Creation of Statement of Total Recognised Gains and Losses (STRGL) |
| | 2000 | FRED22 | Proposes single statement of performance incorporating both P&L account and STRGL |
| Equity v Liabilities | 1993 | FRS4 | Resolved misuse of hybrid instruments |
| | 2000 | DP Share-based payments | Gave recognition & measurement principles |
| Liabilities | 1994 | FRS5 | Previously off-balance sheet transactions brought on balance sheet by applying definition of Liability |
| | 1994<br>1998 | FRS7<br>& FRS8 | Excess or under recognition of liabilities constrained |
| | 1998 | FRS12 | Discounting principles specified |
| | 1999 | DP Leases – a new approach | Gave new principles to recognise lease liabilities |
| | 2000 | FRS17 | Pension reporting started from Balance Sheet rather than P&L account (Current bond rates applied to discount pension liability) |
| | 2000 | FRS19 | Recognised deferred tax as a liability (a timing difference), not a valuation adjustment (a 'temporary' difference) |
| ***Recognition and measurement*** | | | |
| Assets | 1999 | FRS15 | Valuation and depreciation |
| | 1999 | DP Leases – a new approach | Gave new principles to recognise leased assets |
| | 2000 | FRS17 | MV valuation of pension scheme assets |

| | | | |
|---|---|---|---|
| Financial Instruments | 1996 | DP Derivatives and other financial instruments | Discussed measurement and hedge accounting principles |
| | 1998 | FRS13 | Though only dealing with Disclosures, this FRS was part of an ongoing project conducted internationally to improve on IAS32 and 39 |
| ***Reporting entity*** | | | |
| Presentation | 1996 | FRS1(revised) | New, improved information re cash flows |
| ***Interests in other entities*** | | | |
| Control | 1992 | FRS2 | Necessary part of Statement of Principles, though immediate reason for project was new UK legislation |
| Joint Control | 1997 | FRS9 | Regularised current practice by reference to principles<br>Required new, improved information and presentation re joint-venture entities |
| Associates | 1997 | FRS9 | Warned that an investor might have little influence over an associate |
| Business Combinations | 1994<br>1997<br>1998 | FRS6<br>FRS10<br>FRS11 | Little guidance from Statement of Principles but a necessary component of financial reporting |
| ***Qualitative characteristics*** | 2000 | FRS18 | Translated key concepts into accounting standards, superseding 'fundamental accounting concepts' of SSAP2 (1971) |

## Other projects

*Accounting Standards:*

FRS8 Related party disclosures (1995)
FRS14 Earnings per share (1998)
FRS16 Current tax (1999)
FRSSE Financial Reporting Standard for Smaller Entities (1997)

*Statements:*

Operating and financial review (1993)
Interim reports (1997)
Preliminary announcements (1998)
Year-end financial reports: improving communication (Discussion Paper 2000)

*Other Publications:*

Discounting in financial reporting (Working Paper 1997)

# 10 Review

*Geoff Meeks*

This book was foretold a quarter century ago when Whittington was interviewed by Accountancy Magazine (April 1997, p.21):

> ...if Professor Whittington has his way, Sir David will finally get a chance to unburden his feelings. "When we're sitting in the old folks' home, we want to have our chairs wheeled into the same room, and we'll get all the old ASB minutes out and ponder on the history of what happened in those 10 years or so. And we want to write it up – our view of what happened, what the problems were, what we did that we think was good. That's the thing to do when it's over, though, not now. But we must get our oar in before Ron [Paterson] does."

As it turns out, the Cook, Tweedie, Whittington trio are not in an old folks home but are hale, hearty, and as interested as ever in accounting standards all this time later. Also, as this write-up started just before the COVID pandemic, they have not been able to ponder together in the same room. But Zoom – unimagined 25 years ago – has allowed the next best meeting place.

Had they been in the old folks' home, they could have asked one of the carers to record their ponderings. I'm the substitute for that assistant – charged with recording and transcribing their words. As I now know those words well, they asked me to pull the strands of the book together in a sort of afterword. Since I was not involved with the ASB, I bring a different perspective. That is not to say that I am independent, neutral – without priors. I've always been sympathetic to forceful regulation of accounting. And also, 50 years ago, Tweedie, Whittington and I all joined the accounting department of Edinburgh University at the same time, and I soon came to admire their thinking, their energy, and their good humour. I only got to know Cook with this current project, but I soon learned that he is similarly impressive.

My bias is mitigated in this chapter by heavy reliance on independent contemporaneous assessments of the ASB's activities. This was a golden age for accounting commentary, with very high quality discussion of accounting problems and reforms by broadsheet journalists, in professional magazines, and in books. These contemporary sources have a further advantage:

DOI: 10.4324/9781003346920-10

it's sometimes difficult just from today's vantage point to recognise the full extent of ASB's contributions. Some abuses of accounting prominent at the time were so effectively curbed by the ASB that they have fallen out of discussion in modern accounting. Reformed practices which we now take for granted – treat as part of the natural order – were fiercely resisted at the time.

This chapter is not a summary of the previous nine chapters. It just highlights, with illustrations, some representative contributions by ASB to financial reporting – both shrewd firefighting within the inherited accounting model, and more fundamental innovations in the model. To convey the scale of the contributions, it is helpful to outline the resistance they had to overcome in securing their reforms – for example, from finance directors over goodwill, from some parts of the accounting profession nostalgic for the permissive 1980s, from libertarians hostile to any intervention in markets, from lawyers concerned with the letter of the law rather than the spirit of the true and fair view, from actuaries over the valuation of pension liabilities, or from government over off balance sheet financing. The chapter also touches on a topic of interest beyond accounting – how to make work an innovative model of 'self-regulation with statutory backing,'[1] something in between the self-regulation of the ASC, which preceded the ASB, and had in important respects failed, and pure state, top-down regulation, which some proposed at the time. On this topic, it would have been good to include in the discussion Ron Dearing, who designed this hybrid regulatory structure and helped build it. But sadly he is no longer with us.

Some of the commentary quoted below appears to identify the achievements of ASB as those of Tweedie alone: "...many see Sir David as the man who rescued the UK from the cancer of creative accounting", wrote one commentator (Financial Director, 1999). This is not how Tweedie sees it: he emphasises the collective effort of the ASB team. Bruce (1997) notes that alongside Tweedie's first mentor, David Flint, the distinguished Scottish accountant, "the second influence he would cite is Geoff Whittington... who was professor at Edinburgh University when Tweedie, freshly qualified, became a lecturer there". The two worked together continually over the years: a paper they published in 1990 spelled out an agenda for accounting reform much of which the ASB went on to enact. Their partnership continued with Whittington first the ASB's academic adviser and then a Board member. Then Financial Director (1999) emphasised a second partnership: "The double act of Sir David, as chairman and frontman, and Allan Cook, the technical director and back room guru, has been crucial". And this trio made the reform programme attract and retain highly expert and influential members of the Board, as well as talented and committed professional staff. Aware of the collective responsibility for the ASB, Tweedie objected to being named as first author of this book but was forced to yield to a majority vote of the authors. In any plaudits below directed at 'Tweedie' he would want you to understand a collective 'Cook, Tweedie and Whittington', or more widely the 'ASB'. Similarly, he would no doubt be willing to share less flattering descriptions such as a newspaper's headline: 'most hated accountant in Britain'![2]

## Firefighting

Tweedie and Whittington published in 1990 the lengthy article just mentioned in an academic journal (written before they joined the ASB), giving their account of the principal weaknesses in company accounts at that time. Later that year, three months from the start of the ASB, Whittington, and Cook were invited by ICAS and ICAEW to outline key challenges facing the Board. Their diagnosis corresponded quite closely with that emphasised by the highly respected analyst Terry Smith in his best-selling 1992 book for investors, Accounting for Growth. Smith (1992) illustrated what was, in his words, 'wrong with UK accounting' when the ASB was founded. He suggested the scale of misinformation in the accounts. He gave "examples of companies going bust in this recession which reported 'profits' in their last results and announcements and accounts…" And he went on "…much of the apparent growth in profits which had occurred in the 1980s was the result of accounting sleight of hand rather than genuine economic growth…" (pp.3, 4).

The deceitful devices enumerated by Smith were compliant with the law and with the prevailing, pre-ASB, standards. As Griffiths' early (1986) expose of creative accounting comments: 'the hallmark of [effective] creative accounting is that it does not involve fraud'. Such creative accounting is the analogue of tax avoidance, as contrasted with tax evasion. It attracts sophisticated professionals who frame the activity so that it conforms with the letter (but not the spirit) of the rules (Meeks and Meeks, 2020).

The materiality of the challenge presented by creative accounting to the functioning of financial markets is indicated by the size of the markets which were being misinformed. New issues (shares and loan stocks) by UK industrial and commercial companies were running at around 15 billion pounds a year in the nineties; the secondary market in existing shares was valued at around a trillion pounds; and the M&A market reached 30 billion pounds in some years in that decade (1990s prices; Meeks and Meeks, 2002).

Tweedie explained above that "The first standards were really anti-abuse and attacking the schemes." Chapters 3–5 have reviewed these early standards. By his second edition in 1996, Smith was able to write:

> The foundation of the ASB under Sir David Tweedie was a recognition that there was a great deal wrong with UK accounting. Tweedie has set about correcting this with an almost evangelical zeal. And he tells good jokes. It does not do full justice to his achievements simply to list its published standards. … FRS3 basically outlawed extraordinary items and thereby rendered Chapter 7 in the first edition redundant…all of the techniques described in the old chapters [in Smith's 1992 book] on Off

> Balance Sheet Finance and Convertibles with Put Options and AMPs have effectively been dealt with by FRS2, FRS4 and FRS5.
>
> ...There is little doubt that the ASB has achieved a great deal in making UK accounting more rigorous.
>
> (pp.9–11)

And elsewhere in the book he mentions other achievements in those early years. In the balance sheet, these included providing robust definitions of assets and liabilities and bringing previously hidden debt onto the balance sheet. In reporting of the accounting period's flows, the information published was transformed – by forcing full disclosure of movements in cash in the new cash flow statement, making transparent other gains and losses in the new STRGL, and disaggregating continuing and discontinued activities in the P&L.

Looking back at the firefighting programme in 1997, Sergeant wrote

> At the start of the decade, when the powerless old Accounting Standards Committee was wound up, things were very different. Company accounts were a laughing stock and the profession was at bay. Smart finance directors and their advisers had found the bean-counter's stone: cookbooks on how to turn losses into profits and liabilities into assets. Empires were built by creative accounting allowed by loose rules, lax enforcement and weak-minded auditors.
>
> ...FRS10 virtually completes the reform of accounting rules set in train to end the scandals of the last boom and slump. It has been a rare success in state-sponsored, self-led regulation.

Bruce (1996b) was similarly appreciative of the reform programme:

> The Tweedie revolution has stopped much of the old 1980s methods of finding a way of disguising management failure.
>
> ...the obvious loopholes have been closed; and, secondly, the rules have focused on forcing people to look harder at what the figures mean.

Not everyone was so enthusiastic to see so many loopholes closed. For example, the investment bankers who (see Chapter 2) taunted Tweedie – then still an audit partner – over his powerlessness to prevent misleading accounting, will have regretted the loss of lucrative creative accounting schemes; likewise, the lawyers who deployed their wisdom and skills to make the schemes safe from challenge. Spare a thought too for those of us toiling to teach accounting in universities. Not for nothing does accounting have a reputation for tedium: double entry book-keeping can induce sleep and resentment in class. But turn to "how to make your profits what you want them to be" (the subtitle of Griffiths' lucid 1986 critique), and how legally to transform the balance sheet with sleight of hand, and the atmosphere in class suddenly becomes lively and enthusiastic. This wasn't boring old accounting, this was suddenly high finance – a possible entry route to lucrative investment banking!

So while I did not feel the 'hatred' felt by some professionals towards Tweedie and his accomplices described by the newspaper, I did feel a little nostalgia for the gift to an accounting lecturer presented by the shenanigans of the 1980s.

## Innovation

### *Goodwill*

The Board's handling of goodwill illustrates both their technical expertise and ambition and their political skill. Chapters 6 and 7 explained the large scale of goodwill in many companies' balance sheets; and its role as "the balancing item in many of the creative accounting deals involved with acquisitions" – meaning often that "you could choose your profit" after acquisitions. There was a wide range of treatments of goodwill in different jurisdictions. An ASB Discussion Paper in 1993 listed no fewer than six possible ways of accounting for it. The arrangements inherited from the ASC allowed three of them: recognition plus amortisation; or recognition plus write-off against reserves; or merger accounting – completely avoiding recognition. 95% opted to write off against reserves, which was encouraged by the ASC (yet not allowed in other jurisdictions).

When the ASB began work, it was widely accepted that accounting for goodwill needed reform. The ASC had issued Exposure Draft 47, suggesting major change. But the draft provoked more responses than any other since the notorious one for current cost accounting; 80% of corporates objected to the proposals.

It was a hot potato. And the ASB put it in the freezer, to be brought out when the Board had established its reputation and authority by tackling urgent, but more tractable, firefighting needs.

Work on goodwill began in earnest with the 1993 Discussion Paper. There followed an extraordinary sustained campaign to reach an understanding – especially with the corporate preparers, who had been so solidly opposed to the ASC's earlier proposals. The campaign included a lengthy public hearing and widespread efforts – formal and informal – to consult and persuade. Tweedie's diary for just 1996 includes no fewer than 278 meetings with/ speeches to outside bodies and individuals.[3] Cook and Whittington, as well as other members of the ASB team also went out to listen and persuade. In addition, the campaign also included field-testing of the major proposed innovations by seven major companies who were big acquirers.

As the proposals took shape, the FT's Lex column (1995) commented:

> The Accounting Standards Board's proposals on accounting for goodwill are a triumph of diplomacy as well as intellectual ingenuity.

> ...Amazingly, given the passions which goodwill accounting provokes, the proposals are likely to meet with widespread approval. This is despite the fact that companies' favoured way of dealing with the substance – writing it off against reserves – is set to be outlawed.
>
> ...If the proposals are adopted, the quality of accounts will be doubly improved. Goodwill will be visible in the accounts, not written off and forgotten. Furthermore, the tests on the value of goodwill seem rigorous and yet not unduly complicated, and will prove a useful discipline for managers.

The exhausting engagement with preparers and other interest groups worked: whereas the ASC's ED47 had met 80% ***objections*** from the corporates, the 1995 working paper attracted ***support*** from 59% of them.

When the new rules were introduced, Lex (1997) went on:

> Investors should welcome the Accounting Standards Board (ASB) ruling on goodwill. No longer able to write off goodwill on acquisitions ... [firms] will finally have to acknowledge it on the balance sheet as capital employed. Writing goodwill off against reserves was unsatisfactory and out of line with international practice. It overstated returns on investments and gave the erroneous impression that the buyer's net worth had been depleted, rendering the balance sheet meaningless.
>
> With managers now accountable for all the costs of buying a business, it will be easier to spot those who overpay. Furthermore, the requirement to amortise should help speed the move away from justifying deals in terms of earnings per share enhancement. The new standard should facilitate scrutiny of whether acquisitions really create value for shareholders.
>
> The ASB's innovation – allowing companies to avoid amortising goodwill and other intangible assets altogether if they can prove in an annual impairment review that is has not been dissipated – could well become the international standard. Clearly some assets, such as the Coca-Cola or Johnny Walker brands, have extremely long economic lives, and should not be amortised over the normal 20 years.'[4]

And there was admiration from experts abroad, for example the former chairman of US FASB wrote:

> These are great improvements to the accounting for business combinations in the UK, and they represent a model that the US board should emulate in its own project.
>
> ...The US board often leads the world on financial reporting improvements. In this case, however, I believe the board should import the improvements developed in the UK.
>
> (Beresford, 1997)

FASB did indeed propose new rules similar in important respects to those initiated by ASB. They proposed in 1999 that goodwill be routinely recognised in the balance sheet and amortised through the income statement. The subsequent hostile lobbying by businesses, whose objections were taken up by Congress, was so intense that FASB abandoned the proposal and instead introduced compulsory recognition plus discretionary impairment (Beresford, 2001; Zeff, 2002).

Why was there such intense opposition to the amortisation of goodwill? With goodwill recognised in the balance sheet, analysts could if they wished readily impute an amortisation charge to adjust reported earnings; so amortisation would seem to be irrelevant to valuation. What, then, motivated the angst of the opponents of amortisation, one senior executive arguing in Congress that FASB's proposed standard would "stifle technology development, impede capital formation and slow job creation"?[5]

One possible explanation may be found in senior executives' remuneration contracts. High-powered incentive schemes have become more widespread in recent decades. The increased power is reflected in evidence on the ratio of chief executive pay to that of the typical worker in a population of US companies reported by the *Financial Times* (2022): from 20-to-1 in 1965 to 399-to-1 in 2021.

Earnings per share (EPS), the 'all important'[6] metric followed by investors, has been an important driver of these schemes (along with greater size – rapidly achieved through M&A).[7] Typically EPS was written on net income (after goodwill write-offs (Murphy, 1999)). And Chapter 6 above gives an illustration of the potential effect of amortisation on this metric: BP's reported annual earnings would have been depressed by as much as 37% if it had been required to amortise the putative goodwill associated with its combination with Amoco (Li, 2007).

Relevant to the link between pay and performance, a major statistical study by Harford and Li (2007) concluded that "Even in mergers where bidding shareholders are worse off, bidding CEOs are better off three quarters of the time". And the bidding shareholders have frequently been 'worse off': a McKinsey report (2010) concluded that 'Anyone who has researched merger success rates knows that roughly 70% fail'; and peer-reviewed academic studies reported by Meeks and Meeks (2022) have mostly found no post-merger operating gains on average.

In these circumstances, it is not surprising that executives might resist having reported profit diminished explicitly – via amortisation – the diminution of the nebulous, often wasting, asset goodwill purchased with shareholders' funds. There is then a stewardship challenge for accounting in relation to the $4 trillion[8] or so spent globally on M&A in a typical year.[9]

Defenders of the – no amortisation – resolution forced on FASB might argue that the diminution of purchased goodwill was better represented by estimated impairment than by the mechanical device of amortisation. But a problem with this is that anyway, and especially in the FASB version, impairment is vulnerable to manipulation. The FASB version did not incorporate the monitoring safeguards included in the ASB's 'hybrid' or 'twin instrument' version which combines amortisation with impairment.[10] Comiskey and Mulford (2010), Ramanna and Watts (2012), and KPMG (2014) report that in practice, impairment estimates relied excessively on managers' judgements concerning valuation models, cash flow forecasts, and discount rates; that those assumptions were inconsistent across firms; that distinguishing internally generated goodwill from purchased goodwill was challenging; and that the subjectivity is far greater for this than for most other asset classes. Unless a firm was obviously in serious distress it was generally fairly easy for managers to avoid recognising the depletion of goodwill in an impairment charge. ASB had recognised such difficulties with impairment, and in FRS10 imposed much tougher constraints. In the five years after acquisition, cash flows attributable to goodwill had to be compared with the acquirer's ex ante budgets; and if that revealed an impairment, the acquirer had to report it in the published accounts. After five years, constraints were imposed on the growth rate that could be assumed (see Chapter 7).

FASB has not been blind to this evidence on the shortcomings of their standard. And, for one sector – private companies – FASB reverted to its original (ASB-like) position in 2014, allowing private companies to amortise goodwill (FASB, 2014). As most discussion of standard-setting has focused on publicly listed companies, this may seem trivial – but it is perhaps more significant in view of the attrition of companies on the US and UK stock exchanges and the rising share of M&A conducted by private equity.[11]

Then, in 2020, FASB seemed to be aiming for a similar change for companies on the stock exchange. Lugo (2020) reported that "FASB tentatively said it would require public companies to amortize goodwill over a 10-year period on a straight-line basis only, without exception". It was noted in a subsequent IASB Discussion (November 2022) that, in consultations with IASB, 6 out of 7 FASB members favoured including amortisation in the rules.

Similarly, IASB (2020) addressed the problem and invited views on the possibility of restoring amortisation, noting that Board members were divided concerning its merits, the chairman minded to favour its inclusion in the standard.[12]

The UK Endorsement Board, which "influences, endorses and adopts new or amended international accounting standards issued by the International Accounting Standards Board (IASB) for use by UK companies", has expressed itself in support of a 'hybrid', 'twin instrument' model similar to the ASB's, combining amortisation with impairment (UKEB, 2022).

But then there has followed a development which feels increasingly like Groundhog Day – a re-run of the retreat experienced around the millennium. Lugo reported (2022) that

> the board [FASB] had leaned toward requiring that entities apply an impairment with amortization model, where an entity would amortize goodwill over a 10-year default period that would be limited to a 25-year cap.

But "on June 15, 2022, [FASB] unanimously voted to drop its project on identifiable intangible assets and the subsequent accounting of goodwill... The decision came as a huge surprise to market watchers".

Had the executives and their lobbyists been at work again, as two decades earlier – anxious that perceptions of their mergers, and their compensation packages, might suffer if amortisation was demanded?

In November 2022, IASB again followed FASB, rejecting any move towards the ASB's hybrid model incorporating amortisation alongside impairment.[13] IASB did propose some extra disclosures designed to improve accountability for firms' expenditures on purchased goodwill, but these exempted vast amounts of purchased goodwill and specified the additional disclosures in ways which lend themselves to manipulation, with none of the rigour prescribed by the ASB.[14]

### *Pensions*

A similar, patient stepwise approach by the ASB to a controversial and innovative standard is evident also in the development of the pensions standard, FRS17, which replaced the actuarial approach of the ASC's SSAP24 with a radically different fair value, or balance sheet approach. In Chapter 8 of TCW, Tweedie explains how FRS17 built on the foundations installed in the ASB's earlier standards: bringing all the assets and liabilities on balance sheet (FRS5), showing the different components of income (FRS3) and "telling it as it is" with liabilities (FRS4). Moreover, FRS17's general approach to valuing the pension fund asset/liability had already secured approval in FRS7 when valuing an acquiree. However, the new standard promised to overturn the approach favoured and implemented by the actuarial profession. When the first Discussion Paper containing the proposal was issued, only one actuary supported it. After a programme of consultation and persuasion, only one actuary did not support the second Discussion Paper. In Tweedie's words, "there was a complete swing".

Tweedie persuaded the G4 too, at least to the extent that they wrote "we think the way the ASB is going about this is probably the right way to go in the future". UK companies too came to accept and support it, and lobbied (successfully) for permission to retain the ASB model when they became subject to the IASB regime. Finally, years later, in Tweedie's last month as Chair of the IASB, that body adopted the ASB model.[15]

## 'Blue on blue' attacks: opposition from within the accounting profession

The last section traced the conversion of finance directors from outright hostility to losing their favoured accounting treatment of goodwill to supporting just that – a "triumph of diplomacy as well as intellectual ingenuity". Likewise, consultation and persuasion (along with some influential support from within the profession) achieved a volte-face by actuaries, in favour of the Board's innovative accounting.

But, as has been repeatedly mentioned in earlier chapters, through much of the 1990s the ASB faced sustained public attacks from one of the Big Six accounting firms, Ernst & Young (EY). In some respects, EY were important contributors to the reform programme. Their senior partner at the time, Elwyn Eilledge, was a distinguished and enthusiastic founding member of the Board. The work of the Senior Technical Partner, Ron Paterson, on accounting practice is cited earlier in this book. And the firm's substantial review of practice, UKGAAP, is a highly respected standard reference work. However in important respects, EY was not aligned with the ASB and with the other major accounting firms.

Hostility to the ASB mission was already evident before the Board had started work: EY attacked Terry Smith's acclaimed critique of misleading accounting practices. Smith recounted in the second edition of that book that EY "were the only firm which had gone on record at the time of publication to condemn the book as "dangerous and irresponsible"". (Smith, 1996, p.4)

Subsequently they (especially technical partner Ron Paterson) wrote a string of hostile articles in the professional magazines, and an extended critique mailed to the finance directors of all major companies.

I have read many of these articles and attended a talk by Mr Paterson in an effort to understand their concerns. I still do not have a very clear understanding; but I think their objections include:

1 The ASB is held to accord primacy of the balance sheet over the profit and loss account; but the latter, reporting the periodic flows, is thought more important to users of the accounts than the snapshot of assets and liabilities on one day.
2 The ASB is aiming to reintroduce current cost accounting by stealth – by requiring current values for some balance sheet variables.
3 The ASB is deaf to arguments which do not coincide with their agenda.

I am puzzled by such complaints. In relation to number 1, my perception, reinforced by the previous nine chapters of this book, was that the ASB gave very high priority to reporting flows, not only by making the P&L more reliable by curbing creative accounting, but also by substantially expanding the information available on flows through the new cash flow statement and the statement of recognised gains and losses. These modifications and additions by the ASB were partly prompted by the question Terry Smith said he encountered from investors: "XYZ company went bust last week, but it was making profits. How can that happen?"

Then in relation to the attention given by the ASB to the balance sheet, I thought this was prompted by the previously loose definitions of assets and liabilities, which made comparison between companies more difficult, and, because of their implications for measuring income, created opportunities (then being actively exploited) for distortionary creative accounting. As Dechow et al. (2011) observed: "…the more assets on the balance sheet that are subject to changes in assumptions and forecasts, the greater the manager's flexibility to manage short-term earnings". Manipulation of the balance sheet undermined the reliability of the P&L.

As for concern 2, my understanding is that the ASB had no intention to reintroduce current cost accounting. But some components of the balance sheet such as the burgeoning derivatives did not have a 'cost'; and market values for some components were of particular value to users.

And I cannot reconcile concern 3 – deafness to disagreement – with the remarkable efforts described above, which were sustained over several years, to find a robust treatment of goodwill acceptable to preparers and users, or to reach agreement on the major change in accounting for pensions.

But I may not have done justice to EY's arguments, so I have consulted contemporaneous comments.

On the one side, EY sent a critique of the ASB's discussion draft on the future of company reporting to the media and the top 350 companies in Britain. They described the ASB framework as 'pernicious', 'open to abuse', and 'fundamentally misguided'. It 'strives for an accounting model that we do not believe is desirable, based on principles we do not believe to be workable' (European Accountant, 1996).

But all five of the other Big Six firms took a different view. For example, in a letter to the *Financial Times*, John Roques, Senior Partner and Chief Executive, Deloitte, and Touche, wrote:

> In the interests of good financial reporting, the false picture portrayed by the Ernst and Young document criticizing the Accounting Standards Board cannot go unchallenged.
>
> Despite its disclaimers, the document amounts to an attack on the very existence of the ASB itself. I strongly deplore the false implication that the ASB is out of touch and does not reflect the needs of users.
>
> On the contrary, it is to the ASB's great credit that the accounting standards it has produced so far (which are based on the principles contained in its draft statement of principles[decried by EY]) have done much to raise the quality of financial reporting. Do we really want to return to the accounting of the late 1980s?
>
> …Although I do not always agree with the ASB, I strongly support the open and reasoned way it approaches its tasks and I cannot allow its substantial achievements to be undone by an unthinking hankering after yesterday's accounting…

This response to the EY attack was published in the *Financial Times*, on 27 February 1996, along with letters strongly supportive of the ASB from Coopers and Lybrand, KPMG, and Price Waterhouse. On the following day, Arthur Andersen issued a comment along similar lines.

The broadsheet newspapers also responded vigorously.

Robert Bruce of *The Times* first quoted the EY Senior Partner Nick Land's foreword to the EY booklet, Time to Decide:

> Some of its [the ASB's] proposals are theoretical to the point that they are scarcely comprehensible by most accountants and other businessmen. Accounting, traditionally the language of business, is at risk of being taken over by the rhetoric of theorists.

And then Bruce offered his own interpretation:

> It is possible, perhaps, to read between the lines here. Company directors are conservative and dislike new rules. Finance directors find it painful to confront them with Tweedie's new realities. There is commercial advantage in being an accounting firm that seems to support the harassed company director against the bogey of radical accounting theorists.
>
> (Bruce, 1996a)

The *Financial Times'* Jim Kelly (1996) also sensed ulterior motives on EY's part:

> There are two sharply different explanations of the firm's policy. It either springs from a series of genuine and heartfelt differences of opinion with the ASB or is a marketing stance designed to set it apart amid the uniformity of the Big Six market.

And the Independent (1996) was more forthright still:

> The problem [for EY] is that just about everybody else sees the attack as opportunistic marketing that threatens to undo the progress that Sir David and his colleagues have made since the late 1980s.

Then the magisterial FT Leader (1996) issued a strong rebuke to EY:

> The tone of the [EY] paper is harsher than is warranted. It is unfair to accuse the board of unworldliness; Sir David Tweedie, its chairman, has made clear that its "preference" for a change could not be implemented without widespread support. It is also melodramatic to accuse the board of stealth, when its statement was a highly public attempt to stimulate debate. The board makes clear that it wants evolution not revolution.

## Relations with the legal profession

In a discussion of regulation, Gillian Tett (2019) of the FT outlined:

> ...three different regulatory systems in the world, at least when it came to finance.

> In some countries, most notably the US, everything that was not explicitly banned by specific laws was permitted. In others, such as Japan, everything that was not explicitly permitted was considered banned. Then there was a third category of countries (including the UK) that had 'principles'- based systems: instead of relying on the letter of the law, these regimes preferred to outline general principles and apply them using precedent.[16]
>
> (FT, 8 June 2019)

Much of investment banking in London was by 1990 owned by US banks used to operating under the first regime described by Tett above. This had led the US standard-setters to respond by writing ever more detailed rules, in a game of catch-up. Chapter 2 above described Tweedie's exasperation in the 1980s – as technical partner in a major audit firm – with the scornful attitude of investment bankers who were constantly finding (and selling for lavish fees) creative accounting devices which were (just) compliant with the letter of the law and standards, but palpably at odds with the substance of those rules, the principles underlying the rules. Tweedie recalled one of the investment bankers telling him: "You'll never stop us".

Robert Bruce (2000) described the ASB's preference for the third way in Tett's scheme:

> In the past we seemed to be moving towards the American model. That meant a game of ever-tighter and more detailed rules as corporate entities found ways to leapfrog them. But the Tweedie approach cuts its way out of that. If you emphasise the basic principles, you can then enforce the details, not through rules, but through the force of argument which results in peer and market pressure.
>
> ...What is required, as Isobel Sharp [of Arthur Andersen] puts it is that the company law changes "should enshrine principles in law and leave the detail for elsewhere".

The legal profession thought otherwise. Chapter 2 quotes the Law Society:

> We think therefore that the wish expressed by the Release [on off balance sheet finance] to substitute substance for form is a dangerous and undesirable one. More importantly ... we consider that...what is proposed is contrary to the law.
>
> (The Law Society, 1986)

The FT picked up the dispute. Their editorial said (August 1987):

> The argument over off balance sheet finance has demonstrated the frailty of the accountants' 'true and fair' concept in the face of the determined

defence by the legal profession of rigid statutes and the opportunistic exploitation of artificial schemes by merchant banks.

In Chapter 2, Tweedie explains how the Dearing architecture supported the ASB by combining a legal framework with regulators' judgement. The Review Panel assessed accounts which appeared to contravene the spirit of the ASB's standards and was able to demand that – if the company was at fault – it issue revised accounts. The offending company could appeal to the court. But, in Tweedie's words, "as a lawyer would say to them: you'll win on a legal technicality if you win at all; but your peers have judged your accounts not to give a true and fair view. And that is damning". In the case Tweedie cites, the top executives lost their jobs after a damaging decision by the Panel.

Presumably a lawyer would argue that if there were instances where the letter of the law had failed to secure compliance with its spirit, it was for the regulators to promote an updated law. A recent example in an adjacent area of regulation – audit and governance – illustrates one drawback of such an approach. In May 2022 the British government decided not to submit to Parliament in the subsequent year a draft bill on audit reform. "This, despite four years, three major reviews and a white paper, as well as rare consensus between regulators, companies and audit firms that new rules are needed, urgently". (FT Leader, 2022) Why did the government hold back this reform for at least a further year? In the FT's words, "Apparently, government advisers think reforming the UK's corporate governance and audit market is 'boring'".

A lag of five or six years between identifying a loophole in the law and legislating against it provides ample time for investment bankers and their legal advisers to profit from it and to explore further devices to replace any that are outlawed.

## Relations with government

The UK government was very supportive at the birth of the ASB. It was active in setting up the Board and enhancing its authority in the 1989 Companies Act. It engaged constructively through a senior official from The Department of Trade and Industry who had an observer role at the Board. But in the later years of the decade tension developed with the most powerful of government departments, the Treasury – over the reporting of liabilities incurred by government with investments under the Private Finance Initiative. The process was seen by the ASB as tantamount to off balance sheet finance, which the ASB had mandated in FRS5 should be brought back onto the balance sheets of companies. The press relished the prospect of a fight in the London arena between two formidable Scotsmen, Gordon Brown, and David Tweedie.[17] The newspaper commentaries suggest that there may have been considerable betting on the outcome of the fight.

Robert Bruce (1998) observed in *The Times*:

> ...growing arguments over the accounting treatment of the Government's Private Finance Initiative (PFI). The efforts to remove new hospitals, roads and prisons from the public sector borrowing requirement comes close to what, in the bad old corporate days of creative accounting, was known as off balance sheet financing.

Accountancy Age thought this was a fight where the ASB was unlikely to prevail:

> [The ASB] 'has dared to challenge the practice of off-balance sheet accounting for PFI...
>
> According to a Treasury spokesman, several of the banks have already given their backing to the government.
>
> ...The opposition to on-the-balance-sheet PFI is too powerful. There is too much riding on this particular accounting standard. It would seriously jeopardise the government's tight spending restrictions. As a consequence, Sir David is likely to be cut down to size by the Treasury's iron chancellor.'
>
> (Bloom, 1998, pp.14, 15)

On the other side, the *Financial Times* fancied Tweedie and his ASB:

> The ASB under Sir David Tweedie has established a reputation and standing that no government could challenge lightly.
>
> (Kelly, 1998a)

However, the odds on a Tweedie victory lengthened when the politicians sent a shot across the ASB's bows:

> Ministers have publicly warned that if the board, under the leadership of Sir David Tweedie, persists in its views they will simply allow them to be overruled by the Treasury...
>
> (Kelly, 1998b)

In the end, those lengthened odds benefitted those who had bet on Tweedie. Three months later the Daily Telegraph (1998) reported:

> The government has backed down in a dispute with the Accounting Standards Board that threatened its flagship private finance initiative.
>
> Guidelines produced by the board today mean the government will bear the liabilities involved in large scale contracts such as prisons, hospitals and some roads, rather than the private sector.

## Cost-benefit analysis

At the end of 130,000 words on accounting, many of them discussing how to make the P&L more reliable, the reader might reasonably ask in this concluding chapter for a 'P&L' for the 1990s ASB – a statement of the benefits and costs. This request might seem all the more reasonable in view of the ASB's own sixth Fundamental Guideline:

> To issue accounting standards only when the expected benefits exceed the perceived costs.

And the reader familiar with the US literature might have low expectations of the net benefits in view of the contention of a well-known US academic commentator on accounting and financial standards, George Benston (1982), who opined:

> The cost of an accounting standard, ex ante, is likely to exceed its benefits to shareholders

And as *The Times* wrote halfway through the ASB's reform programme, Benston's views were not confined to the US:

> Britain's new accounting standards have two main enemies: auditors who do not like the chosen treatment and companies whose financial engineering is thwarted. Both want to keep a choice of different accounting methods. In America, there is a third group that believes any official regulation beyond property rights is malign, destroying choice and sapping the vigour of market forces. Professor David Myddelton combines the two in a call for a bonfire of accounting standards, the Financial Reporting Council, and all its works.
>
> (Pennington, 1995)

Perhaps this libertarian strand of thinking influenced Ernst and Young in their denunciations of the ASB.

Benston's allegation that the costs exceed the benefits of standards is significant in view of the then ASB's Fundamental Guideline. However, that Guideline continued with a caveat: "The Board recognizes that reliable cost/benefit calculations are seldom possible".[18] Nevertheless, since the profession is devoted to holding participants in the rest of the economy to account for the costs they incur, perhaps the challenge from sceptics such as Benston and Myddelton, does deserve some consideration in a chapter aiming to review the ASB's work: have we no quantitative information about the benefits and costs of the programme of more rigorous accounting standards such as the ASB introduced?

Perhaps the most obvious potential benefit for shareholders is avoiding losses of wealth arising from managers' creative accounting. In one example of such loss of wealth cited earlier, Smith (1992) analysed the activities of the serial acquirer Coloroll in the years immediately preceding the founding of the ASB. It exploited many of the permitted accounting abuses described in Chapters 3–7, which were curbed by the Standards of the nineties: spurious restructuring provisions, unwarranted asset write-downs, manipulation of goodwill, misrepresentation of gearing, … Just before it collapsed, almost worthless, it reported profits some ten times their likely true level.[19] The market value of shareholders' stake fell from over 400 mn pounds to almost nothing.

But economists have argued that the harm from an overly permissive regulatory regime is not limited to – and often greatly exceeds – such losses of shareholder wealth. Nobel Laureate Akerlof (1970) wrote in his classic 'Market for lemons' paper (p.495):

> Consider a market in which goods are sold honestly or dishonestly: quality may be represented, or it may be misrepresented. The purchaser's problem, of course, is to identify quality. The presence of people in the market who are willing to offer inferior goods tends to drive the market out of existence. …It is this possibility that represents the major costs of dishonesty –for dishonest dealings tend to drive honest dealings out of the market. There may be potential buyers of good quality products and there may be potential sellers of such products in the appropriate price range; however, the presence of people who wish to pawn bad wares as good wares tends to drive out the legitimate business. The cost of dishonesty, therefore, lies not only in the amount by which the purchaser is cheated; the cost must also include the loss incurred from driving legitimate business out of existence.

Lev (1988, p.7) applies the argument to the equity market:

> At the extreme, suspecting gross information asymmetries, uninformed investors may quite rationally withdraw from trading …altogether…A massive withdrawal of uninformed investors from the market …will deprive the economy of the allocational and risk-sharing benefits of large and efficient capital markets.

Such benefits are hard to quantify. But suggestive evidence that they can be material comes from a number of sources. Shleifer and Vishny (1997) reported the assets of Russian oil companies being valued at a 99% discount to those of their Western counterparts; and they attribute this in part to the potential plunder of assets by managers, because of weak monitoring and control arrangements, including accounting standards. Gwiliam et al. (2005) traced the growth of the Lloyds of London insurance market after a new regulatory regime was introduced incorporating modern standards of accounting and audit. This was prompted by scandalous abuse by insider agents of asymmetric information resulting in ruin for many ill-informed investors (who in this case did not enjoy limited liability). The new regime was followed by strong growth in the market (20% p.a. in the following five years). In another sector, UK manufacturing, Swann et al. (1996) estimated the impact on the foreign demand for an industry's products when the British Standards Institute published standards for its products – export growth of towards 50% in one of their models.

Meeks and Swann (2009) suggested two other potential benefits from effective accounting regulation. One was reduced search costs when investors or their agents are collecting financial data to inform stock market investment decisions. The study made a (qualified) estimate of the total search costs incurred by investors and their agents in managing the 1,200 billion pounds worth of shares of UK listed companies: around 2 billion pounds. Modest reductions in such costs as a result of greater or better disclosures could then be material. A second potential source of benefit they attributed to effective standards was in reducing contracting costs. Scott and Upton (1991, p.5) illustrate for debt contracts:

> Without a body of [accounting] standards, lenders would be forced to negotiate each set of contracts "from scratch". [Those contracting] would have to create their own comprehensive set of accounting rules rather than simply identifying supplemental rules or departures from GAAP.

The benefit of 'off the peg' accounting measures can come not only in writing contracts but also in enforcing them (Whittington, 1993).

So much for the potential benefits of effective standards. What about the costs of a regulatory regime such as the ASB?

The direct cost of the ASB in this period was about 2 mn pounds a year.[20] To put this in perspective, this was about one tenth of 1% of another component of expenditure on monitoring UK businesses: the audit bill for UK companies at that time (Meeks and Meeks, 2002).

Of course, standards impose additional compliance costs on preparers, and some (fairly heroic) estimates reported in Meeks and Meeks suggest an order of magnitude for these compliance costs of around twice the direct costs incurred by the regulator. One of the studies on which these data are based, by Carsberg and Page (1984), on the highly contentious complex current cost accounting standard SSAP 16, concluded that "the costs of preparing current cost information are quite low...hardly great enough to explain the strong opposition that some preparers show to current cost accounting" (p.176). Another study examined the compliance costs associated with the new accounting system at Lloyds of London mentioned above: compliance and audit costs were of the order of twice the (very modest) direct costs of regulation (Gwiliam et al., 2005). As noted above, the ASB field tested their proposals for goodwill accounting; and the resulting small estimates of preparation costs by the participating companies[21] helped win over finance directors to the new standard.

This is a tentative, incomplete, and imprecise approach to assessing costs and benefits. It does not yield a neat bottom line. But I hope that, in the spirit of FRS3 (Chapter 3 above), such an information set, rather than a single number, helps the reader to take a view – in relation to the ASB's work – on Benston's proposition: "The cost of an accounting standard, ex ante, is likely to exceed its benefits to shareholders".

## The demise of the ASB – Globalisation

Somewhat paradoxically, in two respects the ASB's success made a significant contribution to its own demise. The ASB's work stimulated greater demand for cross-border investment in UK equities, and hence for internationally consistent accounting standards; and it contributed significantly to the supply of such standards.

### *Demand*

First, it is arguable that the Board's restoration of trust in the accounts of British companies contributed – as Akerlof would predict – to the growth of the international market in shares. For example, as the Foreword noted, between 1994, when the ASB was picking up speed in its reform programme, and 2000, when Tweedie and Whittington departed, inward portfolio investment in UK equities recorded a 20-fold increase. And London played a disproportionate role in international M&A (Meeks, 2003).

Just as market developments in the 1980s led to demands for more consistency and comparability in domestic reporting (see Chapter 1), so also the increased internationalisation of business (stimulated by the ASB) increased the demand for harmonisation of accounting across jurisdictions.

That need is illustrated by the experience reported by Nobes (1997) of Daimler Benz when it was the first German company to list on the New York Stock Exchange. It therefore had to report its income using US accounting conventions, alongside the German ones it had been employing. The former (German) figure for 1993 was a surplus of DM615mn; the latter (US) figure was a loss of DM1, 839 mn. There was no suggestion of creative accounting: the company, and audit and financial regulation in its home country enjoyed a deservedly high reputation. The difference arose simply from different (defensible) accounting rules. But they obviously represented an obstacle to international integration.

### *Supply*

The second reason the ASB contributed to its own demise was that it engaged energetically and constructively with efforts to harmonise reporting standards across national borders. Tweedie, Cook and Whittington were very well-informed about the harmonisation challenge. Tweedie had been partner of one of the biggest international accounting firms; and he had been a very active member of G4+1 and the IASC (International Accounting Standards Committee); Cook's corporate posts had been in major multinationals, and he had worked with OECD as well as having a spell as Secretary of IASC; Whittington collaborated with researchers around the world.

A very significant fillip to harmonisation came with the European Commission's move to require listed companies in the EU to use IFRSs in their consolidated accounts from 2005: the ASB's role would then be limited to promulgating UK standards for non-listed companies and giving advice to the IASB. A number of attempts were made to foster liaison between the IASB and national standard-setters, but it proved hard to construct effective liaison arrangements, and as one of over a hundred participating countries, the UK could play only a minor role. As Cook wrote to me, "The days of a powerful, independent UK Standard Setter with a major say in the development of international accounting standards were over".

It can be seen as a compliment to the state of UK accounting in 2000 – compared with its international 'laughing stock' status when the ASB was founded – that the IASB was headquartered in London, and that Tweedie, Cook, and Whittington were hired by the new body.[22] The development was inevitable if accounting was effectively to serve the globalising market. But in the preceding chapters, there are moments of regret about the diminished role of the ASB. As Tweedie commented in Chapter 2, at ASB 'we set out with consent to get the 100 Group (of finance directors) on board, the technical partners on board, and the analysts on side, with separate meetings. If we got all three of those we had a fair chance of getting the standard through. We didn't always make it, but that was the way we approached it. It was so much more difficult with IASB, because that happened in every blooming country'. And also, the strong representation of the US on the IASB increased the pressure to rely more on detailed rules than on the underlying principles.

## *Last words*

*Financial Director* wrote, "There is no single explanation as to why the ASB has been so universally hailed as a success: support of the profession; the time in the economic and political cycle when it was set up; the architecture of British standard-setting created by Sir Ron, now Lord, Dearing; and the fact that the team assembled stuck to the task".[23]

If the trio of authors of this book had been asked to provide an explanation of the success of the ASB, they would have given much of the credit to the very talented and highly committed Board members and staff they worked with. Had they possessed records of meetings and correspondence from the time, they would have liked to include a systematic account of the wider team's contributions.

The comment in *Financial Director* was right that "the time in the economic and political cycle when it was set up" must have helped:

> In the 1980s, finance directors and auditors lost their way, seduced by financial engineering and creative accounting.
>
> When the ASB took on its work, financial reporting was fast becoming a laughing stock. Companies reporting record profits and then collapsing shortly afterwards were not untypical. Now the UK is a major player globally on the financial reporting scene.[24]

As usual, after a crisis, there was an appetite for change. And the authors have acknowledged warmly the ingenuity of Dearing in creating effective structures to support change. But contemporary accounts are almost unanimous in emphasising the critical role in delivering change of the actual people leading the ASB. Bruce in his Foreword recalls his 1997 column offering explanations of factors in the Chairman's success:

> Sir David has great clarity of mind and an amiable disposition. It means that he is able to tell people that they are wrong without them taking too much offence.
>
> But beyond the charm lies the toughness. You do not manage to reform a whole range of financial reporting rules through which the finance directors of some of the country's finest companies had been managing to drive a coach and horses on the basis of a good repertoire of jokes and a pleasant manner. Sir David's secret lies in the combination of two factors. He is academically brighter than most accountants and he is, to most in the largest accountancy firms, an outsider. That combination allows him to note things that those who are more dependent on the culture of the Big Six would rather not. And it allows him to refute the arguments of others in a logical way.

But as the introduction to this chapter emphasised, the ASB was not a one-man show. *Accountancy* (2000) pointed out that:

> ...in the background Sir David has been blessed with the perfect back-room genius, technical director Allan Cook.
>
> The two often disagree but the partnership has thrived on a recognition that they bring different things to the party.
>
> (Accountancy, 2000)

And Williams (2004) agreed:

> Along with the more outgoing one-time chairman Sir David Tweedie, Cook can claim credit for the reputation that UK accounting standards enjoy today.

Their partner, Geoffrey Whittington, brought complementary attributes. He is always at pains to emphasise that, in contrast with Cook and Tweedie, his contribution was only part-time and lesser. But this member, "among the world's leading academic accountants", was described as "one of the most awkward and thoughtful standard-setters of the time".[25] When he followed Tweedie in receiving the Founding Societies Award, "the accountancy profession's equivalent of the Nobel Prize, though without its money" (Bruce, 1997), the citation said he "played a pivotal role in the development of accounting standards…[and]…has played a major part in forming our world class standards".

It is not surprising therefore, that although they had been labelled in the press– directly or indirectly – as "the most hated accountants in Britain", the Queen chose to honour all three – Tweedie with a knighthood, Cook and Whittington as CBE. Always on the lookout for a smart hire, Her Majesty also made Tweedie her auditor.[26]

## Notes

1 The description by Sir Sydney Lipworth QC, Chairman of the FRC after Dearing, in World Accounting Report (1995), Standard-setters Conference, December/January 1995.
2 Actually, the headline ends in a question mark – perhaps another accountant was even more hated?
3 Other standard-setters: 47; press: 61; institutes: 47; auditors: 53; industry: 37; academics: 27; analysts: 13. These were over and above all the internal meetings at ASB.
4 While the ASB was ready to challenge the status quo with innovations in many aspects of M&A accounting, its success in securing consent and compliance owed something to a readiness to compromise when an option they preferred was too great a change for the constituency. The authors mention in Chapter 7 their preference for 'fresh start' accounting with business combinations, but their awareness that it was a 'non-starter' with their constituency, and they did not waste political capital on pursuing it.
5 Dennis Powell, quoted in Beresford (2001).
6 Gryta and Mann (2020) in their study of the then biggest corporation in the world, GE, which made some 1,700 acquisitions over 36 years, before disintegrating (Dissanaike et al., 2022), and which, in the words of the director of the Securities and Exchange Commission's enforcement division, "bent the accounting rules beyond the breaking point" (Edgecliffe-Johnson et al., 2021).
7 See Meeks and Meeks (2022, chapter 2) for a detailed discussion of incentives for senior executives.
8 See Meeks and Meeks (2022, chapter 1) for a detailed discussion of statistics on the scale and outcome of M&A.
9 As well as protecting executives from scrutiny of their spending on goodwill, forbidding amortization distorts investment decisions. Meeks and Meeks (2022) ask: under the regime secured by the business lobbyists, why would the CEO of a tech firm with funds to create intangibles spend years depressing reported earnings by generating the intangibles internally when she could just buy them 'ready-made' in an acquisition, with no hit [from amortization] to reported profit? (p.87).

10 Amel-Zadeh et al. (2020) report statistical analysis which turns out supportive to the ASB version.
11 Tepper and Hearn (2019) note for the US that between 1996 and 2016 the number of listed stocks in the US fell by about half. Meeks and Whittington (2021) also report a rapid attrition of companies on the UK exchanges. Private equity is accounting for a high and rising proportion of M&A activity, with its frequent private purchases and sales of companies (KKR's private equity funds alone currently employ over 800,000 people (Gara and Vandevelde, 2021)).
12 My response to that invitation – strongly in support of amortization – is recorded in Meeks (2020).
13 Based on the IASB Discussion in November 2022 and the IFRS Foundation Monthly News Summary for November 20222.
14 The proposals only affected acquisitions equal in size to 10% or more of the acquirer – i.e. excluding very substantial purchases of goodwill when the acquirer was a giant, and effectively exempting the massive continual spending on goodwill by many serial acquirers – a category responsible for so much dysfunctional merger activity (Meeks and Meeks, 2022, 2023). And the proposals permitted executives of acquirers to choose which metrics to disclose – a gift to 'creative' accountants, enabling them to select ones which showed their deals in the most favourable possible light (Meeks, 2020).
15 This is the only ASB standard about which I have reservations –not about the underlying principles or recognition, but about measurement. Even those sympathetic to the efficient market hypothesis recognize the fragility of share prices on any particular day. Fischer Black (1986), President of the American Finance Association, wrote:

> [We] might define an efficient market as one in which price is within a factor of 2 of value, i.e., the price is more than half of value and less than twice value. The factor of 2 is arbitrary, of course. Intuitively, though, it seems reasonable to me, in the light of sources of uncertainty about value and the strength of the forces tending to cause price to return to value. By this definition, I think almost all markets are efficient almost all of the time. "Almost all" means at least 90 per cent.

Nobel Laureate Shiller (2015) has assembled compelling evidence that the fluctuations in stock market prices are indeed much greater than is warranted by the variation in subsequent real dividends which they would reflect in a market which was fundamentally valuation efficient.

I find single day observations of such prices an uncomfortable basis for measurement of pension fund assets in relation to assessing the progress of transactions (pension contracts) lasting up to 60 years.

Then the use of the AA corporate bond rate to discount liabilities is troublesome when that rate is determined not by free market forces but by central bank intervention in pursuit of macroeconomic objectives. When the Bank of England drove down the rate by two percentage points in 2010, the present value of a pension liability 60 years ahead increased three-fold overnight (Meeks, 2017).

16 In similar fashion (and with characteristic irreverence), Tweedie used to joke: "in the UK everything is permitted unless it is prohibited; in Germany everything is prohibited unless it is permitted; in the Netherlands everything is prohibited even if it is permitted; in France everything is permitted especially if it is prohibited."
17 Who happen to be alumni of the same university, Edinburgh, and to own homes not far apart from one another on either side of the Firth of Forth.

18 The Board does not abandon the objective:

> However, it will always assess the need for standards in terms of the significance and extent of the problem being addressed and will choose the standard which appears to be most effective in cost/benefit terms.

19 Statistical studies of share price movements do find evidence of shareholders being misled by opaque forms of creative accounting – e.g. Botsari and Meeks (2018).
20 This is for the Financial Reporting Council in total, and is net of income from publications (Financial Reporting Council, 2000, p.76). It excludes the pay of staff members seconded to the ASB by their employers.
21 Guinness (which had substantial goodwill) found the test could be completed in two to three days by a recently qualified accountant; and that the test gave credible results (they had available independent, complex data on the value of their intangibles).
22 As Chairman, IFRIC Coordinator, and Board member, respectively.
23 Financial Director (1999, p.24), November.
24 From the citation when Tweedie was given the Founding Societies Award (Accountancy Age, 1997) 5 June.
25 In, respectively, Accountancy Age (1995), 12 October; Citation for award of Honorary Degree of Doctor of Science, University of Edinburgh, 16 July 1998; and commentary by Robert Bruce (source lost).
26 Chair of the Royal Household Audit Committee for the Sovereign Grant.

## References

### *Books and articles*

Accountancy Age (1995). Commentary, October.

Accountancy Age (1997). Commentary, June 5.

Accountancy (2000). CBE for Cook, 24 June 2000.

Akerlof, G. (1970). The market for "lemons": Quality uncertainty and the market mechanism. *Quarterly Journal of Economics*, 84, 488–500.

Amel-Zadeh, A., Faasse, J., Li, K. and Meeks, G. (2020). Stewardship and value-relevance in accounting for the depletion of purchased goodwill, in Amel-Zadeh and Meeks (eds.) *Accounting for M&A: Uses and Abuses of Accounting in Monitoring and Promoting Merger*, Abingdon and New York: Routledge, pp.79–112.

Benston, G. (1982). An analysis of the role of accounting standards for enhancing corporate governance and social responsibility. *Journal of Accounting and Public Policy*, 1(1), 5–17.

Beresford, D. (1997). US should import UK improvements, *Accountancy*, 4 December 1997.

Beresford, D.R. (2001). Congress looks at accounting for business combinations, *Accounting Horizons*, 15(1), 73–86, https://doi.org/10.2308/acch.2001.15.1.73.

Black, F. (1986). Noise. *Journal of Finance*, 41, 529–43.

Bloom, J. (1998). A battle to the debt, *Accountancy Age*, 15 January 1998, pp.14, 15.

Botsari, A. and Meeks, G. (2018). Acquirers' earnings management ahead of stock for stock bids in 'hot' and 'cold' markets. *Journal of Accounting and Public Policy*, 37, 355–375, https://doi.org/10.1016/j.jaccpubpol.2018.09.007.

Bruce, R. (1996a). The issues are now out in the open, *The Times*, 22 February 1996.

Bruce, R. (1996b). Changes spurring the exercise of judgment, *The Times*, 18 July 1996.

Bruce, R. (1997). Unconventional road leads Tweedie to the top, *The Times*, 20 March 1997.

Bruce, R. (1998). In the Government'[s] own backyard, *The Times*, 12 March, 1998.

Bruce, R. (2000). Reviewing company law from a time-warp, *The Times*, 4 May 2000.

Carsberg, B. and Page, M. (1984). The cost of preparing current cost accounts, in Carsberg and Page (eds.) *Current Cost Accounting: The Benefits and the Costs*, London: ICAEW.

Comiskey, E. and Mulford, C. (2010). Goodwill, triggering events, and impairment accounting. *Managerial Finance*, 36(9), 746–767, https://doi.org/10.1108/03074351011064436.

Daily Telegraph. (1998). State backs down over PFI guidelines, 10 September 1998.

Dechow, P., Ge, W., Larson, C. and Sloan, R. (2011). Predicting material accounting misstatements, *Contemporary Accounting Research*, 28, 17–82, https://doi.org/10.1111/j.1911-3846.2010.01041.x.

Dissanaike, G., Jayasekera, R. and Meeks, G. (2022). Why do unsuccessful companies survive? *Business History Review,* https://www.cambridge.org/core/journals/business-history-review/article/why-do-unsuccessful-companies-survive-us-airlines-aircraft-leasing-and-ge-20002008/8EE322645E63347771215BB7E3074142

Edgecliffe-Johnson, A., Silverman, G. and Fontanella-Khan, J. (2021) GE boss bids farewell to industrial complexity', *Financial Times*, 11 November 2021.

European Accountant. (1996). E&Y and ASB row over reporting draft, Issue 64, March 1996.

FASB. (2014). Accounting Standards Update **(ASU) No. 2014-02**, Intangibles—Goodwill and Other (Topic 350): Accounting for Goodwill (A Consensus of the Private Company Council).

Financial Director (1999). Commentary, November.

Financial Reporting Council. (2000). *Annual Review, 2000*, London: FRC.

*Financial Times.* (2022). Pay Gulf, in *Datawatch,* FT, 2 October 2022.

FT Leader. (1996). Accounting for the future, *FT*, 27 February 1996.

FT Leader. (2022). A legislative agenda that favours 'red meat' over real reform, *FT*, 11 May 2022.

Gara, A. and Vandevelde, M. (2021). Kravis and Roberts bequeath a formidable KKR, FT, 12 October 2021.

Griffiths, I. (1986). *Creative Accounting*, London: Unwin.

Gryta, T. and Mann, T. (2020). *Lights Out: Pride, Delusion and the Fall of General Electric,* Boston: Houghton Mifflin Harcourt.

Gwiliam, D., Macve, R. and Meeks, G. (2005). The costs and benefits of increased accounting regulation: a case study of Lloyd's of London, *Accounting and Business Research*, 35(2), 129–146.

Harford, J. and Li, K. (2007). Decoupling CEO wealth and firm performance: The case of acquiring CEOs, *Journal of Finance*, 62(2), 917–949, https://doi.org/10.1111/j.1540-6261.2007.01227.x.

IASB. (2020). *Business Combinations—Disclosures, Goodwill and Impairment*, London: International Accounting Standards Board, 19 March 2020, https://www.ifrs.org/content/dam/ifrs/publications/discussion-papers/english/2020/-updated-dp-business-combinations-disclosures-goodwill-and-impairment.pdf.

Independent. (1996). Robust language in the world of accountancy, 27 February 1996.

Kelly, J. (1996). Rebels against the revolution, *FT*, 29 February 1996.

Kelly, J. (1998a). Public and private sector: harmony from contradiction? *FT*, March 1998.

Kelly, J. (1998b). Watchdog defends draft rules on PFI accounting, *FT*, 15 June 1998.

KPMG (2014). *Who Cares about Goodwill Impairment?* London: KPMG.

Law Society (1986). *Off Balance Sheet Financing and Window Dressing,* London: The Law Society.

Lev, B. (1988). Toward a theory of equitable and efficient accounting policy. *The Accounting Review*, 63, 1–22.

Lex (1995). Goodwill, *FT*, 15 June 1995.

Lex (1997). Goodwill, *FT*, 4 December 1997.

Li, K. (2007). *Goodwill*, unpublished doctoral dissertation, University of Cambridge.

Lugo, D. (2020). FASB to reintroduce amortization of goodwill for public companies, 18 December 2020, https://tax.thomsonreuters.com/news/fasb-to-reintroduce-amortization-of-goodwill-for-public-companies/.

Lugo, D. (2022). In a surprising move, FASB drops project on subsequent accounting of goodwill, https://tax.thomsonreuters.com/news/in-a-surprising-move-fasb-drops-project-on-subsequent-accounting-of-goodwill/.

McKInsey & Company. (2010). *Perspectives on Merger Integration*, June 2010, https://www.mckinsey.com/client_service/organization/latest_thinking/~/media/1002A11EEA4045899124B917EAC7404C.ashx.

Meeks, G. (2003). Reporting to shareholders: the proposals in the Company Law Review, *Journal of Corporate Law Studies*, 3(1), 191–200.

Meeks, G. (2017). Understanding pension obligation figures, http://eprints.lse.ac.uk/84689.

Meeks, G. (2020). Contribution to IASB consultation http://eifrs.ifrs.org/eifrs/comment_letters//561/561_26715_GeoffMeeksUniversityofCambridge_0_IASBDP-2020Meeksresponse15920.pdf.

Meeks, G. and Meeks, J.G. (2002). *Towards a Cost-benefit Analysis of Accounting Regulation*, London: ICAEW.

Meeks, G. and Meeks, J.G. (2020). Managing earnings through M&A, in Amel-Zadeh, A. and Meeks, G. (eds.) *Accounting for M&A: Uses and Abuses of Accounting in Monitoring and Promoting Merger*, Abingdon and New York: Routledge, pp.172–188.

Meeks, G. and Meeks, J.G. (2022). *The Merger Mystery: Why Spend Ever More on Mergers When So Many Fail?* Cambridge: Open Book Publishers.

Meeks, G. and Meeks, J.G. (2023). Inefficient strategies of serial acquisition: glamour, earnings management, financial engineering, and industrial concentration, https://papers.ssrn.com/sol3/papers.cfm?abstract_id=4375502.

Meeks, G. and Swann, P. (2009). Accounting standards and the economics of standards, *Accounting and Business Research*, 39, 191–210.

Meeks, G. and Whittington, G. (2021). Death on the Stock Exchange: The fate of the 1948 population of large UK quoted companies, 1948–2018, *Business History*, https://doi.org/10.1080/00076791.2021.1893696.

Murphy, K. (1999). Executive compensation, in Ashenfelter, O. and Carl, D. (eds.) *Handbook of Labor Economics*, Amsterdam: North Holland, pp.2485–563.

Nobes, C. (1997). *German Accounting Explained: Reducing the Barriers to Measuring Company Performance in Europe's Largest Economy*, London: FT Finance, Pearson Professional.

Pennington. (1995). A right muddle from Myddelton, *The Times*, 2 November 1995.

Ramanna, K. and Watts, R. (2012). Evidence on the use of unverifiable estimates in required goodwill impairment. *Review of Accounting Studies*, 17(4), 749–780, https://doi.org/10.1007/s11142-012-9188-5.

Scott, D. and Upton, W. (1991). The role of cost-benefit considerations in the FASB's standards-setting process, in FASB, *Benefits, Costs and Consequences of Financial Accounting Standards,* Norwalk: Financial Accounting Standards Board.

Sergeant, G. (1997). No news is good news for Sir David, *The Times*, 4 December 1997.

Shiller, R. (2015). *Irrational Exuberance*, Princeton: Princeton University Press.

Shleifer, A. and Vishny, R. (1997). A survey of corporate governance, *Journal of Finance*, 52, pp.737–783.

Smith, T. (1992). *Accounting for Growth: Stripping the Camouflage from Company Accounts* (First edition), London: Century.

Smith, T. (1996). *Accounting for Growth: Stripping the Camouflage from Company Accounts* (Second edition), London: Century.

Swann, P., Temple, P. and Shurmer, M. (1996). Standards and trade performance: the UK experience, *Economic Journal*, 106, 1297–1313.

Tepper, J. and Hearn, D. (2019). *The Myth of Capitalism: Monopolies and the Death of Competition*, Hoboken: Wiley.

Tett, G. (2019). Commentary, *FT*, 8 June 2019.

Tweedie, D. and Whittington, G. (1990). Financial reporting: current problems and their implications for systematic reform. *Accounting and Business Research*, 21, 87–102.

UKEB (2022). https://www.endorsement-board.uk/goodwill-research-project/project-page.

Whittington, G. (1993). Corporate governance and the regulation of financial reporting. *Accounting and Business Research*, 23, 311–319.

Williams. (2004). Only One Cook, Financial Director.com 1 March 2004.

World Accounting Report. (1995). Standard-setters Conference, December/January 1995.

Zeff, S.A. (2002). "Political" Lobbying on Proposed Standards: A Challenge to the IASB, *Accounting Horizons*, 16(1), 43–54, https://doi.org/10.2308/acch.2002.16.1.43.

### *Standard setters' publications*

FRS3 (1992). *Reporting Financial Performance*, ASB.

FRS4 (1993). *Capital Instruments*, ASB.

FRS5 (1994). *Reporting the Substance of Transactions*, ASB.

FRS7 (1994). *Fair Values in Acquisition Accounting*, ASB.

FRS17 (2000). *Retirement Benefits*, ASB.

SSAP24 (1988). *Accounting for Pension Costs*, ASC.

# Appendix

# List of Board members, 1990–2000

This list attributes dates of service only as far as 2000 and gives the job titles held at the time of each member's appointment to the ASB.

David Allvey, 1994–2000, Group Finance Director, BAT Industries Plc
Robert Bradfield, 1990–1995, Head of UK Equity Investment Research, Cazenove & Co
Ian Brindle, 1993–2000, Senior Partner, Price Waterhouse
Dr John Buchanan, 1997–2000, Managing Director and Chief Financial Officer, The British Petroleum Company Plc
Sir Bryan Carsberg, Vice Chairman 1990–1994, Director-General OFTEL
John Coombe, 1996–2000, Group Finance Director of Glaxo Wellcome Plc
Allan Cook – Full-time
Elwyn Eilledge, 1990–1992, Senior Partner, Ernst and Young
Michael Garner, 1990–1995, Finance Director, TI Group Plc
Richard Goeltz 1995–1996, Group Chief Financial Officer, the Nat West Group
Raymond Hinton, 1994–1999, Chairman, UK Professional Standards, Arthur Andersen
Huw Jones, 1994–2000, Director, Prudential Portfolio Managers Ltd
Donald Main, 1990–1994, Group Finance Director, Forte Plc
Roger Munson, 1990–1993, Senior Technical Partner, Coopers & Lybrand Deloitte
Isobel Sharp, 2000, Technical Partner, Arthur Andersen
Graham Stacy, 1990–1994, Partner, Price Waterhouse
David Tweedie – Full-time
Professor Geoffrey Whittington, 1994–2000, Professor of Financial Accounting, University of Cambridge
Ken Wild, 1994–2000, Accounting Technical Partner, Touche Ross

## Advisers

Academic Adviser: Professor Geoffrey Whittington, 1990–1994
Legal Adviser: Professor Robert Jack, formerly Senior Partner, McGrigor Donald

## Observers

Sarah Brown, 1990–1991 and 1994–1996, Head of Companies Division, Department of Trade and Industry
Alan Hardcastle, 1990–1993, Chief Accounting Adviser to the Treasury and Head of the Government Accountancy Service
Frank Jenkins, 1990–2000, Member, Companies Division Department of Trade and Industry
Professor Andrew Likierman 1994–2000, Chief Accounting Adviser to the Treasury and Head of the Government Accountancy Service
Richard Rogers, 1997–2000, Director, Company Law, Department of Trade and Industry
Arthur Russell, 1991–1994, Head of Companies Division, Department of Trade and Industry, 1991–1994

# Index

Note: **Bold** page numbers refer to tables; *italic* page numbers refer to figures and page numbers followed by "n" denote endnotes.

For Product Safety Concerns and Information please contact our EU
representative GPSR@taylorandfrancis.com
Taylor & Francis Verlag GmbH, Kaufingerstraße 24, 80331 München, Germany

www.ingramcontent.com/pod-product-compliance
Ingram Content Group UK Ltd.
Pitfield, Milton Keynes, MK11 3LW, UK
UKHW020014200926
475702UK00014B/1881
* 9 7 8 1 0 3 2 3 8 8 1 6 8 *